LEITRIM

To Rosemarie, Páraic, Darragh and Nessa

Leitrim

The Irish Revolution, 1912–23

Patrick McGarty

FOUR COURTS PRESS

Set in 10.5 on 12.5 point Ehrhardt for
FOUR COURTS PRESS LTD
7 Malpas Street, Dublin 8, Ireland
www.fourcourtspress.ie
and in North America for
FOUR COURTS PRESS
c/o IPG, 814 N. Franklin St, Chicago, IL 60610.

© Patrick McGarty and Four Courts Press 2020

A catalogue record for this title
is available from the British Library.

ISBN 978–1–84682–850–8

All rights reserved. No part of this publication may be reproduced,
stored in or introduced into a retrieval system, or transmitted,
in any form or by any means (electronic, mechanical,
photocopying, recording or otherwise), without the
prior written permission of both the copyright
owner and the publisher of this book.

Printed in England
by TJ International, Padstow, Cornwall.

Contents

	LIST OF ILLUSTRATIONS	vii
	LIST OF ABBREVIATIONS	ix
	ACKNOWLEDGMENTS	xi
	The Irish Revolution, 1912–23 series	xiii
1	Leitrim in 1912	1
2	'We stand solidly and united behind John Redmond': Leitrim and home rule, 1912–14	12
3	'People of the county unanimously in favour of the British': Leitrim and the First World War, 1914–16	17
4	'The people say they are tired of politics': the 1916 Rising and its aftermath	36
5	'Thoroughly sound for the principle of self-determination': the triumph of Sinn Féin, 1917–18	43
6	'On the last lap of the race for Liberty's goal': the Dáil counter-state, 1919–21	64
7	'Vengeance was swift and very destructive': War of Independence, 1919–21	76
8	'The opportunity of being mistress in their own house': the transition to self-government, 1921–2	103
9	'There is this particular type of madness amongst a section of the people': Civil War, 1922–3	110
10	Revolution?	131
	NOTES	136
	SELECT BIBLIOGRAPHY	154
	INDEX	165

Illustrations

PLATES

1. Leitrim Rifles Militia at Carrick in the 1880s.
2. Charles Dolan, Sinn Féin candidate in the 1908 North Leitrim by-election.
3. Thomas Smyth, Irish Parliamentary Party MP for South Leitrim from 1906 to 1918.
4. Mohill, c.1912.
5. Drumshanbo Fife and Drum band, 1912.
6. Irish Volunteers at Manorhamilton in 1914.
7. National Volunteers at Ballinamore in 1914.
8. Poster advertising Bornacoola parade of Irish Volunteers, August 1914.
9. Locals with RIC officer at Drumshanbo, c.1915.
10. Fr Patrick Clancy, British army chaplain and curate in Drumshanbo, 1908–16.
11. Captain Thomas Gordon, Mohill, Royal Army Veterinary Corps.
12. Captain John O'Donel, recruiter for the British army, 1914–18.
13. Seán Mac Diarmada, native of Kiltyclogher and executed 1916 leader.
14. Paul Galligan, Volunteer organizer in Leitrim.
15. Labour activist Jimmy Gralton with his sister, Mary Anne, in America, 1915.
16. Jimmy Gralton in later life.
17. Leitrim's first TD, James N. Dolan.
18. The aftermath of the burning of Dowra barracks by the IRA on the Cavan/Leitrim border in 1920.
19. Graffiti left by the Crown forces on Meehan's shop in Mohill.
20. Cumann na mBan activist Margaret Sweeney.
21. Joe Nangle, a member of the IRA ambush party at Sheemore in March 1921
22. Michael Geoghegan, a member of the IRA ambush party at Sheemore in March 1921.
23. Volunteer Joe Beirne, killed at Selton Hill, March 1921.
24. Volunteer Paddy Guckian, a survivor of the Selton Hill ambush at Gorvagh.
25. William Latimer, shot as an alleged informer at Gorvagh in 1921.
26. Dr Charles Pentland in his Royal Army Medical Corps uniform, 1915.
27. North Leitrim IRA leader Martin Bernard McGowan.
28. Volunteer James McGlynn who was accidentally shot dead while enforcing the Belfast boycott at Drumshanbo in April 1921.

29 RIC District Inspector Thomas Gore Hickman.
30 Memorial card of Commandant Phil Gilgunn, killed in November 1922 during an attack on Manorhamilton.
31 Charles McGoohan in ceremonial National army uniform.
32 British troops departing Carrick for the last time, January 1922.
33 Dr Patrick Muldoon, killed in Mohill in March 1922.
34 Commandant Harry McKeon, National army commander in south Leitrim in 1922.
35 Seán Mitchell, IRA O/C of IRA's South Leitrim Brigade on his wedding day.
36 Members of the February 1922 Northern Command raiding party on Enniskillen, following their release from prison: Frank Reilly (Ballinamuck, Co. Longford), Charlie Reynolds (Gortlettragh, Co. Leitrim), John Kiernan (Newtowngore, Co. Leitrim), Bernie Sweeney (Ballinamore, Co. Leitrim), Seán Flood (Dublin), William Reilly (Longford), John Joe Griffin (Gortlettragh, Co. Leitrim), J. Lee (Longford), Joe Reynolds (Aghacashel, Co. Leitrim), Jim Davis (Derry).
37 Commandant Seán Mitchell with National army troops at Finner Camp, County Donegal.

Credits
1, 7, 8, 18, 32: Leitrim County Library; 2, 17: *Leitrim Guardian*; 3: Denis Glennon; 4, 13: National Library of Ireland; 5, 9: Noel McPartland; 6: Jackie McGoldrick; 10: the Clancy family; 11: Peter Gordon; 12: Prionn Duignan; 14: the Galligan family; 15, 16: John Rooney; 19: Christopher Meehan; 20: Ann Grainger; 21: Doreen Farrelly; 22: Míchael Geoghegan; 23: Des Guckian; 24: Sinead Guckian; 25: Pádraig Leyden; 26: Terry Ingles for the Pentland/Lindsay families; 27: the McGowan family; 28: Patricia Fitzgerald; 29: Irish Military Archives; 30: Dominic Rooney; 31: Liam and Helen Brennan; 33: the Boyle and Muldoon families; 34: Harry McKeon; 35: Seán Mitchell; 36: Eileen Barry; 37: Pat Joe Mitchell.

MAPS

1 Places mentioned in the text	xiv
2 Local government divisions	4
3 Parliamentary constituencies in 1910	7
4 Distribution of the Crown forces	82

Abbreviations

AC	*Anglo-Celt*
AOH	Ancient Order of Hibernians
ASU	Active Service Unit
BMH	Bureau of Military History
CCORI	Central Council for the Organisation of Recruiting in Ireland
CI	County Inspector, RIC
CO	Colonial Office, TNA
CSB	Crime Special Branch
DI	District Inspector, RIC
DORA	Defence of the Realm Act
DRI	Department of Recruiting for Ireland
FH	*Fermanagh Herald*
FJ	*Freeman's Journal*
GAA	Gaelic Athletic Association
Hansard	House of Commons debates
IFU	Irish Farmers' Union
IMA	Irish Military Archives
INAAVDF	Irish National Aid Association and Volunteer Dependants' Fund
INF	Irish National Foresters
IRA	Irish Republican Army
IRB	Irish Republican Brotherhood
IPP	Irish Parliamentary Party
ITGWU	Irish Transport and General Workers' Union
LA	*Leitrim Advertiser*
LGB	Local Government Board
LO	*Leitrim Observer*
MSPC	Military Service Pension Collection
NAI	National Archives of Ireland
NLI	National Library of Ireland
PRONI	Public Records Office of Northern Ireland
RDC	Rural District Council
RH	*Roscommon Herald*
RIC	Royal Irish Constabulary
RUC	Royal Ulster Constabulary
SC	*Sligo Champion*
SF	Sinn Féin
SIC	Special Infantry Corps

TNA	National Archives, London
TTL	Town Tenants' League
UIL	United Irish League
UVF	Ulster Volunteer Force
WS	Witness Statement to Bureau of Military History

Acknowledgments

This book is based on my doctoral dissertation completed at the School of History and Geography, Dublin City University. Throughout that journey, the expert guidance, support and encouragement that I received from Dr William Murphy, my supervisor, was vital, and for this I am eternally grateful.

My sincere thanks to the staffs of the National Archives of Ireland, National Library of Ireland, Irish Military Archives, University College Dublin Archives, Representative Church Body Library, National Archives, London, Public Records Office of Northern Ireland, the Diocesan Archives of Ardagh/Clonmacnoise and Kilmore, Dublin City University Library, Trinity College Dublin Library, University College Dublin Library, Institute of Technology Tralee Library, Kerry County Library, Sligo County Library, Longford County Library and Roscommon County Library. A special word of thanks to Mary Conefrey, Kim Taylor and the staff of Leitrim County Library for all their assistance over the years.

Dr John Logan, Seán Ó Súilleabháin, Fr Tom Murray, Margaret Connolly and Dominic Rooney contributed their expert knowledge on an ongoing basis – thank you all so much.

Sincere thanks to my editors Dr Daithí Ó Corráin and Professor Mary Ann Lyons for their professionalism, expertise and guidance through each stage of the process. I am indebted also to Dr Mike Brennan for creating the maps for this book.

The following people have helped in many different ways on the long journey to publish this book: Ken Boyle, Chris Bradshaw, Mary Brosnan, Michael Casey, Dr Marie Coleman, Kieran Conaty, Patrick Creamer, Frank Darcy, Rosemarie Dempsey, Mary Dolan, Joe and Rosaleen Dolan, Quincey Dougan, Prionn Duignan, Frank Fagan, Oliver Fallon, Liam Farrell, Dr Michael Farry, Cathal Flynn, Roddy Gaynor, Mícheál Geoghegan, Pádraig Gilbride, Peter Gordon, Dr Michael Hopkinson, Oliver Kelliher, Gerry Kilraine, Mervyn Lloyd, David Logan, Thomas Melia, Christopher Meehan, Miriam Moffitt, Gabriel Moran, Padraig Mulligan, Thomas Mulligan, Gerry Mulvey, Gerard MacAtasney, Michael McDowell, David McEllin, Feargal McGill, Bernard McGurn, Noel McPartland, Gerry Nangle, Professor Muiris Ó Laoire, Cormac Ó Súilleabháin, Dr John Pender, Bernard and Mary Reynolds and Dr Michael Wheatley.

Finally, to my wife, Rosemarie, my children, Páraic, Darragh and Nessa, my late parents, Josie and Frank – thank you so much for your love, encouragement and support throughout the never-ending journey of learning.

The Irish Revolution, 1912–23 series

Since the turn of the century, a growing number of scholars have been actively researching this seminal period in modern Irish history. More recently, propelled by the increasing availability of new archival material, this endeavour has intensified. This series brings together for the first time the various strands of this exciting and fresh scholarship within a nuanced interpretative framework, making available concise, accessible, scholarly studies of the Irish Revolution experience at a local level to a wide audience.

The approach adopted is both thematic and chronological, addressing the key developments and major issues that occurred at a county level during the tumultuous 1912–23 period. Beginning with an overview of the social, economic and political milieu in the county in 1912, each volume assesses the strength of the home rule movement and unionism, as well as levels of labour and feminist activism. The genesis and organization of paramilitarism from 1913 are traced; responses to the outbreak of the First World War and its impact on politics at a county level are explored; and the significance of the 1916 Rising is assessed. The varying fortunes of constitutional and separatist nationalism are examined. The local experience of the War of Independence, reaction to the truce and Anglo-Irish Treaty and the course and consequences of the Civil War are subject to detailed examination and analysis. The result is a compelling account of life in Ireland in this formative era.

Mary Ann Lyons *Daithí Ó Corráin*
Department of History *School of History & Geography*
Maynooth University *Dublin City University*

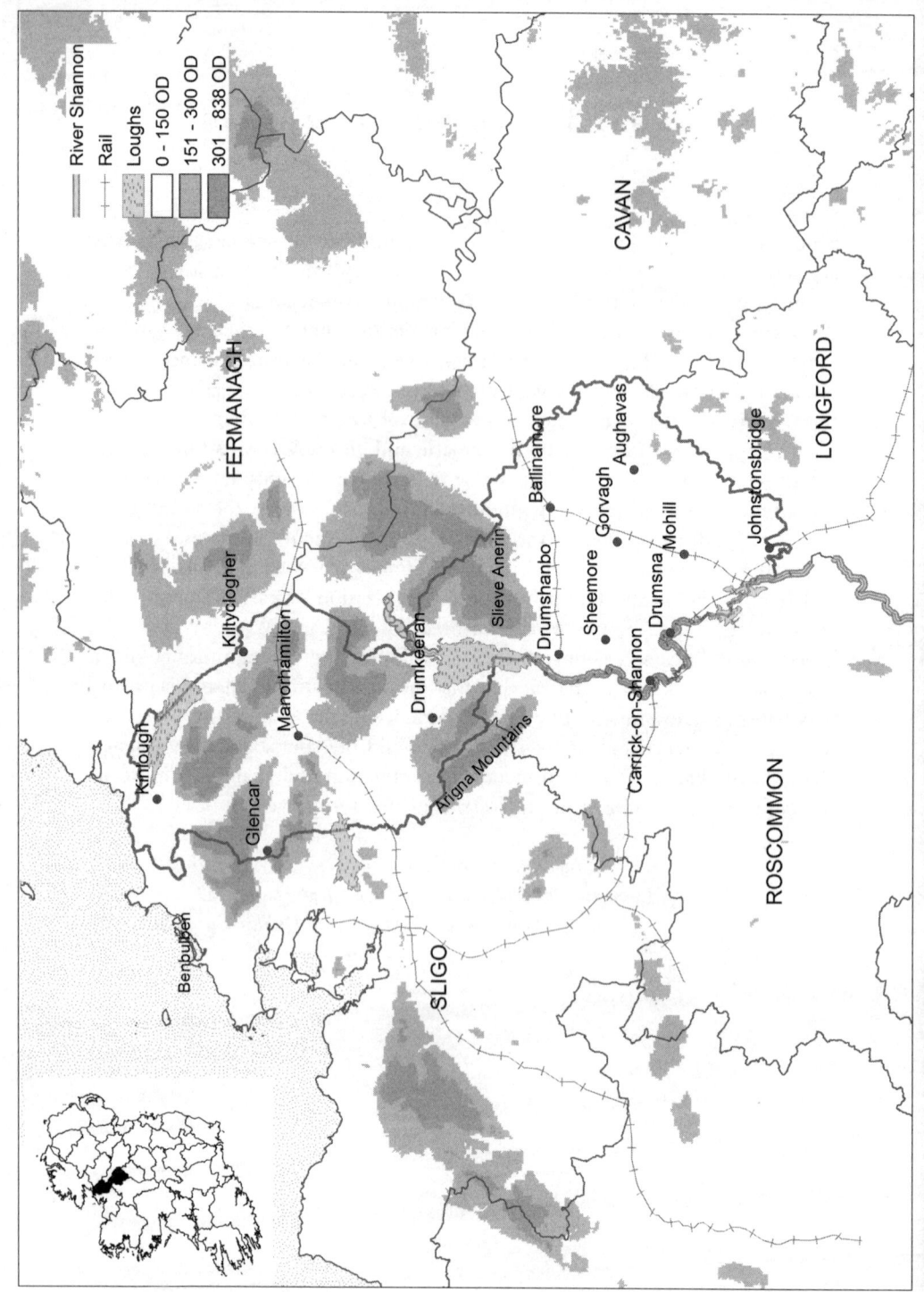

1 Places mentioned in the text

1 Leitrim in 1912

Travelling through Leitrim during the Land War in the spring of 1882, Canadian journalist Margaret Dixon McDougall wrote: 'I listened to one tale after another of harassment, misery and thoughtless oppression in Kiltyclogher till my heart was sick'.[1] Such incidents were not unique in Leitrim, a county that witnessed widespread evictions, and had one of the highest levels of agrarian violence nationally during this period.[2] Remarkably, less than twenty years later, Leitrim's Royal Irish Constabulary (RIC) County Inspector (CI) claimed that 'the inhabitants of the county are well to do and there is no real poverty'.[3] By 1920 the lives of Leitrim's smallholders had been transformed and the intervening years had witnessed successive governments responding to the land question with a series of land acts. While this legislation transferred landownership from the county's landlord class to its smallholder tenant farmers, the national question remained unresolved. However, following the 1910 general election, the Irish Parliamentary Party (IPP) held the balance of power in the House of Commons, making home rule a certainty in the eyes of Leitrim's nationalists. But, resistance from their Ulster unionist neighbours to Irish self-government, a world war, a republican insurrection and subsequent British government ineptitude and incompetence all contributed to a transfer of political allegiance from constitutional to advanced nationalism within the county. Far from signalling a significant political transformation, the county that emerged in a new and independent Ireland showed a striking resemblance in its structures and culture to the political order of old.

The 1911 census revealed that Leitrim had a total population of 69,343 people, a fall of nearly 6,000 from that recorded in 1901. Like many other regions along the western seaboard, the county suffered the consequences of emigration with 82,629 of its sons and daughters having departed since 1851. By 1911, 91.5 per cent of its inhabitants were Roman Catholic, 7.4 per cent were members of the Church of Ireland, and the remainder were of the Methodist and Presbyterian faiths. The predominant role of agriculture was reflected in the census with 19,034 of the 24,486 individuals in employment (78 per cent) stating that their occupation involved working on the land. Of the remainder, 2,996 were employed in industry, primarily textiles, and coal mining at Arigna; 1,137 were members of the domestic class; and 1,022 were described as professionals. Only 297 people were employed in the commercial sector, divided into 124 employed in commercial occupations and the remainder working in the 'conveyance of men, goods and messages'.[4]

The county comprised 392,381 statute acres occupying 1.9 per cent of the land mass of Ireland. Leitrim was a poor county, primarily composed of marginal land with ninety per cent of farm holdings in the county under fifty acres in size.[5] Nearly eighty-four per cent of residents on holdings/agricultural holdings, the second-highest percentage in Ireland, lived on holdings with a rateable valuation of less than £15 per annum.[6] Only fifty-seven farm holdings were in excess of 200 acres in 1911 and sections of the northern part of the county were part of the region administered by the Congested Districts Board.[7]

Leitrim had the unique distinction of being the only county in Ireland without a town with a population in excess of 2,000 people. The largest was Carrick-on-Shannon (Carrick), the county town, with a population of 906. Ninety-four per cent of the population, the largest proportion in an Irish county, lived outside of towns with 500 inhabitants or more.[8] The remaining principal towns of Manorhamilton, Mohill, Ballinamore and Drumshanbo were served by either the Cavan–Leitrim narrow guage railway, or the Great Northern or Midland Western railway network which facilitated the export of cattle, agricultural produce and coal (see map 1).

In common with all rural areas of Ireland, land was the driving force of revolution in late nineteenth-century Leitrim as the campaign for landownership was aligned with the national question.[9] Although the British government initially reacted with a series of reforms, much of the early legislation created large ranch-type grazier holdings to the detriment of many smallholders and landless families. Responding to their sense of grievance, nationalist MP William O'Brien founded the United Irish League (UIL) in 1898, and the organization grew rapidly. It had seven branches and 472 members in Leitrim by January 1899; within five months seventeen branches with a membership of 2,530 were recorded in the county. By December 1900 the police reported the existence of thirty-one branches and 7,602 members in Leitrim compared to only thirteen branches in neighbouring Sligo.[10]

In 1900, following the UIL's merger with a re-united IPP led by Waterford MP John Redmond, the twin forces of land agitation and nationalism re-ignited. Almost immediately, the UIL established itself as both the local constituency organization for the IPP and a driving force of land agitation for smallholders. Renewed calls for land reform were met by further land acts in 1903 and 1909, facilitating the transfer of land to tenant farmers. Attempts to break up large grazier farms across Ireland preoccupied the UIL. While the 'Ranch War' (1906–9) was widespread in the neighbouring counties of Roscommon and Longford, agitation against graziers in Leitrim was non-existent in a county dominated by small farm holdings and few grazier farms.[11] Nevertheless, the UIL was active and when agitation did occur it was directed at families who occupied evicted farms, or assisted those facing eviction. In the Mohill district in June 1907, the police reported the boycotting of an elderly man named McGarry because his daughter married the occupant of an evicted farm. The only incident of any significance in the county was a protracted dispute involving two Protestant brothers named McNeill who occupied an evicted farm at Aughavas on the Cavan/Leitrim border.[12] UIL branches in both counties orchestrated a boycott campaign that prevented any shops in nearby towns supplying goods to the men. Thomas Smyth, IPP MP for South Leitrim, was active in the campaign against the McNeills. The CI reported that in his calls to boycott the men, the MP used 'most vicious and criminal language'.[13] Despite occasional disturbances, police reports indicated that the county was peaceful with high levels of land purchase by tenant farmers.[14] In May 1911 the CI noted that local farmers 'appear thrifty and contented and on the whole pay their instalments regularly. This extensive land purchase has had a marked beneficial effect on the welfare of the tenants.'[15]

The RIC occupied twenty-nine barracks in Leitrim in 1914 and also had administrative responsibility for Dowra barracks in County Cavan. The force's strength of CI Ross Carthy Rainsford, four district inspectors based at Carrick, Mohill, Ballinamore and Manorhamilton, and 141 men was considerably less than the 230 men of all ranks that occupied the county in 1891. Rainsford, a Trinity College graduate from Louth, had entered the force as an officer cadet and transferred to Leitrim from Mayo in 1912, where he served until his retirement in 1920.[16] The county was unique in having no British army base prior to 1920.

Only two newspapers were published in the county: the *Leitrim Observer* at Carrick, edited by Pat Dunne, and the *Leitrim Advertiser* at Mohill, edited by Robert Turner. Both newspapers were strong supporters of the IPP, and in the post-1916 period the *Observer* was sympathetic to Sinn Féin (SF). The *Sligo Independent* was the only unionist publication in the region, and together with the *Sligo Champion* and *Fermanagh Herald* it provided extensive news coverage of events in the north of the county. In addition to Leitrim's two local newspapers, events in the south of the county received coverage in the *Longford Leader*, the *Anglo-Celt*, and the *Roscommon Herald*. Although the political affiliation of the majority of the newspapers was pro-IPP, the *Herald*, owned by dissident nationalist, Jasper Tully, provided widespread coverage of events in Leitrim and an alternative perspective on both national and local politics.

The profoundly inward-looking nature of local politics could be most clearly seen in the proliferation of local political elites and their attendant rivalries. Patrick Flynn, town landlord, large farmer, and a leading wholesale and retail merchant, controlled the Carrick UIL branch. He was also a member of a plethora of local bodies, including the county and rural district council (RDC) and county grand jury. Local nationalist opposition to Flynn was centred on Michael McGrath, a draper, auctioneer and leader of the town's Ancient Order of Hibernians (AOH). Tensions between Flynn and McGrath were a regular feature of the local political environment.[17] Other prominent nationalist leaders

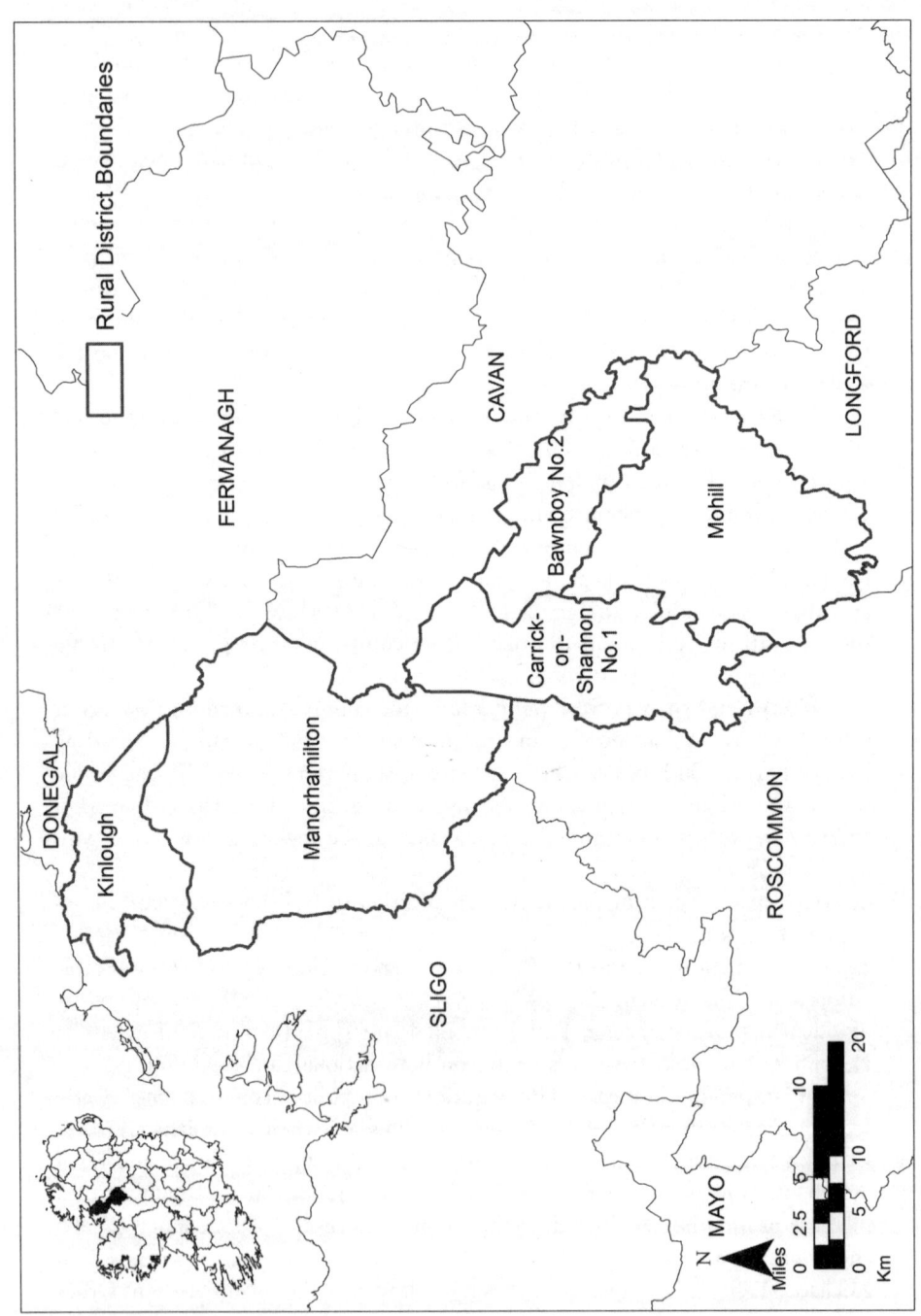

2 Local government divisions

in the county included Manorhamilton's Francis Meehan, MP, publican and grocer, who dominated local politics in north Leitrim.

Alongside the UIL, the AOH served as a local support organization for the IPP and it too was active in land agitation. Emerging at the end of the nineteenth century as a counter-force to the Orange Order, police reports indicated that this overtly sectarian oath-bound organization was strong in Ulster and in counties Sligo, Leitrim and Cavan.[18] Membership of both the UIL and AOH was common, and both organizations often operated together in land agitation and boycott campaigns.[19] In 1908 the CI wrote of 'the terror which the UIL and AOH inspire in the minds of the people, deterring magistrates and juries from enforcing the law in cases where agrarian matters are involved'.[20] With its roots in the Defender and Ribbon organizations, the AOH was perceived as the more militant of the two groups. By 1910 police reports revealed that the AOH dominated the UIL in the county.[21]

One of the main reasons for the increasing influence of the AOH was its Belfast-based leader Joe Devlin's success in ensuring that the AOH became an approved society under the National Insurance Act of 1911. This legislation provided state health insurance for low- and middle-income wage earners, making membership very attractive for a large element of the population. Although the IPP lacked clearly defined policies or ideology on a range of social issues as a result of trying to balance the interests of its various political groupings, this innovative social legislation gave the AOH a substantial membership boost. Nationally, membership increased from 10,000 in 1905 to 170,000 by 1914.[22] In Leitrim, AOH divisions increased from thirty-five in 1910 to forty-one in 1912, and by 1916 there were 4,283 registered members in the county.[23] Numbers also increased in neighbouring counties with Sligo, Roscommon and Longford recording membership numbers of 2,373, 2,201 and 945 respectively, demonstrating the strength of the Hibernians in the region.[24]

While one of its main functions was serving as a local political support group for the IPP, the AOH was active in providing a range of social activities for its members. An infusion of government funding to the AOH's insurance section to secure premises meant that these buildings were also used as AOH halls.[25] Increased funding resulted in the opening of halls in Mohill, Lough Allen, Annaduff, Gorvagh and Drumsna where local political leaders never lost an opportunity for speechmaking in favour of home rule. Social events at these halls reflected the ethos of the Hibernians and were always of an exclusively Irish nature. Before speeches commenced at the official opening of Lough Allen hall in April 1912, the assembled audience were entertained by 'a selection of Irish airs on a gramophone'.[26]

Although both the AOH and UIL dominated local politics, other organizations such as the Irish National Foresters (INF) and the Town Tenants' League (TTL) had a spasmodic existence in the county. Like the AOH, the

INF was a Catholic benefit society and social organization under the umbrella of the IPP. While overlapping membership between organizations was common, no strong network of the INF emerged in Leitrim. Only three branches ever existed in the south of the county at Dromod, Ballinamore and Carrick. It was not until August 1916 that the Carrick branch was formed. Among its aims was the provision of social facilities for the town's young people. The main promoters were Michael McGrath and parish priest Canon Thomas O'Reilly who believed that having access to such facilities would overcome 'the many other evils and temptations, which at present confront them, and uplift the social status of and life of Carrick, which in recent years has greatly deteriorated in quality and rank'.[27] By December 1916 INF membership in the three branches totalled 143, smaller than neighbouring Longford, which had four branches and 160 members.[28]

The advancement of land purchase legislation triggered the foundation of the TTL in 1904. It campaigned for the rights of the tenants of town land and property. Branches were formed at Carrick, Mohill, Drumshanbo, Manorhamilton and Drumkeeran, and co-operation between local organizations was common. AOH halls were provided on a regular basis for Town Tenants' meetings, and both organizations were involved in a number of tenancy issues. The Carrick branch was the most active in the county and constantly campaigned on behalf of town tenants, particularly in its attempts to have town lands included in the sale of the local Whyte estate.[29] Advocating for members in rent disputes and leading campaigns on a range of issues, including a lack of sanitary facilities in town houses, was a feature of branch activity. The TTL was also involved in preventing outsiders bidding against existing tenants of properties placed for sale by local landlords.[30]

The Gaelic Athletic Association (GAA) was founded in the county in 1889 with Thomas Fallon elected as its first chairman. Like many of his GAA counterparts, Fallon, a veteran of the Land League campaign, was imprisoned for his participation in land agitation in 1881. Despite the presence of eleven GAA clubs in the county by 1891, 'all under Fenian control' according to the police, the association in the county was disorganized and riven with internal disputes.[31] Controlled at national and provincial levels by the Irish Republican Brotherhood (IRB), the organization also attracted the wrath of the clergy with priests at Carrigallen in 1889 actively discouraging people from attending games.[32] Throughout the 1890s occasional tournaments constituted the only form of GAA activity and no county board was in existence for most of the decade. Despite the re-establishment of a county board structure in 1904 and the election of Thomas Smyth as chairman in 1905, attempts to reorganize championship football in the county proved difficult. Only six teams competed in the 1910 senior championship, but club activity increased in the following years. By 1911 the RIC reported that the

Leitrim in 1912

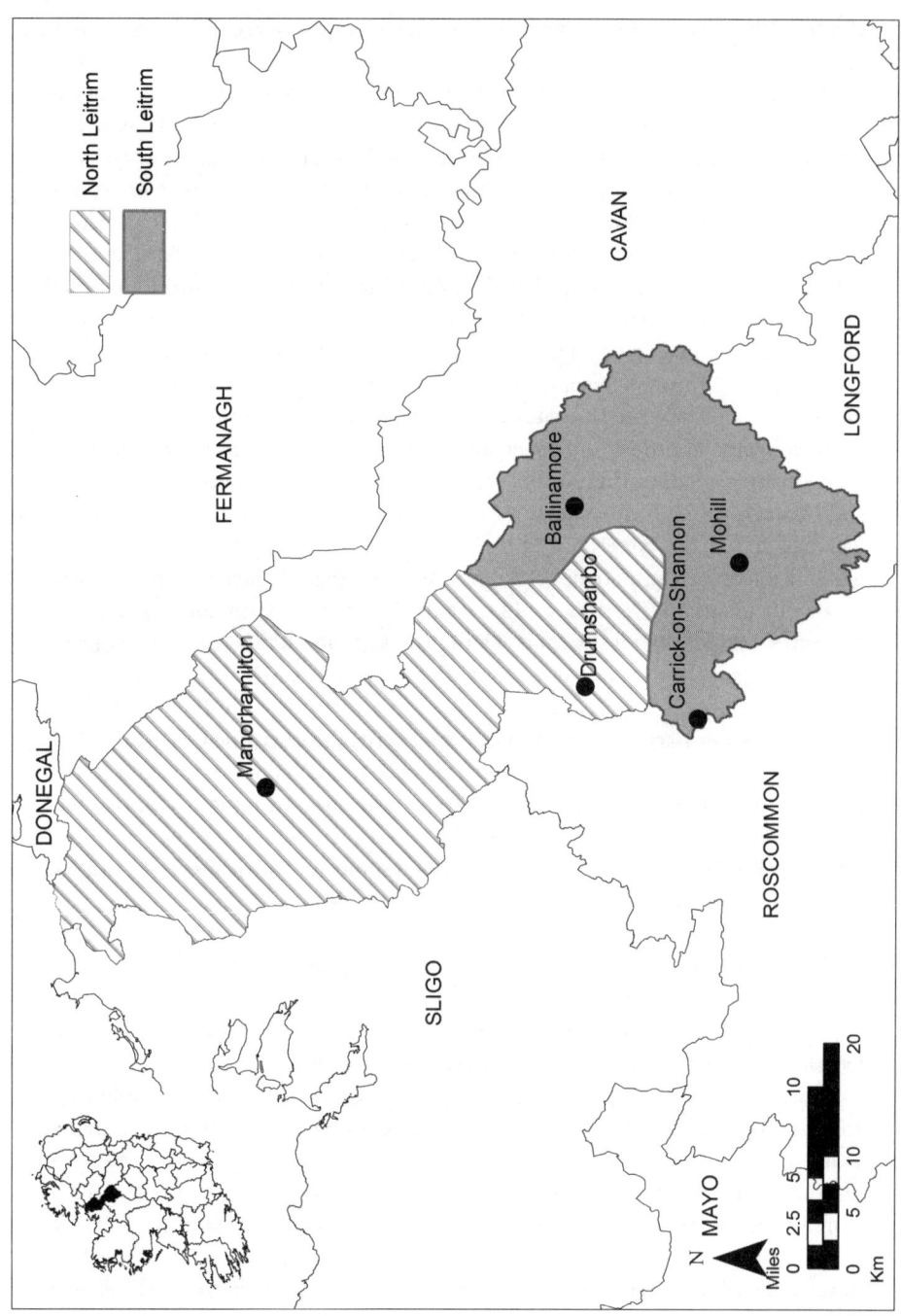

3 Parliamentary constituencies in 1910

eleven clubs that existed were 'solely for athletic purposes and have no IRB connection'.³³

Established in 1893 to counter the increasing Anglicization of Irish society and to conserve and revive Irish as a spoken language, the Gaelic League had mixed fortunes in a number of counties, including Leitrim.³⁴ After a phase of growth in the early 1900s, the League's branch numbers declined in Ireland from 964 in 1906 to 388 by 1913.³⁵ Success was evident for a brief period in south Leitrim due to the efforts of a local organizer, Seán Ó Ruadháin, and the appointment of a travelling teacher, Kathleen McGowan. While police reported the existence of eleven branches in south Leitrim in 1911, the departure of McGowan resulted in a decline to six branches by November 1912.³⁶ The League passed through several phases of growth and decline during the early decades of the twentieth century and the organization was not strong in Leitrim, meriting little or no coverage in police reports and local newspapers.³⁷

Leitrim was administered by two Catholic dioceses: Kilmore in the north and Ardagh and Clonmacnoise (Ardagh) in the south. Church of Ireland parishes in Leitrim were part of the diocese of Kilmore, Elphin and Ardagh, while Leitrim's Methodists were part of the Sligo District Synod of the Methodist Church of Ireland. Unlike many of their Protestant counterparts, the Roman Catholic hierarchy and clergy played an active role in politics. Following the split in nationalist ranks after the Charles Stewart Parnell divorce case, the Catholic Church did not hesitate in attempting to influence political opinion. Bishop Bartholomew Woodlock of Ardagh proclaimed that accepting Parnell as their leader 'would condone his crime as an adulterer'.³⁸ At a public meeting in Manorhamilton in June 1891, parish priest Fr John Maguire told the assembled crowd that 'Ireland would deserve the ridicule of the world if it tolerated Parnell as leader.'³⁹ Following the establishment of the UIL and the subsequent re-unification of the IPP, UIL branches were organized in every parish. While the clergy were supportive of the League, the church viewed the AOH with suspicion given its perceived militancy and its origins in the secret agrarian societies of the nineteenth century.⁴⁰ At Drumkeeran in 1905, the establishment of a local AOH division was so strongly opposed by the local parish priest that the division's president had to resign.⁴¹

Although a home rule parliament had not been established in Dublin, the Local Government (Ireland) Act (1898) did replace the ascendancy-dominated grand jury system of local government with locally elected county and rural district councils. In Leitrim, in addition to a county council, the act established five RDCs located in Ballinamore (Bawnboy), Mohill, Carrick, Manorhamilton and Kinlough (see map 2). Together with the Poor Law unions/board of guardians, and financed by a budget from the Local Government Board and local ratepayers, these bodies were responsible for an array of local services, including road maintenance, water supply, housing and sanitation. Management of the county's three workhouses at Carrick, Mohill and Manorhamilton, together with seven dispensaries, was the responsibility of locally elected boards of guardians.[42] With no strong advanced nationalist tradition in the county, politics in Leitrim was dominated by the IPP and its local party political machine, which immediately controlled the newly established councils and boards of guardians.

Lough Allen divided the county into two distinct units, north and south, each with its own separate parliamentary constituency between 1884 and 1918 (see map 3). P.A. McHugh represented North Leitrim and Jasper Tully South Leitrim until 1906. At the 1906 general election, McHugh transferred to the neighbouring North Sligo constituency and was replaced unopposed by Charles Dolan from Manorhamilton. Thomas Smyth, a Mohill-based auctioneer, replaced Tully in South Leitrim and also faced no opposition at the ballot box. After only fifteen months representing the IPP at Westminster, Dolan announced his intention to resign his seat and stand for re-election for the recently established Sinn Féin (SF) party because of the perceived futility of the IPP's position on the home rule question. This new entity, led by pacifist and economic nationalist Arthur Griffith, advocated withdrawal from Westminster and the establishment of an Irish parliament in Dublin. Not only did the IPP face embarrassment with Dolan's defection, but the RIC also reported in June 1907 that the North Leitrim executive of the UIL had 'passed a resolution in favour of the Sinn Féin policy by 37 votes to 13'.[43]

The campaign in North Leitrim throughout the winter of 1907–8 was a protracted, violent and bitter affair. With Dolan's fellow Manorhamilton townsman, Francis Meehan, emerging as the IPP candidate, divisions in the ranks of the UIL soon emerged.[44] At a UIL meeting on 11 February 1908 Killargue's parish priest, Fr Charles Flynn, accused Dolan and 'his little Hungarian band of faction mongers' of living in 'a fool's paradise', and of 'insulting the clergy and the intelligent people of Leitrim'.[45] Throughout the campaign, large numbers of election workers from across Ireland travelled to the county to support both candidates. Although no IRB presence within the county appeared in police reports, the CI observed in 1907 that 'the county is being stumped by orators including Bulmer Hobson and J. McDermott of Belfast'.[46] MacDermott, a native of Kiltyclogher, became Dolan's election agent, and as Seán Mac Diarmada eight years later, would be executed as one of the leaders of the Easter 1916 Rising. Both Hobson and Mac Diarmada were active IRB organizers and travelled the constituency in support of Dolan. Hobson's Quaker background was soon highlighted: he was denounced in church and described in one newspaper as being 'a Salvation Army preacher from Belfast and an Orangeman'.[47]

In its fight against SF, the IPP used its extensive UIL and AOH support bases in north Leitrim. In addition, Joe Devlin employed his organizational skills to transport men from Belfast to disrupt SF meetings and violence became widespread.[48] In spite of these obstacles, Dolan performed relatively well, polling 1,157 votes to Meehan's 3,103. Despite the loss, SF leader Arthur Griffith wrote that 'Ireland's resurrection would be dated from the day when 1,200 Irishmen in the poorest and most remote county in Ireland voted for Sinn Féin'.[49] The vote in North Leitrim was as much a vote of censure against the IPP for its failure to win home rule as a vote for SF.[50]

Both nationally and locally, SF declined rapidly in the years following the North Leitrim by-election. By 1909 nearly half of the 106 branches in Ireland had failed to pay affiliation fees and only 581 members had paid the annual subscription of 1s.[51] Only one of six SF candidates, John O'Rourke, was elected in the 1908 Manorhamilton RDC electoral area, and the party's sole candidate in the county council elections was defeated. The *Sligo Champion* reported that 'the chief feature in connection with the elections in the Manorhamilton district was the sweeping defeat of the Sinn Féin candidates'.[52] Despite its closeness geographically to north Leitrim, no strong SF presence existed in Sligo.[53] Only one branch existed in Longford with no SF presence in Roscommon.[54] In Leitrim, activity in the county's twelve branches rapidly dissipated and by January 1910 the RIC reported that 'no interest is now taken in this organization'.[55] Following the 1908 by-election, Charles Dolan left politics and emigrated to America, briefly returning to Ireland in 1911 to establish a shoe factory. When it failed he returned to America, practiced law in Missouri and died in 1960.[56]

The absence of advanced nationalist activity alongside minimal levels of land agitation meant that the IPP and its local support organizations dominated political life in the county.[57] A relatively seamless transfer of landownership from landlords to tenant farmers meant that in rural Leitrim 'politics appeared comatose in this period'.[58] Nevertheless, inter-factional rivalry was a regular feature among IPP supporters. Newly-elected MP Francis Meehan was among its first victims when he was defeated at the 1908 county council elections by local AOH leader John O'Donel. Commenting on the result, Meehan claimed that 'Sinn Féin and conservatism ruled against him'.[59] During the 1911 county council elections, UIL/AOH rivalry was widespread throughout the campaign, which witnessed Michael Carter, AOH county president, defeat Pat McManus, a prominent UIL councillor, in the Drumshanbo electoral area.[60] In spite of such divisions, county council chairman Thomas Fallon demonstrated a unified front at the first meeting of the incoming council. He declared that 'faction had no hold in their county and they were all true to the principles of the United Irish Party [*sic*]'.[61]

This book explores the Irish Revolution through an analysis of events at a regional level in County Leitrim between the years 1912 and 1923. Both political behaviour and military activity are examined from the introduction of the home rule bill to the end of the Irish Civil War, a time of extraordinary upheaval and unrest at a national level. Aside from the 1919–23 period of intense conflict, the eleven years between 1912 and 1923 witnessed a massive political transformation with the collapse of the hegemonic IPP and the rise of SF. This book examines the party machines and interconnections of constitutional and advanced nationalism at local level, and assesses whether the political motivations and operations of both factions were based on narrow parochial and personal interests rather than social class or ideology. The intervention of the First World War had a major bearing on the political transformation of Ireland and Leitrim in this period. This was followed by the local experience of a republican counter-state and political violence between 1919 and 1923. The chapters that follow chart the impact on local politics and society of the linked national and international conflicts of the period, and examine the consequences of the Irish Revolution for a small rural community in the north-west of Ireland.

2 'We stand solidly and united behind John Redmond': Leitrim and home rule, 1912–14

Renewed optimism among Irish nationalists emerged following the 1910 general election, when the IPP led by John Redmond held the balance of power in the House of Commons. It subsequently supported Herbert Asquith's Liberal government based on an assurance that home rule would be implemented and that, consequently, an Irish parliament would sit in Dublin for the first time since 1800. Given Redmond's position as the power broker at Westminster and Asquith's plans to introduce a home rule bill to the House of Commons, the IPP and its supporters saw home rule as inevitable. In its second edition of 1912, the *Leitrim Observer* was confident about the dawn of a new era, declaring that 'the New Year comes with a brighter prospect for Ireland than many she has known through many a decade of her sad history. It comes with the prospect of victory certain, and soon for the cause of Ireland'.[1] The *Cork Examiner* was equally optimistic, predicting that 'home rule is as certain as Church disestablishment, land reform and franchise extension'.[2] The course of events during what became known as the third home rule crisis would prove otherwise.

Redmond's alliance with Asquith had also resulted in the Parliament Act in 1911 which paved the way for an easier passage for home rule legislation. The act removed the House of Lords' right to veto bills passed in the Commons and limited its power to delay such bills to two years. Plans to propose self-government for Ireland did not go unnoticed in nearby Ulster, where the unionist population adopted a two-pronged campaign of resistance: allying itself with the Tory opposition at Westminster and threatening political violence in Ireland. Under the leadership of Edward Carson, a paramilitary group, the Ulster Volunteer Force (UVF), was established and armed in January 1913 to resist home rule. In response, Gaelic League activist Eoin MacNeill founded the Irish Volunteers as a nationalist counter organization in November 1913, to pressurize Britain into fulfilling its political promise of Irish self-government.

Ironically, despite its powerful position in British politics, the IPP was not strong at a local level in the years prior to the First World War.[3] With an element of certainty about the achievement of home rule, a mood of complacency and political apathy emerged among many Irish nationalists. In his May 1912 monthly report, the RIC Inspector-General observed that 'the Irish government is not much discussed by the people who seem to care little where parliament is'.[4] Across Ireland, an increasingly conservative and stable countryside was prevalent as the progress of land reform became more and more marked.[5] In Leitrim, police reports consistently noted a peaceful countryside with no mention of cattle drives taking place throughout 1912.[6] Following the land acts of 1903 and 1909, approximately seventy per cent of land was now owned by former tenant farmers, which contributed to political stability. Observing the prevailing political environment in much of rural Ireland, the novelist Canon Patrick Sheehan wrote that

> so long as there was a Cromwellian landlord to be fought and conquered, there remained before the eyes of the people some image of the country. Now the fight is over, and they are sinking down into the abject and awful condition of the French peasant who doesn't care for king or country and only asks who is going to reduce the rates.[7]

The absence of active political participation was noted at a series of poorly attended UIL meetings across Leitrim. At one such meeting of the UIL South Leitrim executive at Fenagh in September 1912, when questioned about the absence of delegates, an angry Patrick Briody, the secretary, retorted that 'when they wanted a bit of bog they came here'.[8]

Recognizing the need to reinvigorate an inactive party structure, a renewed impetus from the UIL nationally, spearheaded by John Dillon, came about, which resulted in the reorganization of branches across Leitrim. At a meeting of the UIL North Leitrim executive in February 1915 Meehan declared that 'never before within living memory were the prospects of the Irish people more bright or more full of hope. Apathy and dissension were the only thing[s] that would destroy these prospects'.[9] Despite numerous attempts at reorganization, UIL branch meetings were very infrequent across the county. Only five branches from south Leitrim were affiliated to the UIL national directory in December 1915.[10]

The TTL continued to remain active in the county. Although affiliated to the IPP, it failed to attract the support of the political establishment for the cause of town tenants. Given that many prominent IPP members were town landlords, there was an ambiguity at the heart of the movement because of the desire of local branches to remain respectable in the eyes of ratepayers.[11] Nevertheless, the Carrick branch openly rebelled against the IPP by refusing to subscribe to the home rule fund because two of the fund's collectors were local landlords. The local TTL chairman, Michael McGrath, condemned the stance of the IPP in relation to town tenants, claiming that they had done nothing for 'the poor rack-rented town tenants'.[12] Despite some local successes in aiding purchases of town properties, the League had become increasingly irrelevant as it struggled to find a place in the large number of organizations under the umbrella of nationalism.[13]

Leitrim was relatively peaceful compared to many of its neighbours. Yet, one factor revived political agitation among Leitrim farmers – the local rates levy. The dispute centred around the presence of the Cavan and Leitrim

Railway running through the county and the increasing level of rates imposed on Leitrim ratepayers to subsidize the privately owned and Protestant-controlled railway company. The establishment of both the Farmers' Protection Association and the Ratepayers' Protection Association revived agitation among Leitrim farmers who vehemently opposed any increase in rates. Members of both the UIL and the AOH were active in these organizations. The agitation was directed by two local farmers, James Geoghegan and Pat Gaffney, and by Michael Carter, AOH county president. While both local MPs supported the ratepayers, they also argued that the presence of the railway provided an opportunity for economic development and employment through the development of Leitrim's coal and mineral resources.[14] By early 1913 the agitation had subsided and Leitrim returned to its political slumber when the county council reduced its rail subsidy and agreed not to increase rates. By December 1913 CI Rainsford reported that, barring a few cases of rent being withheld, Leitrim 'was in a peaceful and orderly state during the year and practically free from agrarian trouble.'[15]

A key feature of IPP culture in the pre-war period was the curtailment of its parliamentary backbenchers and strong centralized control by the party leadership.[16] While the *Leitrim Observer* reported that 'Mr Francis E. Meehan was every day becoming a more popular member of the IPP and is at present very busy addressing meetings not alone in Leitrim but throughout Ireland', there is little evidence to suggest that he was an influential representative at a national level.[17] Like many of his colleagues, Meehan's role as an MP revolved around addressing local meetings and home rule demonstrations, and attending to constituency issues. Thomas Smyth fulfilled a similar role for south Leitrim. When pressed by a member of Mohill Union at its meeting in September 1912 on the status of the home rule bill, Smyth appeared to demonstrate his influence in the party by stating that 'those who might be expected to be in the know, Messrs Redmond, Dillon and Devlin seem to be quite hopeful and when they are hopeful and have reasons for being so, so we should be satisfied'.[18]

In November 1912 Smyth was one of twenty-one IPP members who were not present at a vote on the home rule bill, resulting in defeat in the House of Commons. The members of Leitrim County Council demonstrated their unhappiness with Smyth by passing a resolution condemning 'in the strongest manner the actions of those members of the IPP who absented themselves on the division on the home rule bill'. The meeting called on Smyth to attend to his duties or resign as MP.[19] At a meeting of the South Leitrim executive of the UIL in January 1913, Smyth apologized for his absence and explained that it was the result of a 'snap vote' called by the opposition while he and his colleagues were en route to London. In June 1913, although he was ill with tonsillitis, the *Leitrim Observer* reported that Smyth attended the vote for the home rule bill, accompanied to Westminster by two nurses.[20]

Despite ongoing unionist resistance, most Leitrim nationalists saw 1914 as the year when home rule would be achieved. Addressing a home rule demonstration in Drumkeeran in January 1914, Francis Meehan told the crowd that 'the year 1914 would be a memorable one in the history of their country'.[21] At the same meeting, John O'Donel, president of the Drumkeeran AOH, was equally optimistic when he stated that 'in the year they were just entered upon, they would see the hopes and prayers of the heroes who died 'in '98, '48 and '67 realised'.[22] In May 1914, seven months after the formation of the Irish Volunteers in Dublin, the first Volunteer corps was established in Leitrim at Manorhamilton with a reported 250 men under the command of Thomas McGovern, chairman of the local district council.[23] Leitrim followed the national trend as the Irish Volunteers did not become a large body until the summer of 1914 when the IPP took effective control of the organization's executive committee.[24]

With clear support from the IPP, new Volunteer companies began to emerge throughout the county during the summer of 1914. By June large Volunteer companies were established at Carrick, Mohill, Manorhamilton and Drumshanbo with twenty-six companies in total in place countywide. At the founding meeting of the Drumshanbo company, a resolution was passed that 'we stand solidly and united behind John Redmond'.[25] In some instances, local branch meetings of the AOH and UIL facilitated the recruitment of Volunteers. Unlike in neighbouring Sligo, where the IRB was involved in the formation of the Volunteer movement, no advanced nationalist influence was evident in Leitrim, with the main driving forces coming from the ranks of both the AOH and UIL.[26] Throughout the summer of 1914 a feature of many parish sports days and agricultural shows in the county were prizes for the best turned out Volunteer unit. Several clergy, including Fr Thomas Kelly in Manorhamilton and Fr Bartle McCabe in Drumkeeran, were active in the Volunteer movement. The RIC noted the growing strength of the Volunteers and the active involvement of the Catholic clergy, reporting that members were 'very friendly with police'.[27]

Organized unionism also existed, albeit less conspicuously, alongside nationalism in Leitrim. As early as June 1912, Leitrim unionists met at Manorhamilton, where a resolution condemning the home rule bill was passed.[28] Unionist political organization in the county centred on thirteen branches of the Irish Unionist Alliance governed by two constituency executives in the north and south of the county.[29] Like their counterparts across Ireland, Leitrim's unionists were vehemently opposed to home rule. At the Manorhamilton meeting in June, Major James Crofton told the gathering that unionist opposition to Irish self-government was 'doing them (nationalists) a good turn in saving themselves from themselves'.[30] A month later south Leitrim's unionists met in Mohill and condemned the proposed home rule bill and in September 1912 a large group of Leitrim unionists attended Ulster Day celebrations at Enniskillen, where Edward Carson addressed a crowd of 30,000 unionists from the north-west.[31]

According to police reports, four branches of the UVF were established in the county, principally along the border with Cavan at Killegar and near Carrigallen. Attached to the 2nd West Cavan Battalion of the UVF, these units were present at several parades in Cavan in the summer of 1914. At least one UVF inspection took place in Leitrim at the home of Anna Godley at Carrigallen; and men from areas close to the border drilled with UVF units based in south Fermanagh.[32] Nevertheless, many Protestant clergymen, including Bishop Alfred Elliott of Kilmore, Elphin and Ardagh, and Revd Issac Coulter, dean of Kilmore, cautioned against the threat of violent protest in the campaign against home rule. At Bohey in January 1914 Coulter told a gathering of unionists that 'we in the south and west have more faith in prayer and trust in God than in the clash of arms or garments rolled in blood'.[33]

In the face of increasing unionist resistance, the spectre of civil war, and pressure from Asquith, Redmond conceded in March 1914 to the principle of temporary exclusion for Ulster counties from a Dublin parliament. The *Leitrim Observer* reflected the mood of the county's nationalists, reporting that 'keen disappointment has been felt by all who have ever took any part in the struggle for our country's rights at the meagre form of Home Rule outlined in the proposals of government'.[34]

On 25 May 1914 the third reading of the home rule bill was carried in the House of Commons, followed by the introduction of the Government of Ireland (Amendment) bill to the House of Lords in June, which provided for partition. Faced with ongoing tension and what many believed was imminent civil war, King George V took the unprecedented step of inviting all the leaders of nationalism and unionism and the British government to a conference at Buckingham Palace in late July. Within ten days of the talks, which broke down without agreement, Britain declared war on Germany on 4 August. In the two years preceding the commencement of hostilities, the political landscape in Ireland was fragile as the prospects of the very introduction of home rule, and, increasingly, the shape it would take, was unknown. With two armed militias co-existing on the island of Ireland, the European war not only prevented a potential Irish civil war, but gave Asquith a political reprieve in relation to the Irish question. The prime minister's dilemma was colourfully described by his confidante, Venetia Stanley, who likened the situation to 'cutting off one's head to get rid of a headache'.[35] The headache of the Irish question was solved by Asquith announcing the suspension of home rule until the cessation of hostilities in Europe with the additional promise of special provision for Ulster in any future settlement.

3 'People of the county unanimously in favour of the British': Leitrim and the First World War, 1914–16

Immediately following Britain's declaration of war on Germany on 4 August 1914, competing overtures of loyalty to the Empire emanated from the opposing tribes of unionism and nationalism in Ireland. Rather than uniting a nation, however, the war accentuated divisions within Irish nationalism. As this chapter will reveal, the early enthusiasm for the war soon waned in the face of mounting casualties, the prolonged nature of the conflict and the indefinite postponement of home rule. Aside from the economic gains enjoyed by the farming classes of the county, due to the increased demand for agricultural produce, a distant war had little impact on the operation of civil society in Leitrim. Nevertheless, ongoing support for the war by local political and civic leaders and the constant fear of conscription gradually turned a broadly supportive local population into a hostile one and altered Leitrim's political landscape.

Across Leitrim, the immediate effect of the war on the local population was the cancellation of cheap train excursions to Lough Derg and Bundoran. This action was initiated by the authorities because passenger trains were required to transport troops to Dublin for embarkation to England and France.[1] Almost immediately local army reservists were called up to join their regiments. These former soldiers, numbering over 30,000 across Ireland, were required to bolster the British Expeditionary Force in France.[2] At Mohill railway station, departing soldiers were cheered by family and friends, and were each given a packet of cigarettes by Duke Crofton, a retired naval officer and local landowner.[3] Similar scenes took place at Ballinamore, where the *Anglo-Celt* reported a 'hearty send-off' to a party of reservists who were also members of the local Volunteer company. As the train departed the station, 'the Reservists gave three cheers for the Irish Volunteers, home rule and Redmond'.[4]

The *Roscommon Herald* predicted that 'for Ireland, this war should mean big fortunes for the farmers who have bought out their lands'.[5] The economic potential of the war for farmers was immediately felt when George Hewson, a British army purchasing agent, visited fairs at Mohill and Carrick during the early weeks of the war to seek suitable horses.[6] According to Catriona Pennell, the early days of the war were characterized by disruption, dislocation and rising prices.[7] Shoppers at Mohill witnessed an immediate rise in the price of foodstuffs. Sugar doubled in price to 6*d.* a pound within a week and a bag of Indian meal rose from 16*s.* 3*d.* to 27*s.*[8]

The CI reported the 'people of the county unanimously in favour of the British in the war, and hope Germany may be well beaten'.[9] Local newspapers were united in their support for Britain and scathing towards perceived German aggression in Belgium. The *Leitrim Advertiser* suggested that Germany's perception of an imminent civil war in Ireland 'may have led her into the belief that our power for effective intervention would be paralysed. If so, that miscalculation may prove a costly one'.[10]

Almost immediately following the outbreak of hostilities, both Redmond and Carson competed in their overtures of support for Britain's war effort. The war was seen by Redmond and his supporters as an opportunity to display the loyalty of nationalist Ireland to the British Empire in their quest for home rule. They saw the Irish Volunteers as defenders of the island of Ireland which would afford regular British troops based in Ireland the opportunity to fight in Europe. Redmond believed that such a force would also aid recruitment to the British army, where 'the military spirit would rapidly develop amongst them, and volunteers for Foreign Service would speedily become numerous from their ranks'.[11] At Carrigallen in mid-August 1914, Patrick Briody, the local UIL stalwart and Volunteer leader, told the local Volunteers that their training was in order to defend Ireland and that 'no man was asked to go out and fight the Germans who did not wish to do so'.[12]

By September 1914 Redmond's initial offering of a home defence role for the Irish Volunteers had extended to endorsing recruitment and full support for Britain on the battlefields of Europe. Redmond's address to Irish Volunteers at Woodenbridge, County Wicklow, on 20 September 1914, calling on them to go 'wherever the firing line extends', was a demonstration of loyalty in return for Asquith's support for home rule. Following Redmond's Woodenbridge speech, the temporary arrangement whereby the Volunteer movement held together different shades of nationalism began to disintegrate. The majority of the movement backed Redmond and became known as the Irish National Volunteers, while a small minority led by Eoin MacNeill retained the name Irish Volunteers.

Like many other areas of nationalist Ireland, there was no shortage of celebration in Leitrim with the official placement of the home rule bill on the statute book of the House of Commons on 18 September 1914. At Mohill, bonfires were lit and the Irish Volunteers marched through the town.[13] At a public meeting in Manorhamilton, Councillor J.P. McGuinness declared that after seeking independence for 114 years, 'the struggle is ended and victory is ours'.[14] The *Leitrim Observer* was more circumspect in its comments on the home rule bill, observing that 'so we have got home rule at last, or in other words, a bill for the promotion of recruiting for the English army in Ireland'.[15]

Not unlike their unionist opponents in Ulster, Redmond and his supporters endeavoured to adapt to a mixture of paramilitary and parliamentary politics. Arming the Volunteers was tactical and initially seen as a continuation of the home rule struggle by other means.[16] By October 1914, the *Leitrim Observer* advised Volunteers that if they enlisted they needed to be 'firmly resolved to fight for their freedom at home, and preserve the home rule bill from further mutilation, as [sic] if we can silence the German guns, we can certainly silence the Belfast corner-boys, and no matter how the war ends, we must have home rule'.[17]

At a joint AOH/UIL meeting at Carrigallen in October 1914, Patrick Briody told the assembled crowd that the purpose of the Volunteers was to 'defend our shores from invasion'.[18] While reluctant to support actively recruitment, the meeting condemned in the strongest possible terms the action of 'the self-constituted Committee of Dublin factionalists who tried to introduce again their Hungarian policy by issuing a mischievous manifesto to the National Volunteers'.[19] Similar sentiments were expressed by Myles McKenna, president of Drumkeeran UIL, who condemned MacNeill's breakaway faction and pledged the branch's 'whole hearted and undivided support to Mr John Redmond and the IPP in the reorganization of the Volunteers and the regeneration of our country'.[20] Despite such rhetoric, Volunteer activity declined both nationally and locally due to fear of conscription. Nevertheless, Leitrim was unequivocal in its support for Redmond with no evidence of any separatist faction of significance emerging. Of the 4,216 members in forty-one Volunteer companies in the county, only 95 members in Leitrim backed MacNeill.[21]

While emigration from poorer areas of the west of Ireland was a common feature of rural life, the process was accelerated in early October by rumours of impending conscription. The *Roscommon Herald* stated that 'the scare of the Ballot Act is said to have something to do with the exodus'.[22] The *Longford Leader* reported that

> hundreds of young men in Leitrim, Longford and Roscommon at once rushed to the emigration offices to book passages for America. All this week the trains were crowded with these timorous and deluded people rushing from a land in which they have plenty of work and food to a country where there is at present wholesale starvation for want of employment.[23]

The *Leitrim Advertiser* accused the emigrants of cowardice and of leaving 'their old mothers at home to fight the Germans if they came to invade Ireland. Shame on them'.[24] Although less scathing than its rival, the *Leitrim Observer* remarked that

> every sailing day draws numbers of the young men from Leitrim County and if the tide continues very few will be left. It appears the

> country people dread forced service and are flying before it overtakes them. It's a pity an amicable arrangement can't be made to keep a couple of German cruisers in the Atlantic.[25]

Unlike continental European armies, Britain had to rely on voluntary enlistment until the introduction of conscription in January 1916. Nevertheless, while many men in Britain and Ireland were not swept away by wartime enthusiasm, the issue of family welfare encouraged many to enlist. The announcement in late August 1914 that separation allowances would be paid to the dependant relatives of enlistees prompted many from towns and cities to join the colours. In Leitrim by September 1914, the local branch of the Soldiers' and Sailors' Families Association was financially supporting twenty-four families of enlisted men pending the payment of separation allowances. The wife and family of Patrick McGee, a soldier from Carrick, were forced to apply for Poor Law relief from the local board of guardians before a separation allowance of 11s. 10d. per week due to them was received from the War Office.[26]

While backing the war, the *Leitrim Observer* reported that public opinion was still divided and noted

> it's too bad that now when our people were beginning to realise the efforts of forty years of land agitation, and trying to enjoy some of the benefits which have been won by their sacrifices alone, that they should now be called on to give their life in a quarrel which is not of their making.[27]

A letter writer to the newspaper in September 1914 questioned the availability of the RIC for enlistment and asked: 'are the Government so silly as to think that our Irish boys will fight their battles, when you have a body, well fed and trained, having an easy time, while Tommy is having a hot time at the Front?'[28]

The *Leitrim Advertiser* lent unstinting and unquestioned loyalty to the war effort. From the commencement of hostilities, it consistently supported the calls for voluntary recruitment. With increasing demands for more recruits in autumn 1914, the newspaper's editorials exhorted men to join the army by asking: 'would not Irishmen be unworthy of the name of their liberty loving traditions if they did not take their share in the hazards of battle for the empire, particularly so that Ireland will shortly take her place as the newest of the federated self-governing colonies?'[29]

Calls for young men in Leitrim to enlist were answered in the early months of the war. By November 1914 over fifty from Mohill had joined the army, the majority of them were Volunteers, including three drill instructors.[30] Throughout Leitrim, Volunteer corps were still drilling and parading but not in the same large numbers that had been previously reported by police.[31] In late September 1914 Thomas Smyth, MP, received a consignment of fifty rifles for distribution among National Volunteers. Columns of Mohill Volunteers marched through the town with their new rifles. The *Leitrim Advertiser* reported that the Volunteers cheered for Smyth and home rule and 'the men presented a fine military appearance, and some of them wished to get at the Germans'.[32] Similar scenes were witnessed at Manorhamilton, where seventy-five men had enlisted from the town by October 1914. Thus, as elsewhere in Ireland, the response in Leitrim to the outbreak of war was one of 'naïve enthusiasm for war that now seems almost incomprehensible'.[33]

The highest numbers of voluntary enlistees in Ireland were recorded between August 1914 and February 1916. In this period over 95,000 enlisted, compared to only a little in excess of 45,000 for the remainder of the war when conscription was in force in Britain.[34] By the autumn of 1914 the tragic consequences of war began to appear in local newspapers with stories of dead and wounded local men. Parke Dobson of the Royal Munster Fusiliers was the first man from Mohill reported killed in October 1914.[35] By December 1914 ten Mohill men had died in the conflict.[36] During the same period Manorhamilton lost five men and Leitrim's total of war dead reached twenty-six.[37] While nearly 250 men had enlisted by December 1915, figures decreased dramatically in the early months of 1916. By October 1916 only 522 men had been recruited from the county, resulting in Leitrim having the lowest number of men, relative to total population, enlisting in Ireland.[38]

While the IPP was officially endorsing army recruitment, its local party machine was less inclined to follow the party leader's stance. The pre-Woodenbridge positioning of the Irish Volunteers as defenders of Ireland's shores was a constant theme of nationalist political meetings. At a joint AOH/UIL meeting in October 1914 at Manorhamilton, both Meehan and Smyth denied claims that Redmond was a recruiting officer for the British army. The meeting heard that the sole purpose of the Volunteers was to 'defend our shores from invasion'.[39] While both men emphasized home defence, they did not hesitate in condemning the young men of the locality who had left Ireland for fear of conscription.[40]

Although large numbers chose to support Redmond by joining the newly established National Volunteers, the organization's activities and active participants declined at a rapid rate. The intransigence of the War Office in not facilitating Redmond's requests for a territorial army, a prolonged war, increasing casualties and fear of conscription were major factors in the demise of the National Volunteers.[41] At the end of December 1914 the body boasted 156,750 members, but less than twelve months later, it was reported that the 'movement is practically dead in this country'.[42] Leitrim followed the national trend. In January 1915 the *Leitrim Observer* reported the observations of their Jamestown correspondent 'on the alleged depletion in the ranks and the absence of drills which he states are sad features of Carrick-on-Shannon, Gowel and other Corps of the Irish National Volunteers'.[43] A consistent theme of the CI's monthly reports during 1915 was the ongoing depletion of the National Volunteers. Branches were reported to have collapsed across the county in areas such as Gortlettragh, Gorvagh, Newbridge, Bornacoola, Drumreilly, and, most notably, in Carrick. The RIC attributed the collapse to fear of conscription. In January 1915, police noted that there were thirty branches with 3,011 members in the county, but by the end of 1915 only eighteen branches with a nominal membership of 1,747 were still in place.[44] The lack of activity in Leitrim was best reflected when Thomas Smyth returned thirty Mauser rifles in March 1915 to John D. Nugent, AOH national secretary, in Dublin.[45] Although the IPP officially endorsed Redmond's Woodenbridge speech, the majority of IPP MPs did not encourage recruitment.[46] Large elements of the party were divided on the issue of recruitment, with the grassroots more reserved than the Redmondite leadership.[47] In an editorial comment, the *Leitrim Observer* suggested that Asquith 'wants hundreds of thousands of Irishmen to die fighting for England in return for his home rule bill'.[48]

The first attempts at recruitment in Leitrim took place in late August 1914 when a recruiting sergeant visited Mohill, where a 'good many recruits offered themselves for service'.[49] While there was no national or county-wide strategy to encourage recruitment until 1915, all the institutions of state were utilized, albeit in an ad hoc manner, to encourage enlistment. Unlike in Britain, where a parliamentary committee was responsible for recruitment, the army was initially tasked with the promotion of recruitment in Ireland. One of its first actions was the appointment of recruiting officers for each region. James Murphy, a retired army officer, was appointed with the rank of major with responsibility for recruitment in the counties of Roscommon, Sligo and Leitrim. Another Leitrim former soldier, John O'Donel, a member of both the AOH and Leitrim County Council, was commissioned as an officer in the South Irish Horse Regiment and appointed as a recruiting officer for Leitrim. Although no public meetings to promote recruitment took place through the autumn and winter months of 1914, O'Donel used local newspapers to admonish reluctant potential enlistees. In a letter to the *Leitrim Advertiser* in December 1914, he wrote: 'Oh shame on those who are fit to join and don't do so at once; and remember that this was a war that was forced on us and must be fought to a finish, for our freedom depends on its result'.[50] Supporting O'Donel's 'patriotic letter', Captain Duke Crofton from Mohill, an ardent promoter of recruitment and member of the local gentry, noted the difficulties of recruiting in a rural area with high emigration, observing that 'this dearth of young Irishmen in rural places is only too visible in the harvest season of the year, when labour is scarce'.[51]

Leitrim's first public meeting to promote recruitment was held at Dromahair on 19 January 1915. A broad range of speakers, including Thomas Fallon and Francis Meehan, called for young men to enlist in the fight against 'German barbarism'. Local Church of Ireland rector, Dean Coulter, reminded the large crowd that despite political differences between nationalism and unionism, when it came to the defence of their country all Irishmen were united. Coulter observed that 'if 50,000 Germans landed at Galway, Donegal or Rosses Point, they could march to Dublin in a few days and would level all their churches and cathedrals, caring not whether they were Catholic or Protestant'. Meehan told the assembled crowd that all classes and creeds were now united with a common purpose to defeat Germany. Supporting him, Thomas Fallon, chairman of Leitrim County Council, declared that men were needed 'to assist in the great struggle that was going on in Belgium and France. They (Irishmen) had a duty to perform in this crisis'.[52] Unlike many of their IPP colleagues, both Meehan and Smyth endorsed recruitment at public meetings across the county.[53]

While clerics from Protestant denominations played a key role in backing the war effort, the police reported that 'the bishops and senior clergy of the Roman Catholic Church are loyal to Great Britain in [the] present war'.[54] In early 1915, in his attempts to aid recruitment, Bishop Bernard Coyne of Elphin temporarily donated his car to the military to convey recruits to Boyle from parts of Roscommon and Leitrim.[55] Clergymen such as Canon Thomas O'Reilly of Carrick were also active in recruiting campaigns; one of O'Reilly's curates, Fr Patrick Clancy, joined the army in March 1916. Clancy, who previously served in Drumshanbo, was presented with a purse of sovereigns by the people of that town before leaving for France.[56] Although Clancy was the only Leitrim-based priest to volunteer, the police reported few instances of clerical opposition to the war.[57]

The establishment of the Central Council for the Organisation of Recruiting in Ireland (CCORI) in April 1915 was an attempt to assist local committees to co-ordinate recruitment drives. The presence of local dignitaries on recruiting platforms suggested that 'little official encouragement was needed for men of influence to wholeheartedly assist recruiting'.[58] The provision of speakers and travelling recruiting officers was a further attempt to stimulate recruitment among the local population. With no permanent army barracks located in the county, recruitment strategies under the aegis of CCORI consisted of public meetings attended by MPs, public representatives, military personnel and other prominent locals. Recruiters were often accompanied by a military band, and, on occasion, by local soldiers serving in various regiments. The defence of small nations and alleged German atrocities against women, children and members of religious orders were recurrent themes on recruiting platforms.[59]

Meetings like those at Ballinamore and Mohill in April 1915 coincided with fair days, which helped attract large crowds. At Ballinamore on 6 April a well-attended recruitment meeting was supplemented by the pipers band of the Royal Irish Regiment which played Irish national airs and marches throughout the day. Despite a large crowd, Thomas Fallon observed that he did not 'see the same fire in men's eyes that might be in them just now'. He told those assembled to 'remember it is not at home that we ought to get our politics from an odd Sinn Féiner at the corners, but we all should go into the fray with open arms, and say we will fight if wanted'.[60] Local MP Thomas Smyth told the meeting that while Leitrim had played its part, men who could not enlist should join the National Volunteers. Women were urged to aid voluntary associations and encourage their menfolk to enlist.[61] Calling for support for the British army who were said to have been fighting for 'justice and rights', Meehan referred to the 'Curragh Mutiny', where British officers refused to confront unionist resistance in Ulster in 1914. Meehan recalled the actions of the British officers claiming that 'up to this we never had a reliable British army. It was rotten to the core'.[62] His comments were met with a swift public retort from Major Murphy, a fellow speaker.[63]

At a recruitment meeting in Mohill on 22 April 1915, Smyth reminded the crowd that a German victory in the war would result in Ireland witnessing the same atrocities that Belgium had suffered. He asked men who were undecided about enlisting to join the National Volunteers in order to 'defend their own country on their own shores if necessary'. Appealing to all sections of the population, Smyth advised that aged farmers would be doing their duty 'as well as if they went to the front' by increasing tillage on their land.[64] Meehan claimed that 117 men had enlisted from his home town of Manorhamilton and urged men of military age to

> take pattern and join that great body – The Irish Brigade – drill and become equipped and fight for our country in such a noble cause. I hope now young men you will do what your leaders have spoken to you about and when the time comes Leitrim will not be last on the list in connection with the war.[65]

At a recruitment meeting at Manorhamilton on 8 May 1915 Meehan told the crowd that the recent sinking of the passenger liner *Lusitania* off the Irish coast, on which two Manorhamilton natives lost their lives, demonstrated how near the Germans were to Ireland. Speakers called on the young men of Manorhamilton to join Irish regiments in the army and 'assist in crushing despotic German militarism forever'.[66] Recruiting officer Major Murphy warned the crowd that in the event of not enough voluntary recruits enlisting, 'as sure as God was in Heaven above there would be conscription if they did not get the men without it'.[67] Similar warnings were echoed in neighbouring Cavan, where recruitment was also low. By September 1915 the Cavan CI delivered an obvious forewarning of conscription by declaring that 'the young men of this county will not go until they are brought'.[68]

Despite the calls from local MPs and a broad range of local notables, recruitment was slow and sporadic, especially from rural areas.[69] At a recruitment meeting in Manorhamilton in June 1915, Captain Cheevers of the Connaught Rangers asserted that in addition to farmers, there were men who 'were members of the "scissors brigade", men who stand from morning to night behind the counter doing work at which women could be better employed'.[70] All levels of the judiciary and the judicial system lent their support to recruitment. At the spring assizes of 1915 a resolution of the grand jury was passed declaring that 'we fully and cordially appreciate the action of those young men in our county who have joined the forces, and hope their patriotic action will be still more largely followed'.[71] The petty sessions were utilized in a variety of guises to promote the war and to provide men for enlistment. In his capacity as a local magistrate at the Manorhamilton petty sessions, O'Donel commented on the large number of assault cases before the court, stating that 'if they wanted fighting and they went to him he would send them where there was plenty of fighting to be done'.[72] When postman Patrick McDaid was charged with stealing two postal orders, valued at 15s. each, Judge Brown at Carrick quarter sessions bound the defendant to the peace for two years as it was his intention to join the army.[73] Before discharging McDaid, the judge commented: 'I think you may congratulate yourself that you are not in prison garb. When you have undertaken to help your King and country, there is no reason why you may not get a medal for distinguished conduct and so retrieve your character, which to a certain extent has suffered'.[74] The police were also occasionally singled out as suitable recruits by resentful locals. At Mohill petty sessions when local man Patrick Woods was convicted of having no light on his cart, he charged the court to 'look at all the fine police we have here in this peaceable country with nothing else to do but this work – that old women could do – instead of being out now fighting the Germans'.[75]

A fair day meeting at Manorhamilton in September 1915 was unique as it was the first where heckling could be heard. Comments about having the harvest to save and 'put home rule in operation and you will get twenty recruits' came from the assembled crowd.[76] In general, such scenes were uncommon, and, aside from some minor heckling on the non-implementation of home rule, there was no apparent hostility towards recruitment touring parties. The *Leitrim Observer* reported that O'Donel was very popular and was received well locally, despite at first being met 'with a little opposition from a few insignificant Sinn Féiners'.[77]

Throughout 1915 various national and local initiatives were undertaken to increase recruitment. In June 1915 Leitrim County Council established a recruitment committee; its objective, according to Councillor James Kiernan, was 'simply to get as many voluntary recruits as possible', while insisting that conscription would not be introduced.[78] In response to declining recruitment levels from 6,000 per month in March 1915 to 2,000 per month in September 1915, CCORI was replaced in the autumn of 1915 by the Department of Recruiting for Ireland (DRI), headed by Lord Wimborne, the lord lieutenant.[79] According to John Osborne, the reason for the policy change was that 'emotion was no longer productive and that modern warfare demanded modern organization'.[80] Part of Wimborne's new recruitment strategy in October 1915 was a direct postal campaign to men of military age. These letters reportedly caused 'a considerable stir among the people and it is thought a good many of the farming class liable for military service will emigrate to America'.[81]

The next phase of the DRI's campaign to bolster recruitment was the organization of a nationwide tour in late 1915 for war hero and Victoria Cross holder, Lieutenant Michael O'Leary. Accompanied by the band of the 4th Battalion of the Connaught Rangers and a group of recruiting officers, O'Leary visited Leitrim in November 1915. Welcoming him to Carrick, Thomas Fallon declared that the visit was 'an honour conferred on the county'.[82] At Mohill on 18 November O'Leary claimed that in answering the call for recruitment 'the cities have done well, but the farmers' sons had not', and that soon 'we will have to raise a battalion of women to defend Ireland'.[83] Referring to the death of local man, Bernard Reynolds, a member of the Connaught Rangers, Major Murphy told the crowd that 'it was a most glorious death and that in dying for his country, the name of Reynolds will be memorable in Mohill for years to come'.[84] Several days later at Manorhamilton, O'Leary pleaded with the crowd to 'give us the men and we will do the work'. Murphy told the meeting that there would be no conscription 'as long as the Allies got sufficient support from the country'.[85] For many farmers, the war brought major economic benefits with the demand for agricultural produce in wartime Britain. Such a situation meant that men from farming families were discouraged from enlisting owing to the negative impact this would have on communal farm income.[86] Despite travelling to every major town in the county, O'Leary's tour was not a success. The RIC reported that 'some recruits were obtained but not many. Farmers' sons are still slow at joining'.[87]

The failure of the tour was raised at Westminster by Laurence Ginnell, dissident Nationalist MP for Westmeath. He enquired about the cost of the tour, consisting of twenty-four men and officers of the Connaught Rangers, and seven touring cars, and the reason for its failure. Harold Tennant, the undersecretary for war, did not provide costings and claimed that he could not explain the low numbers of men enlisting without 'a more intimate acquaintance with the psychology of the inhabitants'.[88] Criticizing Ginnell, Meehan observed that his parliamentary colleague was being manipulated by 'a small section of Sinn Féiners who have made a catspaw of my honourable friend for the purpose of retarding recruitment in the county'.[89] Ginnell, a fervent critic of recruiting, had earlier posed a parliamentary question in relation to the activities of John O'Donel while recruiting in the county. He asked if the War Office would take responsibility for O'Donel's 'scandalous conduct', whereby he danced in the public street with 'drunken women of ill repute, who were fined at the following petty sessions for drunkenness'.[90]

Despite meetings, countywide tours and an extensive advertising and poster campaign, recruitment numbers did not increase substantially. By December 1915 only 238 men from Leitrim had enlisted.[91] As a result of the low levels of voluntary recruitment, the question of conscription was being discussed during the autumn of 1915 and early 1916. Locally, elected members of councils followed the position of their national leaders by opposing the principle of conscription yet continuously encouraging army recruitment. Thomas Fallon, chairman of Leitrim County Council and an ardent supporter of the recruitment cause, declared that the council was 'all in favour of recruiting, but not in favour of conscription'.[92] At the Carrick board of guardians, UIL stalwart Patrick Flynn described conscription as 'disastrous to the interests of the Empire and Ireland'.[93]

In March 1916, following the introduction of conscription in Britain, Redmond invited MPs to attend a conference to promote recruitment in Ireland. Corresponding with Redmond, Westport-based William Doris, MP for Mayo, outlined the dilemma for many in the IPP, stating that 'as to this western part of the county, I fear we have very little chance of getting recruits, and the calling of public meetings for the purpose would only show our weakness in this respect'.[94] Unlike many of their IPP parliamentary colleagues, Leitrim's two MPs were active in recruitment campaigns throughout the county. At a local level in Leitrim, owing to the failure of the county council's recruitment committee to increase enlistment, a meeting chaired by Canon O'Reilly to establish a wider countywide forum took place in Carrick-on-Shannon in March 1916. The members present included the two local MPs, the military, the RIC, the AOH and UIL, together with a broad representation of the county's middle classes. The meeting appointed Fallon as director of recruiting for the county.[95] A strategy was developed that included the establishment of fifteen committees for each town and district, and the formation of a recruiting officer in every large town. Addressing the meeting, Captain Kelly praised the recruitment work of the two local MPs who 'had done much for the cause of recruiting when it was not fashionable to do so'.[96] The Easter Rising a month later and the suspension of army recruitment tours ended this new initiative.

The dynamics of Ireland's social class structure were reflected in the activities of many communities when sending men to war. Stories of Leitrim's middle-class men being feted by their peers prior to their departure to the front received widespread newspaper coverage. Gifts were presented, suppers served and speeches made praising men who were prepared to serve their king and country. The *Leitrim Observer* praised Thomas Gordon, a veterinary surgeon from Mohill, for 'sacrificing a large and lucrative practice' by choosing to volunteer. Before travelling to England for training, Gordon received a gold wristwatch from Edward Geelan, clerk of Mohill guardians, at a farewell supper in Kelly's Hotel.[97] Similarly, F.R.S. Peters, a cashier at Mohill's Northern Bank, was presented with a purse of sovereigns and a silver cigarette case prior to his departure.[98]

With over 300 Irish medical doctors holding an officer commission in the Royal Army Medical Corps at the turn of the twentieth century, it was no surprise that the medical profession responded favourably to the call for recruits at the outbreak of hostilities.[99] Three Leitrim doctors – Charles Pentland from Mohill, and Samuel Armstrong and P.J. Rooney from Manorhamilton – volunteered. Before leaving Mohill, Pentland was presented with a gold watch, a sword, a gold ring and a service revolver from a variety of local friends, including those in the Masonic Lodge and local RIC, for 'his noble action'.[100] The *Fermanagh Herald* reported that two prominent north Leitrim men – J.P. McGuinness, a district councillor for Manorhamilton, and P.J. McGoey from Glenade – were enlisting. At a farewell supper in the Commercial Hotel, 'speeches were delivered by several prominent citizens who wished both gentlemen every success'. McGuinness claimed 'he came to the conclusion that he was not doing his duty by remaining at home'.[101] The question of social class was also identified by CCORI as hindering recruitment from the farming and commercial strata of Ireland. The committee observed that 'we are satisfied that a much larger number of recruits could be obtained from the classes named were it not for their reluctance to enter upon their training with recruits from the labouring classes. This class prejudice is probably much more pronounced in Ireland that elsewhere in the United Kingdom'.[102]

As in other regions, enlistment in the army was concentrated in Leitrim's major towns with only small numbers joining from rural areas.[103] Reporting on the 117 men from Manorhamilton who enlisted, the *Sligo Champion* noted that 'from the return shown, this is the largest percentage of men who joined the colours from any town of the size and population of Manorhamilton in the United Kingdom'.[104] Unlike many of their farming neighbours, men in rural towns did not benefit from the fruits of a booming agricultural economy. For many of Leitrim's town dwellers, poverty was often the greater motivating factor for enlistment.[105]

The predominance of men in the army from towns and villages, as opposed to rural areas, is reflected in the absent voters' register of October 1918.[106] Of eighty-nine men on the list from the Carrick area, only nineteen were from rural districts, and only three of the nineteen were farmers' sons. Similar patterns emerge in Mohill, with thirty-five of fifty-three soldiers from the town, and Ballinamore, with less than a third of the thirty-one men from rural areas. Manorhamilton was the only district where nearly equal numbers enlisted from the local town and surrounding rural areas.[107]

Although the question of military mobilization remained to the fore, the period also witnessed the growth of voluntary associations supporting the war effort. The scale of this mobilization of civil society was unprecedented. Thousands of non-combatant civilians, mainly women, contributed in a broad variety of ways to aid frontline troops and refugees. Across Ireland, a number of initiatives, ranging from refugee aid to providing tobacco for soldiers, emerged with the formation of local war support committees. Within weeks of the declaration of war, several comfort and relief funds were set up in Leitrim. A Red Cross Society was established in Mohill by Amy Crofton, daughter of Duke Crofton, a local landlord and magistrate. At a meeting in the Church of Ireland Hunt hall, Miss Crofton called for support, stating 'I believe that men of all classes whose duties keep them at home and who cannot sew, will be glad to help by contributions however small, towards the cost of the necessary materials which we women will gladly make up into garments'.[108]

From the beginning of the war, financial appeals to aid soldiers and their families were a regular feature in the local press. Support for the Prince of Wales Relief Fund organized by Leitrim's County Lieutenant Harlech was requested by the *Leitrim Advertiser*, which reported that 'the appeal is a very deserving one, and one which we are sure will meet with a generous response from all creeds and classes in Co. Leitrim'.[109] Funds established to aid the relief of Belgian refugees attracted most public support. A collection by Miss Evelyn Notley for the Belgian Relief Fund received over £24 – with contributions ranging from £1 by Revd Geraghty to numerous 6d. contributions from members of the general public.[110] As with most charitable activities, it was the socially advantaged members of Leitrim's upper-middle classes who were primarily involved in assisting Belgian refugees.[111] Upper- and middle-class women were actively involved in charitable war work in Leitrim. These were largely from the families of the landed gentry and professional classes, and were predominantly members of the Church of Ireland, Presbyterian or Methodist communities. Praising a group of

Manorhamilton women, led by his wife, who knitted socks for Indian soldiers, Francis Meehan claimed that the gesture 'showed how broadminded the people of Manorhamilton were'.[112]

The support of Patrick Finegan, the Catholic bishop of Kilmore, for Belgian relief funds also contributed to the success of public appeals.[113] Leitrim, like other counties in Ireland, provided housing and job opportunities for some of the 3,000 Belgian refugees who arrived in Ireland during the early autumn of 1914. By February 1915 Leitrim County Council had established a Belgian Relief Committee to co-ordinate the work of local committees across the county. The purpose of the committees was to aid the Belgian people who were 'ruthlessly driven from their once happy homes by an implacable and ruthless enemy, who is our enemy also'.[114] Two Belgian families arrived at Ballinamore in May 1915 and were provided with housing and employment at the nearby Arigna mines.[115]

Despite having no hospital, ambulance, or nursing presence in the county, the Red Cross was one of the few charities that received continued support throughout the course of the conflict. A countywide committee was established with Captain Duke Crofton from Mohill acting as county director. At Carrick town hall on 16 September 1914, the local Red Cross held a fundraising dance at which 'all the business people of the town were actively associated with the movement, and did their utmost to make it the success that it was'.[116] Elsie Allen, daughter of Richard Allen, Leitrim's Crown clerk, reported in December 1914 that the £32 7s. 10d. collected had enabled her 'to find materials sufficient to make 372 garments and comforts'.[117] At Manorhamilton a concert to aid the Red Cross ambulance fund in November 1915 was so well attended that many had to be turned away.[118] The popularity of the Red Cross cause was again demonstrated on 21 January 1916 at Leitrim village, where George Peyton, the local Church of Ireland vicar, organized 'one of the best and most successful concerts held for many years'.[119] Despite the changing political environment following the Easter Rising, the Red Cross collected over £534 in Leitrim during its 1917 annual collection, the highest amount in Connacht outside of Galway.[120] The British Red Cross recognized the broad support base that the organization had across Ireland, reporting that 'contributions from Ireland represent all social grades of the people, and all religious denominations'.[121]

Despite many women entering employment in wartime industries in urban areas of Britain and Ireland, in rural Ireland, a woman's role remained that of wife and mother, who were economically dependent on their menfolk. The expansion of employment opportunities for women in rural Ireland was not as dramatic due to the absence of conscription, with traditional patterns of female employment remaining close to pre-war levels.[122] While speakers on recruiting platforms and army recruitment newspaper advertisements requested that 'women of Ireland, do your duty' and influence loved ones to enlist, traditional societal roles for women remained broadly intact.[123] In an effort to increase enlistment John O'Donel advocated the boycotting of businesses employing young men at work that could be undertaken by women.[124] Similar sentiments were expressed at a recruitment meeting at Mohill in November 1915, where Colonel Harrison of the Connaught Rangers criticized young male shop assistants for not doing their duty, declaring that 'there are thousands of women in Ireland who are capable of doing that sort of work'.[125]

Following the introduction of separation allowances in 1914 to support soldiers' dependants, many working-class women received a regular income for the first time in their lives. In Britain and Ireland the independence that this income permitted raised some concerns when 'separation women' appeared before the courts on drunkenness and public order offences. In a period of danger associated with war, the importance of being good wartime mothers was reinforced by propaganda emphasizing the role of motherhood in support of the war effort. Any transgressions of appropriate behaviour were met with widespread disapproval and condemnation.[126] In June 1915 three 'separation women' in Leitrim, Brigid Woods, her daughter Kathleen, and Mary McDonagh, were fined 3s. and costs at Mohill petty sessions for public disorder and drunkenness. The court heard that all three women were drunk and 'abusing each other and using very bad language'.[127] Increasing instances of drunkenness by 'separation women' resulted in the issuing of a circular to resident magistrates threatening the withdrawal of the allowance for repeat offenders.[128] Fining Eliza Manning, Mary Manning and Jane Conboy 2s. 6d. and costs for public drunkenness, local magistrate Captain Duke Crofton admonished the women: 'it is a shame to you behaving like this, drinking your separation allowance while your husbands are away fighting for their country'.[129] After convicting both Mary Foley and Ellen Quinn of being drunk and disorderly in Mohill in May 1916, Crofton issued warnings that separation allowances would be stopped if the women persisted in such conduct.[130]

Across Britain and Ireland the experiences of war varied considerably in both urban and rural communities. Within days of the declaration of war in August 1914 a raft of legislation, including the Aliens Restriction Act, the Defence of the Realm Act, and the British Nationality and Status of Aliens Act, was passed. A demand to intern all 'alien' males of military age surfaced regularly during the war. Among the 'secret enemies in our midst' identified by July 1915 were Germans, syndicalists and the papacy. Fear of a German invasion and an obsession with spies became common during the early months of the war. In Dublin crowds attacked and boycotted a number of German business premises.[131] Within weeks of the commencement of hostilities, two strangers were arrested at Tarmonbarry in Longford, close to the

Leitrim border, on suspicion of being German spies who 'had some evil design on the bridge over the Shannon at the village'. On further investigation, it was discovered that the 'spies' were travelling Russian salesmen.[132] The fear that enemies could be living in the region prompted O'Donel to propose a motion at Leitrim County Council on 27 October 1914 that the government 'give immediate direction to the RIC to detain all Austrians and Germans whether nationalised or not', as they were 'a menace to the Allies and a danger in our district'.[133] In October 1914 the sound of distant artillery gunfire alarmed the population of Carrick who feared imminent invasion. Assuaging the fears of locals, the *Leitrim Observer* reported the source to be a naval training exercise in Clew Bay.[134] Further fears of invasion emerged at Mohill on 21 October 1914 when residents believed that a German airship was hovering above the local railway station. The *Roscommon Herald* later reported that the object was in fact 'a kite which some wags put up for the purpose of surprising some of the townspeople who are in the advanced stages on the war scare, and it was rendered the more conspicuous by two lights being attached'.[135]

At Carrick petty sessions in March 1915, the prosecution and subsequent discharge of William Winter under the Registration of Aliens Act caused a minor sensation in the local press. Winter, a German national and motor mechanic, was employed by Patrick Flynn, a local businessman and UIL leader. In presenting evidence, DI Hussey claimed that Winter 'belongs to that accursed race, and steps should be taken to have them put out of the Kingdom'.[136] Several weeks later Winter was before the courts again on a charge of being in possession of a motor car in Carrick on 5 March 1915. The DI told the court that a German chauffeur could 'do as he wished with a car when in possession of the wheel and do infinite damage blowing up bridges'.[137] The case against Winter was dismissed, although many of his fellow countrymen residing in Ireland were held in jails and internment camps at Arbour Hill in Dublin, Templemore, County Tipperary, and Oldcastle, County Meath.[138]

Whereas the war had a major political impact on nationalist Ireland, its social and economic effects were quite limited in most rural areas. As large towns and cities initially suffered from severe unemployment, Ireland's rural economy prospered during the war due to the British demand for agricultural goods. While some commodities such as bread and alcohol became scarcer and more expensive during the war, the state intervened by introducing price controls and rationing. At Carrick Union, the introduction of margarine to the local workhouse was approved in October 1915 at a saving of 30*s*. a week because, according to Councillor Patrick Flynn, 'the price of butter is gone out of all reason at 1*s*. 6*d*. per lb'.[139] Although the *Leitrim Observer* reported in December 1916 that 'a great scarcity of flour, butter and salt exists in

Carrick and the surrounding districts', the county did not suffer from serious food shortages at any time during the war.[140] In its Christmas message of 1916, the *Leitrim Advertiser* reported a dull festive season marked by 'slackness in business' as a result of 'a scarcity and dearness of many items'.[141] Although food prices rose and the fear of famine escalated in Ireland, there were never any serious food shortages in rural areas.[142] Neither was there an issue with the supply of clothing. Advertisements for various assortments of clothing items appeared continuously throughout the war. In preparation for the 1914 Christmas market, Manorhamilton draper John McGuinness advertised 'the largest consignment of drapery goods ever landed in Manorhamilton'.[143] However, alcohol remained in scarce supply throughout the war with the police reporting declining levels of drunkenness, 'owing to high prices for liquor, and scarcity of same'.[144]

As war raged on mainland Europe, Leitrim's countryside remained peaceful. Crime was confined to a range of minor offences. Among the list of cases before Carrick petty sessions in January 1915 were malicious damage to a sire goat, the sentencing of a tramp to one month's hard labour for abusive language and damage to property, and several cases of locals fined for having no lights on their carts. One defendant, Patrick Heslin, pleaded in defence of having no light, that he was delayed because 'it was a very slow donkey I had that day, in fact I had to drag him part of the way'.[145] In his report to Lord Justice Rowan, the CI reported that 'there is no boycotting, no one getting protection, and the condition of the county is satisfactory'.[146] Only one man, James Kerrigan, was prosecuted under the Defence of the Realm Act (DORA) in August 1915 when he was fined £1 at Manorhamilton petty sessions for interrupting a recruiting meeting in the town 'in a manner calculated to prejudice the appeal for recruits'.[147]

At the outbreak of hostilities, strict censorship laws, focusing primarily on newspaper coverage and postal correspondence, were enacted to control the flow of information through society. Only on one occasion, in December 1916, did a Leitrim newspaper attract the attention of the censor. In correspondence with the editor of the *Leitrim Observer*, the censor advised the newspaper not to insert the names of individual sailing ships in travel advertisements 'in order that the enemy may not be aware what ships are sailing'.[148] Equally, only one Leitrim native, 'John McDermott' (Seán Mac Diarmada), attracted any significant attention from the authorities in the pre-Rising period. His Dublin home at 15 Russell Avenue, Drumcondra, was subjected to ongoing police surveillance and postal censorship. By January 1915 the authorities temporarily ceased the postal censorship of Mac Diarmada's home, and that of his fellow IRB colleague, Thomas J. Clarke, because, according to police, 'evidently these use other addresses, or receive correspondence indirectly fearing censorship'.[149]

Across Britain and Ireland, organized sport was a casuality of war because of the curtailment of fixtures, transport difficulties and men enlisting in the army.[150] In 1915 Drumshanbo GAA club reported that 'many of our members are serving in Kitchener's army'.[151] Among those to die was Jimmy Clyne, an Irish Guardsman from Ballinamore who was killed at Vermelles in October 1915. When his body was recovered, one of the few items found in his possession was his GAA Leitrim senior county championship medal, won in 1913.[152] Private Thomas Dockery, a 21-year-old from Carrick and a member of the Royal Dublin Fusiliers, was another victim of the conflict, 'and prior to joining the colours was a prominent member of the local football club'.[153] Despite members of the GAA enlisting, many stayed at home and incurred the wrath of O'Donel in his attempts to promote recruitment in the county. At Carrick in July 1915, having been denied admission to a GAA football game when he refused to pay the admission fee, O'Donel retorted that he would prefer to throw the money in the River Shannon.[154] At a poorly attended recruitment meeting at Carrick in August, O'Donel condemned young sportsmen who 'were acting the fool rather than enlisting', and added that only conscription would 'bring these laggards out'.[155]

The growth of the GAA during the period was facilitated by many athletic events like those at Carrick in July 1916 being conducted 'under GAA rules'.[156] Despite the war and the Easter Rising, the decade from 1910 to 1920 witnessed major growth in the GAA within the county. In addition to gaelic games, a wide range of other sports including athletics, horse and pony racing, and cycling were part of annual parish sports days. Unlike Britain, which witnessed major disruption to organized sport, local sports events in Leitrim continued to take place during the war. The major impediment to sporting events in the county was not the European war, but the period of martial law declared after the Easter Rising. By July 1916 the *Leitrim Observer* noted that General Maxwell had amended the order banning organized gatherings, which permitted 'sports meetings without written authority'.[157]

Leitrim's local newspapers revealed a seamless continuation through the war of sports events, dances, social events, fair days and agricultural shows. By the summer of 1915 the *Leitrim Observer* reported the resumption of cheap train excursions to the seaside resort of Bundoran but it noted a lack of people at the seaside due to a fear 'of being shelled by German submarines'.[158] While some dances, like that at Carrick Golf Club in February 1916, were organized to raise funds for the British Red Cross, most dances and social events were community gatherings, supporting a variety of local initiatives. The proceeds of a large and successful concert at Mohill in January 1915 went towards the local hall fund. In the same month, Eslin hall hosted 'a dance and cinematograph entertainment' for the people of the parish.[159] Mohill traders organized a commercial ball in October 1916 at the local

Canon Donohue hall, which was reported as 'the largest ever seen at a dance there before'.[160] As normal social life continued across the county, the Catholic hierarchy raised some concerns. In his Lenten pastoral in March 1916, Bishop Joseph Hoare of Ardagh warned parents to protect their children 'against bad and immoral literature of every description, dance houses, and the attending at picture palaces of children and elders to see bad, or indecent, or suggestive pictures that might happen to be shown'.[161]

While the First World War marked a watershed in the redrawing of the map of Europe and the demise of European empires, its political implications for Ireland were equally significant. As mainland Britain and urban areas of Ireland were drawn closer to the realities of war through mass enlistment and maintaining wartime industrial needs, its effect on large tracts of civil society in rural Ireland were minimal. The war was bringing economic benefit to the agricultural classes of Leitrim but the traditional structures of civil society remained largely intact. Apart from those with family members directly involved in the conflict, the effect of the war on most sections of the population was limited. Leitrim, like most parts of rural Ireland, initially actively supported the war effort. This stemmed from a combination of factors, including the promise of home rule, the encouragement of political and religious leaders to support Britain, a sense of duty in the defence of small nations, and alleged German atrocities in Catholic Belgium. However, a prolonged war, increasing casualties and the ever present threat of conscription turned an enthusiastic population into an apathetic and hostile one. While over three hundred Leitrim men lost their lives in the conflict, their comrades returned to an Ireland where their sacrifices on the battlefields of Europe received neither recognition nor appreciation from many of their compatriots.

4 'The people say they are tired of politics': the 1916 Rising and its aftermath

Referring to the membership of Leitrim County Council in November 1915, the *Leitrim Observer* reported Councillor Patrick Flynn's assertion that 'we haven't any pro-Germans or Sinn Féiners on it'.[1] Within twelve months of Flynn's declaration, politics in the county witnessed a significant transformation with widespread support among a broad section of the local population for the cause of advanced nationalism. The change in political sentiment can be explained by the intervention of the Easter Rising in Dublin, led by a small section of the Irish Volunteers and IRB, among them Leitrim native Seán Mac Diarmada. Widespread state repression in the wake of the Rising, including arrests and executions, coupled with perceived government duplicity in the implementation of home rule discredited the cause of constitutional nationalism and provided a platform for the alternative doctrine of radical republicanism.

The first news of the Easter Rising reached Leitrim on 27 April, four days after it began, with scant reports of a 'revolt in Dublin'.[2] The deaths of more than two hundred civilians and the destruction of the centre of Dublin led to widespread condemnation of the rebels from many sections of Irish society. In Leitrim the *Advertiser* condemned James Connolly and Roger Casement and asked 'who are the traitors who have plunged poor Ireland into revolt and rebellion when so many of her sons abroad are now fighting against the cruel Huns for real liberty?'[3] In the north-west, news of local involvement in the Rising was not reported until 13 May 1916 when the arrest of Constance Gore Booth (Countess Markievicz) of Sligo was noted. The *Leitrim Observer* reported that the countess was of 'an artistic and highly strung temperament and was well known in theatrical and literary circles in Dublin'.[4] In the following week's edition, the execution of Seán Mac Diarmada from Kiltyclogher was carried in a short column: 'John McDermott, or Seán Mac Diarmada, aged about 30 and a native of North Leitrim, was well known in Gaelic League circles and was reported as one of the organizers of the Sinn Féin movement and Irish Volunteers, of which he was at one time secretary'.[5]

There was no significant reaction to Mac Diarmada's execution in his native county. The CI's report for April 1916 noted that 'the Sinn Féin insurrection is deplored by most people in the county and has no supporters save a few in the neighbourhood of Manorhamilton who are without leaders or organizers'.[6] Similar themes emanated from the Carrick union when Patrick Flynn declared that 'those who participated were only the dupes of others'.[7] The meeting of the Sligo–Leitrim asylum committee expressed similar sentiments when Leitrim county councillor, Thomas Fallon, declared full confidence in John Redmond, stating that the IPP 'had gained practically everything for the people they represented. Landlordism had been wiped out, but it was not wiped out with the bayonet or sword'.[8] Fallon predicted that 'in due course Sinn Féin would be wiped out by the people who were at the back of the Irish Parliamentary Party'.[9] At the monthly meeting of the petty sessions court in Manorhamilton, a resolution proposed by John O'Donel was passed. It condemned the rebels and called on the government to 'adopt such stringent measures as will at once put an end to lawlessness'.[10] The local clergy also added their voices to the denunciation with Fr John Pinkman, a curate in Mohill, telling his Sunday Mass congregation that 'the insurrectionists were a disgrace to themselves and Ireland'.[11] Although Bishop Hoare of Ardagh and Clonmacnoise described the Rising as 'a mad and sinful adventure', he also appealed to the authorities to refrain from a policy of vengeance and reprisal.[12]

While IPP stalwarts and local magistrates condemned the Rising, a change in public opinion slowly began to emerge. Although not agreeing with the actions of the insurgents, the *Roscommon Herald* blamed its origins on Redmond's support for the war effort. The *Herald* was unequivocal in condemning the activities of army recruiters. In a strongly-worded editorial, it admonished Redmond for allowing recruiters to make 'wicked threats against farmers' sons and shop boys, that they would put petticoats on them and take them by force by conscription were part of the machinery that turned these youths to the evil courses of revolution'.[13]

On 11 May the *Leitrim Advertiser* reported that 'it may not be out of place to note that there are no revolutionary Sinn Féiners in Mohill, nor throughout Leitrim generally. Consequently, there have been no arrests or searches for arms in the county'.[14] However, in the weeks following the Rising, military activity increased across the county with searches and arrests in Carrick, Drumshanbo, Mohill and Manorhamilton. In Carrick, Patrick Dunne, editor of the *Leitrim Observer*, and Sam Holt, assistant clerk of the Carrick union, were detained for a brief period and released. At Manorhamilton, a detachment of the Sherwood Foresters billeted in St Clare's hall were accused of a number of incidents, ranging from criminal damage to pilfering tobacco and grocery provisions in raids and searches in the town. James Dolan (brother of 1908 SF candidate Charles), Thomas Gilgunn, John Daly and Ben Maguire were among those arrested in north Leitrim. In total, there were eleven arrests in Leitrim, although four detainees were released within days. Such arrests, together with the executions of the leaders of the Easter Rising, were critical factors in the transformation of public opinion.

Detecting the changing political mood in the county and increasing sympathy with SF, the CI reported in June that 'Sinn Féin badges are openly worn by many in the county'.[15] While the Catholic Church was slow in formulating a response to the Rising, the *Leitrim Observer* reported Bishop Edward O'Dwyer of Limerick's correspondence with General Sir John Maxwell, commanding officer of British forces in Ireland: 'personally I regard your action with horror, and I believe that it has outraged the conscience of the country'.[16] The changes in public mood were twofold – condemnation of the military proceedings was followed by a re-evaluation of the rebels resulting in ever-increasing sympathy.[17]

While the arrests and executions contributed to a change in public sentiment, Asquith's attempts at a home rule settlement during the summer of 1916 dealt a fatal blow to the political credibility of Redmond and constitutional nationalism. Asquith had sent David Lloyd George, minister of munitions, with a proposal for the immediate implementation of the home rule bill but with the exclusion of six northern counties. Redmond agreed to the plan on the understanding that the exclusion would be temporary. However, Lloyd George had guaranteed Carson that Ulster would not be forced into a self-governing Ireland. On learning of Lloyd George's guarantee, Redmond and the IPP withdrew support for the proposed scheme. Such apparent deception by Lloyd George and the continuing political inaction resulted in the politics of home rule and consent becoming discredited. This created a space in the political landscape for radical alternatives.[18]

Although Leitrim's local councils, controlled by local IPP supporters, continued to pass votes of confidence in Redmond and the IPP, loyalty to the home rule cause was eroding. A reprinted letter in the *Leitrim Observer* of 17 June 1916 from 'an Elphin Man' to the editor of the *Irish Independent* stated:

> In the nefarious swindle, the Irish Party, still true to their wanted subservience, and fed on the hackneyed and hollow votes of confidence of some of our public boards, UIL and AOH branches, bodies composed of men the vast majority of whom cannot see two yards beyond their own noses, and engaging themselves in the devilish work of bartering our country to the Orangemen of Ulster.[19]

Dissidence, albeit on a small scale, soon emerged on local bodies. Thomas Flynn, a member of Carrick's board of guardians, declared that 'the men who died in Dublin for the betterment of their country were as good Irishmen as ever lived'.[20] After a lengthy debate on partition at a meeting of the Carrick RDC in July 1916, the usual vote of confidence in the IPP was passed, but not without one dissenting voice, stating that 'they were sick and tired of passing resolutions of confidence in Mr Redmond and the Irish Party'.[21]

Frustration and disillusionment with the IPP was also voiced by prominent local nationalist supporters. Reflecting a changing political mood, Canon

Thomas O'Reilly in Carrick observed that 'if our country is to be regenerated it must be by a leader of sternness and independence of all political parties'.[22] The canon's fellow townsman, Dr Patrick Doorly, held similar views, declaring that 'everybody in Ireland whose opinion is of value detested partition, and rejoices now that the scheme is at an end. Our leaders in Parliament have landed our affairs in a muddle, from which it appears to me a younger and more enthusiastic group of men will be required to extricate them'.[23] The *Leitrim Observer* reported the stinging criticism by Archbishop William Walsh of Dublin of the IPP and its leadership: 'the Irish home rule cause in Parliament was being led along a line that could only bring it to disaster'.[24] Reflecting on politics since the Easter Rising, the *Roscommon Herald* reported that 'the events of Easter week followed by Lloyd George's intrigue to hand over Ulster to Sir Edward Carson opened the eyes of the Irish people, and they have now discovered that the so called Home Rule Act which remains buried in the Statute Book is only a sham of the worst type'.[25]

Declining levels of support for the UIL were reflected in the dwindling number of Leitrim branches that had paid the £3 annual affiliation fee to the UIL National Directory, with only eight Leitrim branches affiliated in 1915 compared to thirty-one two years earlier. Neighbouring Sligo followed a similar pattern with affiliated branches decreasing from thirty-four to twelve between 1914 and 1915.[26] Like many of his fellow MPs, Meehan was conscious of the changing mood of the people. Recounting his battles with SF at the 1908 North Leitrim by-election, the MP declared that he bore no animosity towards opponents and declared that 'they all regretted the consequences of the rebellion. But it could be fruitful of none but evil results. At the same time he deeply deplored the loss of so many lives and regretted sincerely that a number of his constituents were at present interned in English prisons'.[27]

Despite widespread criticism of constitutional nationalism throughout the summer and autumn of 1916, there was no organized political alternative to the IPP. While the RIC reported growing SF sympathy, advanced nationalist activity was negligible across the county.[28] IPP victories in by-elections during the 1914–16 period broadly signalled a belief that home rule remained a viable political creed across Ireland.[29] The strategy of the IPP was to continue to ensure the reorganization of local branches and to reassure the people that constitutional nationalism had made many political gains. While attempting to reinvigorate his local supporters at a North Leitrim UIL executive meeting, Meehan claimed in July 1916 that 'the farmers of Ireland were never more prosperous than they were at the present time, and if they remained true and loyal to their leaders the Irish question would be settled to the general satisfaction of all Irishmen'.[30]

Although John Keaveney, UIL regional organizer in Connacht, continued in his attempts to reorganize local branches in the county, declining support for the party was evident. Following a reorganization meeting held at Gowel in August 1916, the RIC reported that there was 'little enthusiasm, and the meeting was more or less a failure. The people say they are tired of politics. Mr Redmond and his party are not now thought much of'.[31] At a similar meeting at Drumsna on 10 September 1916, Michael Shanley, a UIL stalwart, attacked the 'treachery of pseudo-nationalists who have been disappointed in their political career, and who endeavour to promote disunion now'.[32] The message at public and party meetings was consistent in attacking advanced nationalism and outlining the political and economic benefits, most notably land reform, gained by the IPP. At Drumsna, Keaveney declared that landlordism had disappeared and that

> at no period of the country's history has the land of the country been more securely vested than at the present. Cottages have been built, grass ranches have been acquired and divided into economic holdings, other reforms have been accomplished, and best of all home rule has been put on the Statute Book. Mr Redmond and his party have triumphantly vindicated themselves by the constitutional movement, while the revolutionary one, futile and disastrous has brought ruin in its train.[33]

Despite the absence of an organized SF structure in Leitrim, sympathy for advanced nationalism was increasing. The police reported that there was 'a great deal of sympathy with the Sinn Féin movement, but there is no open opinion given in favour of it'.[34]

The foundation of the Irish National Aid and Volunteer Dependants' Fund (INAAVDF) played a crucial role in the radicalization of Irish political life following the Rising.[35] While many separatist leaders were dead or jailed, a republican organizational apparatus was established across the country. Although its primary focus was welfare, the fund played a decisive role in shaping the popular memory of the Easter Rising as well as laying the foundations for a reinvigorated political and military campaign after 1917.[36] Initially, Kathleen Clarke's Irish Volunteers Dependants' Fund and George Sigerson's Irish National Aid Association were separate aid organizations with similar goals. The merging of both bodies under the INAAVDF banner in August 1916 gave many nationalists a focal point in the absence of an organized SF structure in Leitrim. The first INAAVDF functions in Leitrim were a series of open air dances in the Cloone area at the end of May 1916, organized by two local women, Katie Healy and Annie Doyle.[37] In Leitrim women were particularly active in the Mohill and Cloone branches, but less so in other districts. In Carrick many AOH and UIL stalwarts such as Patrick Flynn and Michael McGrath were prominent in organizing and contributing to successful fundraising campaigns.[38]

Several of the INAAVDF branches received large contributions from local clergy. At Ballinaglera the local INAAVDF committee acknowledged subscriptions totalling £18 5s., including £1 each from the two local priests, Fr Philip King, and his curate, Fr Philip Cahill.[39] At Mohill the nuns at the local Convent of Mercy and local clergy were the highest contributors to the fund.[40] The support of the clergy indicated the campaign's success among many of the moderate sections of Leitrim society. In addition to providing much-needed funds for impoverished families, the INAAVDF was an alternative vehicle of political expression for sections of nationalist Ireland who were never wholly comfortable with the political philosophy of Redmondism.[41] The broad based nature of support for the INAAVDF in the county was reflected in a Gorvagh parish collection in July 1916. Donations ranging from 10s. to 6d. came from all socio-economic groups, including the local priest, grocer and national school teacher; the majority of donations were from small farmers in the area. Two of the donors were members of the Methodist and Church of Ireland congregations, and one was an RIC pensioner.[42]

In November 1916 Leitrim witnessed the first public demonstrations of collective sympathy for advanced nationalism with the celebration of a High Mass for Seán Mac Diarmada in his local parish church in Kiltyclogher. Large crowds from north Leitrim and the neighbouring counties of Sligo, Cavan and Fermanagh attended the Mass which had over twenty priests as choir members and chanters.[43]

While the activities of the British political and military establishment contributed to the demise of constitutional nationalism, the threat of conscription during the autumn of 1916 gave the IPP a temporary political reprieve. The party's strident opposition, together with a call for the release of all untried prisoners still in detention following the Easter Rising, was an attempt to claim back some of the political ground lost to advanced nationalism. Commenting on the potential implementation of conscription, the *Leitrim Observer* had more confidence than most in the IPP. It declared that 'the Irish people are against the application of such a system to this country, and in the hands of the Irish Parliamentary Party we are certain their wishes will not be fraught [sic] against'.[44] Police reports from Leitrim in November 1916 noted strong opposition to conscription and increasing SF sympathies.[45] The government's decision not to introduce conscription in Ireland allowed the IPP regain some political credibility but the threat of conscription remained a constant. In a further attempt at political rehabilitation, Redmond lobbied for the release of prisoners incarcerated after the Rising. Assessing the situation in Ireland, the IPP leader informed Asquith that while he understood the dangers of releasing the prisoners into the current political climate, they would do 'much more harm as prisoners in Frongoch than at liberty in Ireland'.[46]

Not only did the Easter Rising promote the cause of advanced nationalists, it also forced the authorities to suspend recruitment tours and public meetings to aid the war effort. While 238 men enlisted in Leitrim in 1915, only fifty-one joined the colours from March to December 1916. The period between April and December 1916 was one of political transition and transformation that saw increasing sympathy for the cause of the Easter rebels. Despite the continued incarceration of its surviving leaders, the decisive role played by a fledgling political welfare organization in the form of the INAAVDF provided a focus around which advanced nationalists could reorganize themselves. In this changing political climate, the *Leitrim Observer* did not directly refer to the Easter Rising in its end of year review of 1916. Instead, the last edition of the year carried stories of local soldiers home from Europe on Christmas leave.[47] The editorial gave a general welcome to the release of the Easter Rising internees by Britain's new prime minister, Lloyd George, and proclaimed the hope was that this act was 'an indication of greater things in anticipation by them for the material prosperity and advancement of Ireland'.[48] The death of James J. O'Kelly, IPP MP for North Roscommon, was also reported. The resulting by-election provided the first opportunity for advanced nationalists to challenge the IPP and give Irish nationalism a new lead. It signalled a reinvigorated and changing political climate.

5 'Thoroughly sound for the principle of self-determination': the triumph of Sinn Féin, 1917–18

As Irish republican internees detained in the post-Rising arrests arrived home at Christmas 1916, they returned to an Ireland more sympathetic to the cause of advanced nationalism. Their places of detention in prison camps across Britain became 'universities of new nationalism', with many of the 'graduates' becoming indoctrinated and committed to a more radical means of resistance to British rule in Ireland.[1] Almost immediately, these men and women set about reorganizing the political and military arms of advanced nationalism, which transformed the face of Irish nationalist politics. Over the next two years, a highly organized, younger and more energetic group of idealists wrested control of Irish nationalism with relative ease from an ageing and disorganized IPP. Nevertheless, the close resemblance of the different strands of Irish nationalism in Leitrim was reflected in the seamless transfer of political allegiance from constitutional to advanced nationalism. As in the past, the republican cause was ably assisted by ongoing government ineptitude, including a conscription crisis and continuous state repression. Such a volatile political environment ultimately saw the people of Leitrim elect its first TD in December 1918 with the largest Sinn Féin majority in Ireland.

Local political issues dominated the early months of 1917 with a call for government aid for farmers to alleviate damage caused by floods on the River Shannon. At a mass meeting of farmers in Carrick on 7 January 1917, Patrick Flynn pledged support for the agitated farmers and declared that the community strongly supported the IPP, which had handled their grievances effectively over the past thirty-five years.[2] In its first edition of 1917, the *Leitrim Observer* reported the speculation in the Dublin press about a successor for the recently deceased North Roscommon MP, James J. O'Kelly. The newspaper stated that 'the Sinn Féiners would nominate a man now serving a term of penal servitude in England for his connection with the recent Rebellion'.[3] While a prisoner was not chosen to contest the election, the eventual selection of Count Plunkett, father of the executed 1916 leader Joseph Mary Plunkett, proved a wise choice. Although not an official SF candidate, Plunkett was the representative of advanced nationalism and the first opponent of the IPP in the constituency since the 1890s. Polling took place on 3 February 1917 and Plunkett received 3,022 votes, compared to 1,708 for the IPP's Thomas Devine and 687 votes for Jasper Tully who ran as an independent. SF's success in North Roscommon was celebrated in Leitrim with victory parades at Mohill,

Ballinamore, Drumshanbo and Ballinaglera. At a celebration in the Bush Hotel in Carrick, Arthur Griffith deemed the result 'the greatest victory since Clare returned Dan O'Connell'.[4] The local division of the AOH at Drumlion congratulated Plunkett and thanked 'the young men of Carrick-on-Shannon for the admirable work they did during the recent election'.[5] Commenting on the Roscommon result, the *Leitrim Observer* noted that it was a timely warning for the IPP. It was further suggested that 'the disregard by the Liberals and Tories of Ireland's demand for self-government and the belief in the "wait and see" policy by Mr Redmond and his Party were amongst the reasons for North Roscommon deciding by so big a majority'.[6]

Commenting on the growing popularity of SF, the RIC Inspector-General reported in March 1917 that the party consisted 'for the greater part of idealists, including many Roman Catholic curates, and of young men who find in its doctrines convenient excuses for shirking their duty in the trenches'.[7] By early 1917 Leitrim was following the national trend of increasing sympathy for SF. On 15 April 1917 two former Frongoch internees, James Dolan and Ben Maguire, established Leitrim's first post-Rising SF club at Manorhamilton. Dolan and Maguire were regarded by the RIC as instrumental in the formation of SF clubs throughout the county in the months that followed.[8] In April 1917 republican flags were hoisted and subsequently removed by police in Dromod and Carrick.[9]

In March 1917 Count Plunkett issued a manifesto proposing abstention from Westminster and an invitation to all members of county and district councils to meet at Dublin's Mansion House. These were not well received by the IPP-dominated local councils across Ireland. Referring to Plunkett's previous position as director of the National Museum, Councillor Bernard Connolly declared at a meeting of Kinlough RDC that the manifesto should be burned and he called Plunkett 'a discredited Castle hack, who never did a day's work in the service of Ireland'.[10] In rejecting Plunkett's overtures, Manorhamilton RDC followed the trend of many councils by passing a resolution renewing confidence in Redmond and the IPP.[11]

In nearby South Longford the impending by-election caused by the death of John Phillips, MP, gave a fresh impetus to advanced nationalism.[12] The South Longford constituency had no history of advanced nationalism and the IPP campaigned strongly to retain its parliamentary seat. Both of Leitrim's MPs, Meehan and Smyth, played prominent roles in the IPP campaign during the by-election, the first contested election in the constituency since 1892. Both constitutional and advanced nationalist supporters travelled from all parts of Ireland to campaign for their respective candidates. Joe McGuinness's victory for SF by just thirty-seven votes led to celebrations across neighbouring Leitrim. SF flags were flown from buildings in Ballinamore and crowds thronged the streets. A torchlight procession headed by the Drumreilly and

Aughnasheelin pipe bands led the marchers through the town. In reference to Smyth's support for recruitment for the war effort, shouts were heard from the crowd that 'we want no recruiting sergeants representing us in South Leitrim'.[13] McGuinness's victory in South Longford was significant given the dominance of the IPP in an area with no tradition of advanced nationalism. Both Éamon de Valera's victory at a by-election in East Clare and William Cosgrave's victory in Kilkenny in July 1917 gave further impetus to the growth of SF. The *Sligo Champion* recognized the significance of de Valera's victory and warned that if something was not done promptly by the government to conciliate Irish sentiment, 'Sinn Féin will take the place of constitutionalism, and the fires which flared on the hills of Clare in honour of the victory of Eamon de Valera, will be ablaze in every part of Ireland'.[14]

By July 1917 sixteen SF clubs with a membership of 728 had been established in Leitrim. Numbers were also increasing in neighbouring counties with fourteen branches and 1,255 members in Longford and twenty-two branches and 1,113 members in Roscommon.[15] Large public meetings organized by SF were held in Ballinamore and Mohill that month. At Ballinamore a resolution was passed congratulating the electors of East Clare for returning de Valera and for 'striking a blow at the deceivers of the Irish people who carried on nothing but jobbery and bossism'.[16] An anti-recruiting theme was evident at Ballinaglera on 19 August when the meeting, under the auspices of the local SF club, heard maverick MP, Laurence Ginnell, and James Dolan declare that the £400 per annum salary made MPs more English than the English themselves. The meeting condemned Redmond for espousing the cause of England and noted that 'his representatives went around the country as recruiting sergeants'.[17]

New SF clubs were formed on a continual basis throughout the late summer of 1917; many were named after executed 1916 leaders. At the inaugural meeting of the Seán Mac Diarmada SF club in Carrick on 19 August, Michael Collins was the main speaker. He urged clubs to be formed in every district in order to gain power at local council level, with the ultimate goal of capturing the parliamentary seat. Earlier that day, Collins had attended Mass in Gowel and spoke at the local Roger Casement SF club where he outlined SF's main policies.[18]

Aeraíochtaí (open-air Irish concerts) were common features of SF gatherings in the county, and that at Ballinamore on Sunday 2 September 1917 was 'one of the biggest gatherings of people ever witnessed in any part of south Leitrim'. They gathered to welcome Joe McGuinness and Harry Boland to Leitrim.[19] On the journey to Ballinamore the previous night, hundreds of people gathered at Mohill, Gorvagh and Fenagh to welcome the SF MP to the county. Dismissing claims that SF was a new phenomenon that would disappear quickly, McGuinness stated that it was a political party with a policy 'that was advocated for seven hundred and fifty years and was not a new movement'.[20] He called on the people to ensure that SF represented them on local councils and to make their local clubs intellectual centres where Irish language and history would be taught. In supporting the meeting's demand for Thomas Smyth's resignation, McGuinness condemned Smyth's record and the lack of development of the Cavan and Leitrim Railway, and the nearby Arigna coal mines. By the end of September 1917 SF had established two executive structures for the north and south of the county, comprising over twenty-eight clubs with a membership of nearly fifteen hundred people.[21] James Dolan presided over the North Leitrim SF executive, while Michael Murphy, a former UIL member and long-serving councillor from Gorvagh, presided over its southern counterpart.

From early 1917 republican strategy across Ireland revolved around building Irish Volunteer structures in every area to co-exist alongside the SF party. While SF's membership base and party structures grew extensively in Leitrim, this was not matched by growth in Volunteer numbers. The first post-Rising Volunteer companies were formed at Ballinamore and Aughnasheelin in spring 1917. Hugh Brady recalled that 'our drill parades were held in public for the first six months or so and we were a source of amusement and jibes for a lot of the locals who I suppose thought we were mad or fanatics'.[22] Patrick J. Hargaden remembered similar experiences in the Gorvagh and Mohill areas during the summer of 1917, recounting the formation of small numbers of men into units with no arms or ammunition:

> it was realised that when a few men in Dublin city and other centres could stand up to the might of the British Empire and give their lives for their country, then surely if the whole country was united in one effort there was a bigger chance of succeeding. In this way, when the young men met in groups, they would discuss such matters.[23]

Despite their establishment, only on one occasion did police mention a Volunteer presence in the county with drilling reported at an unspecified location in October 1917. No prosecution was recommended by the CI.[24]

The role of Cumann na mBan in the post-1916 environment mirrored that of the Irish Volunteers, with most activity devoted to assisting SF in voter registration and political campaigns. Brigid Mullane from Sligo, a Cumann na mBan organizer, was responsible for much of the movement's development in south Leitrim during 1918.[25] Owing to the efforts of Mullane and Kate Healy from Cloone, sixteen branches were established in the county by early 1918.[26]

Bernard Sweeney recalled a mobilization of republicans at Aghoo Bridge during the East Cavan by-election in May 1918 to organize an electoral campaign team to support Arthur Griffith. Sweeney recounted the trip to Cavan:

At Bailieboro a party of military attacked us and smashed up our cycles and they took the hurling sticks we were carrying. Despite this interference, however, we succeeded in getting to our destination. There were about two hundred Leitrim men on this job.[27]

Family involvement in political activism motivated many to join the Volunteers and Cumann na mBan.[28] Hugh Brady recalled that his father was a former Fenian 'and was always a separatist, and it was from him that I developed my rebel tendencies'.[29] Lily Freyne, a member of Cumann na mBan from Rooskey on the Leitrim–Roscommon border, also recounted a history of political activism in her family: 'I was brought up in Fenianism, my uncle was a Fenian poet, all belonging to me were Fenian. It was all I heard at home'.[30]

The death of Thomas Ashe in Mountjoy Jail in September 1917, from force-feeding while on hunger strike, drew widespread condemnation across Ireland. The thousands who attended Ashe's funeral demonstrated the strength of popular support for advanced nationalism. In Leitrim, condemnations of the nature of Ashe's death and expressions of sympathy to his family were passed by SF clubs throughout the county. Within the ranks of constitutional nationalism, the local AOH division in Annaduff described Ashe as 'a martyr for Ireland, done to death at the hands of the unscrupulous rulers of this country'.[31] A similar motion was passed by the Carrick branch of the INF on 14 October 1917.[32] Popular sympathy for Ashe continued into October 1917. Memorial Masses were held in Mohill and Carrick, where shops were closed as an expression of sympathy.

Over eighteen hundred people attended an aeríocht at Carrigallen on 7 October 1917 to hear Arthur Griffith speak. Reminiscing about the 1908 North Leitrim by-election, he told the crowd that the IPP then had large resources available to defeat SF but a decade later the situation was reversed. A similar theme was evident in Griffith's address at Manorhamilton on 1 November when he reminded the large crowd that Manorhamilton was the first town in Ireland spanned by arches bearing the motto: 'No London Parliament'. He added that 'in the future history of the Sinn Féin movement, the name of Leitrim would be forever associated as the vanguard and pioneer of the movement'.[33] Prominent national speakers continued to visit the county, including William Cosgrave and Darrell Figgis who spoke at an aeríocht in Dromod.[34] Similarly, in nearby Longford, the work of local organizers was boosted by that of prominent national figures in SF and the Volunteers who travelled around Ireland during the summer of 1917.[35]

Newly elected SF president, Éamon de Valera, and Harry Boland spoke as part of an aeríocht organized by the local Edward Daly SF club in Mohill on 18 November 1917. Arriving the previous evening, the visitors were escorted by thirty horsemen and a torchlight procession to a reception in the local Canon Donohue hall. At the beginning of the public meeting, de Valera thanked the local board of guardians for their formal welcome and identified the changing political loyalties across Ireland in many local councils, 'because they show clearly that these bodies, although the people had not yet the chance of electing these bodies, have changed, or should he say have changed in their allegiance to a Party that was running the country to ruin'.[36] In his speech to the thousands of people gathered, de Valera referred to the European war as a battle for England's trade supremacy and declared that 'John Bull with the bible in one hand and the sword in the other has brought more ruin on this earth than any other nation'.[37] At Mohill, he condemned SF's political opponents, who, he claimed, 'try to brand this movement of ours which is as pure and good a National movement as there ever was in any country, they try to brand it as immoral'.[38] At a meeting in Drumcong the following week, James Dolan conveyed a similar message: 'it is said that Sinn Féin is out for red ruin and revolution. Nothing of the kind. Sinn Féin is the policy laid down by Parnell when he declared that no man was to set the boundary to the onward march of a nation'.[39]

Throughout 1917 many IPP supporters transferred allegiance to SF and a demand for a republic. Following a countrywide tour in early 1917, Maurice Moore, inspector-general of the National Volunteers, claimed that most young people were SF supporters, and while some farmers and shopkeepers remained loyal to the IPP, both groups were moving towards SF.[40] On public bodies a transfer of loyalty, albeit incremental, was also evident. As early as March 1917 Mohill District Councillor John Mulligan condemned Redmond for endorsing recruitment to the British army. Fellow councillor, Patrick Woods, rebuked Mulligan, declared that English law was the best in the world, and suggested that if people had not joined the army 'the Turks would be here now'.[41] At a Leitrim County Council meeting on 30 May 1917, a heated discussion ensued when Thomas McGivney and Michael Murphy proposed a motion congratulating McGuinness on his election victory.[42] Both Murphy and McGivney were UIL stalwarts and long standing members of the county council. While the resolution was defeated by eleven votes to five, it demonstrated that division had emerged on a public body that had hitherto consistently supported the IPP. When Patrick Flynn was re-elected chairman of Carrick RDC he issued a conciliatory statement. He called for a new policy to reunite the different strands of nationalism and declared that 'it was sad enough to think unfortunate differences existed in the Nationalist ranks'.[43]

Leitrim was following a pattern of neighbouring counties where political loyalty was freely transferred from the local IPP machine to SF.[44] After SF's Longford by-election victory, the AOH Gorvagh division passed a motion congratulating the electors of South Longford on having elected

McGuinness.⁴⁵ According to the *Leitrim Observer*, it was notable that at an aeríocht at Eslin in September 1917 'some of the flags carried by the contingents were those which were used in the days when the IPP was the leading light of the Irish people'.⁴⁶ At Drumsna the local AOH division decided to dissolve and, having paid all monies due, transferred its funds to the local SF club. When the question of the use of the local AOH hall was discussed, the chairman did not foresee any issue 'as the same party would be in charge'.⁴⁷ The village of Cloone witnessed a similar development when the local AOH division unanimously decided to dissolve and join the local SF club.⁴⁸ While some AOH members transferred their political allegiance freely, others such as the Gowel AOH division resolved to continue to support Hibernianism but passed a motion wishing 'the Gowel Sinn Féin Club every success, as we believe we are working for the same noble cause'.⁴⁹

In an attempt to thwart the advance of SF, Lloyd George sought to reconcile the different strands of political thought in Ireland with the establishment of the Irish Convention, which met in July 1917. Consisting of representatives of the IPP, southern Unionists, Ulster Unionists and some independents, the forum attempted unsuccessfully to propose a system of self-government for Ireland. Alvin Jackson argues that SF's decision not to take part in the nine-month deliberations gave it an opportunity to further consolidate its political support.⁵⁰ At a SF public meeting at Ballinamore in July 1917, the IPP's support for the Irish Convention was condemned. Calling on Thomas Smyth to resign, the meeting also advised Thomas Fallon, who had been nominated as IPP delegate, 'not to go to the bogus Convention as representing the people of Leitrim, as we do not approve of recruiting orators representing us'.⁵¹

Attacks on political opponents were not the sole preserve of advanced nationalists. Commenting on the growth of SF, Fallon declared that 'the young men of this country were being misguided and misled by a certain clanned party in Dublin that were never any good for anything'.⁵² At a UIL reorganization meeting in Glencar on 24 June 1917, Francis Meehan described both Count Plunkett and Laurence Ginnell 'as the very dregs of place hunting'.⁵³ Meehan claimed that he had fought against Plunkett and McGuinness in the Longford and Roscommon by-election campaigns in order 'to withstand those who, however good their motives might be, were wreckers and disturbers'.⁵⁴ Tensions were also present in some areas between the different strands of nationalism. Newspapers reported that SF members had been heckled in Newtownmanor and refused lifts unless they removed Thomas Ashe badges from their clothing.⁵⁵ Members of the newly formed Drumshanbo SF club warned members 'not to be drawn into street brawls or rows by parties opposed to Sinn Féin'.⁵⁶

By the end of 1917, forty-three SF clubs, with a membership of almost 2,300, were established in Leitrim, the second-largest number of clubs per head of population in Ireland. In charting the growth of SF in 1917 and early 1918, the transfer of political loyalty from constitutional to advanced nationalism was evident throughout the county. While the AOH still had a large membership and support base, the thin line between both strands of nationalism and an underlying culture of Anglophobia was evident. The growth of SF can be explained by a growing disillusionment with the old order and an active cadre of party organizers across the county. A continuous series of aeraíochtaí and public meetings, supplemented by a range of high-profile national speakers, contributed to the increasing support for republicanism in the county.

As it had done so often in the past, land agitation once again became a political issue during the early months of 1918. Although the land acts of 1903 and 1909 had ensured that an estimated two-thirds to three-quarters of former tenant farmers owned their land by 1914, a new hunger for land developed in early 1918 that was exacerbated by the cessation of emigration during the war.[57] Concern over wartime food supplies and the inadequate response of large farmers to compulsory tillage orders gave the impetus for land takeover by smallholders and landless men.[58] SF, previously devoid of an agrarian policy, quickly took the political initiative and attracted support from a land-hungry rural population to commandeer land in the name of the Irish republic.[59] While this campaign was an attempt to campaign for the sale and division of grasslands, its background was a fear of famine brought about by the demands of warfare.[60] From late 1917 SF had established a food committee that campaigned to halt exports of a wide range of farm produce. The intrusion of the state on Irish food production was seen by critics as serving British imperial needs rather than those of the Irish people. As early as August 1917 the North Leitrim SF executive condemned the level of food restrictions being imposed by the food controller and demanded the establishment of an Irish mercantile marine fleet.[61] In Leitrim, as elsewhere, politically SF exploited the fear of famine and land hunger to garner support. While in some instances agreement was reached with landowners to rent land on a conacre basis, by late February 1918 farms at Manorhamilton, Dromahair and Kiltoghert were forcibly taken over by local people without agreement and with local SF support. At a farm takeover at Dromahair, James Dolan argued that conserving food was important in order to protect the country from famine.[62] A similar theme emerged at Fearglass, when the local SF club urged the public not to sell their farm produce to England, reminding people that 'if you sell your food to England now, you cannot satisfy your hunger later with the paper money you got in exchange, so hold the harvest and remember '46 and '47.'[63]

One of the more prominent land seizures in the county involved the occupation of a forty-acre farm at Kiltoghert, the property of J.A. Ormsby

Lawder, a member of the Leitrim grand jury. After the owner refused a request from the Drumsna and Gowel SF clubs to discuss a letting agreement, the land was seized by a large crowd on 23 February 1918 'in the name of the Irish Republic'.[64] The close relationship between elements of SF and the AOH was evident at Kiltoghert as the *Leitrim Observer* reported that prominent members 'of the AOH and enthusiasts in the UIL joined the Sinn Féiners in the commandeering of the farm'.[65] In the week after the Kiltoghert incident, the RIC took a more hardline approach when a large police and military presence prevented seizures at Cashel, Emlagh, and Woodbrook. At Woodbrook the Drumlion band were not permitted to play their instruments and the crowd was prevented from marching in military formation.[66] At Manorhamilton seventy extra police were drafted into the town on 28 February 1918 in anticipation of a land raid by the local SF club.

By contrast with land seizures in neighbouring counties such as Roscommon and Sligo, which had large numbers of grazier farms, the seizures in Leitrim were few and minor. There were only five attempted seizures countywide. Police reports recorded the negotiated and consensual nature of many of the land transfers but observed that 'there are indications that the more responsible people are beginning to tire of this practice, and the prospect of having to pay large sums in compensation will have an effect'.[67] Calls for a firmer administration of justice came from some large landowners. At the spring assizes in Carrick on 5 March 1918, J.A. Ormbsy Lawder and Captain John O'Donel proposed a resolution to direct the government to restore 'law and order, unless they wish to turn this country into another Russia'.[68]

As a result of the seizure of the Lawder farm at Kiltoghert, Thomas Duignan, secretary of Gowel SF club, Michael Lynch, Thomas Keaveney, T.P. McNabola, J. Murray and Michael Carter were convicted and bound to the peace at Carrick assizes. The trials of the six men attracted large crowds and a strong police presence at the courthouse. CI Rainsford testified that no further land seizures had taken place since the February incidents and he was confident that none would occur in the future. Despite requests from their defence solicitor that they be released under the First Offender's Act, five of the six defendants told the court that they would go to jail instead of paying a fine. Persuaded by their solicitor, the men finally agreed to pay the sureties and were released to loud cheering. Councillor Patrick Flynn claimed that 'it was owing to the tempest which swept the country that these young men were carried away, and he believed there would be no more such acts'.[69]

Despite calls from SF meetings for his resignation, Meehan remained in his role as MP and continued to advocate on land issues. At a meeting in Tullaghan on 7 October 1917, organized to discuss the sale of the Dickson and Reynolds estates in that vicinity, Meehan warned about land grabbers and urged the locals to form a committee under the auspices of the local UIL.

Condemning SF, he claimed that 'they had no policy except that of destruction, bluff and flag waving'.[70]

While the land question remained of paramount importance, attempts were also made to organize labour in the county during 1918. The impetus came from the Sligo office of the Irish Transport and General Workers' Union (ITGWU) and the appointment of William Reilly, a local councillor and tailor, as a full-time secretary and organizer in March 1918. Reilly established Leitrim's first branch in Manorhamilton in April 1918. At the inaugural meeting he urged all workers to join the union. It took nearly another six months to form the county's second branch in Carrick on 16 September 1918. Reilly addressed a large meeting in the town hall, declaring that

> they could not see why the workers of Carrick-on-Shannon should not be as well paid for their labours as the men of Sligo and elsewhere. The conditions of the workers as he understood them was of the slave status, but they had now he was glad to see resolved that they would be free men and not slaves and take their place in a free Ireland.[71]

The newly formed branch in Carrick attracted both skilled and unskilled workers, and by November 1918 the branch reported that membership had increased 'into three figures'.[72] The union continued to grow across the county. In March 1919 the CI reported that SF and the ITGWU were the only active political organizations in the county, with a union membership of 281 in four branches.[73] With a low industrial base and few farm labourers, organized labour would never reach a position of influence within the political structures of the county.

As the war in Europe progressed, the major dangers confronting belligerent governments and military commands were declining morale and a counter mobilization in favour of peace, and even revolution which would challenge the war effort directly.[74] This counter mobilization took place at a rapid pace throughout Ireland during 1917 and 1918 with an ongoing anti-conscription message ensuring increasing support for advanced nationalists. The rising tide of political support for SF throughout 1917 greatly diminished Ireland's backing for Britain's war effort, with only forty-two Leitrim men enlisting in 1917.[75] This trend continued throughout 1918 with ten men enlisting during the first four months of the year.[76]

While a series of by-election victories for the IPP in South Armagh, East Tyrone and Waterford City during the early months of 1918 temporarily slowed SF's momentum, the results were not representative of Irish public opinion. The election victory of IPP candidate Patrick Donnelly in Armagh in February 1918, with support from sections of the unionist population, gave IPP supporters a rare opportunity to celebrate. At Manorhamilton RDC on 14 February 1918, a motion was passed congratulating 'Mr Donnelly on his magnificent victory in Armagh over the powers of disruption and anarchism'.[77] At a large SF rally in Elphin, County Roscommon, on 3 February 1918, Carrick SF leader Sam Holt attributed Donnelly's victory to 'an unholy and unnatural alliance founded on political perfidy and doomed to national repudiation'.[78]

On 6 March 1918, after a short illness, John Redmond died in London. Throughout Ireland, votes of sympathy were passed by IPP-dominated district councils and boards of guardians on the death of the leader of constitutional nationalism. At Manorhamilton, the local AOH branch meeting described Redmond's death as a 'national calamity'.[79] Mohill board of guardians passed a resolution of sympathy, but Patrick Woods cautioned that 'if they don't elect a leader in his place who will see [that] the Convention will get us home rule, I am afraid it will make Sinn Féiners of us all'.[80] The assessment of Redmond's legacy in local newspapers varied from praise to criticism of a man who 'failed to rise to the occasion'.[81] Following the election of John Dillon as Redmond's successor, the *Sligo Champion* called for unity between SF and the IPP and advised that 'if the one and only objective be full Colonial self-government, without prejudice to the means and methods, the Ulster barrier would collapse, and in the present condition of England, the Irish demand would be irresistible'.[82] The by-election in Waterford caused by Redmond's death was won by his son, William, a serving British army officer. Commenting on Redmond's victory, Gorvagh's Seán Mac Diarmada SF club condemned 'the voters of Waterford in returning Captain Redmond as their MP, a man in khaki that sought his votes like the IPP for conscription'.[83] Reporting on the Waterford result, the *Leitrim Observer* noted: 'considering that the Sinn Féiner had to fight the issue against the unionist and nationalist vote combined, a powerful fight was made'.[84]

Less than two weeks after Redmond's death, the contrasting fortunes of advanced and constitutional nationalism were evident in Leitrim at a series of public meetings on St Patrick's Day. At Drumkeeran a UIL/AOH meeting, with Leitrim's two MPs as the main speakers, condemned proposed attempts at introducing conscription and called on the IPP 'to use all means in their power in not having a compulsory military service scheme applied to this little almost depopulated country of ours'.[85] Meehan called on the people to support constitutional nationalism and advised that 'there was really no use running their heads against stone walls – it was enough for the Revolutionary Party to be doing that'.[86] Adopting a more conciliatory tone, Thomas Smyth outlined all the concessions that the IPP had received for Ireland. He told the crowd that 'he did not blame these people who were connected to the Revolutionary Party because he had always maintained that everybody was entitled to his or her own opinion, but Ireland could never be made free by physical force'.[87] Less than ten miles away at Dromahair, 1,200 people attended a SF meeting addressed by Seán O'Reilly from Dublin. The RIC reported that the result of the Dromahair meeting 'will be probably to strengthen Sinn Féin in the neighbourhood'.[88] In the south of the county the largest political gathering on St Patrick's Day 1918 was at an aeríocht at Cloone where 4,000 people attended to hear Rory O'Connor from Dublin, Paul Galligan from Cavan, and local SF activist, John McDonald. Commenting on the shifting political loyalties locally, O'Connor told the assembled crowd:

> I am very glad to know that the AOH has joined and fallen into line with the Sinn Féin movement, and I am very glad to be able to tell you that Mr McDonald and one of the recent secretaries of the United Irish League not far from this district have informed me that the League and Hibernians have transferred funds.[89]

From the outbreak of the First World War, the conscription of the Irish civilian population was deemed unacceptable to all shades of Irish nationalism. The issue arose periodically during the course of the conflict but legislation was never enacted. By early 1918, as a result of increasing military losses in France and Belgium following a new German offensive, the British government proposed extending conscription to Ireland and parliament passed the Military Service bill on 10 April 1918. A sense of outrage swept Ireland and the IPP MPs returned from the House of Commons to join the opposition to conscription at home. At an all-party anti-conscription conference in the Mansion House, the legislation was condemned, a one-day national strike organized, and an anti-conscription pledge was formulated by the Catholic hierarchy. The support and approval of the pledge by the Catholic hierarchy, which was to be taken in every parish after Sunday Mass, ensured the formation of a nationwide movement of opposition. While SF was part of a wide coalition of opposition, the party did not lose the opportunity to gain political advantage. SF statements in local newspapers claimed 'the decision of the English government to enforce conscription on Ireland in defiance of the expressed will of the nation has demonstrated beyond dispute the futility of the policy of Irish representation at Westminster'.[90]

One of the first actions of SF in Leitrim after the conscription announcement was the South Leitrim executive's order that 'no dances will be permitted to be held during the present crisis through which the country is passing, and no club meetings are to be summoned or reported in the Press without the sanction of the Executive'.[91] Almost immediately, Volunteer companies throughout Leitrim saw an influx of recruits.[92] Heated responses to conscription were evident at meetings of local councils and boards of guardians. Carrick board of guardians believed it would 'lead to bloodshed, disaster and the ruination of all the success achieved here for the past two years in food production'.[93] Across the county prayers were said at all Masses 'that God might save this country from inevitable ruin and destruction which would follow its enforcement'.[94]

At Bornacoola on 14 April 1918 a crowd of nearly 5000 people attended an aeríocht with Frank McGuinness from Longford as the main speaker. He appealed to both unionist and nationalist opponents to join the anti-conscription cause. He declared his willingness 'to allow them into our ranks and ... to never say a word that will give one of them offence'.[95] The local INF branch at Dromod reacted with caution to the plea for unity, observing that 'we have heard talk recently of burying the hatchet. Coming as it does from those who have always been using the hatchet, we would be inclined to take it as an indication of repentance'.[96]

At a large meeting in Carrick town hall on 16 April 1918 a campaign of passive resistance was proposed. Canon Thomas O'Reilly, the parish priest, called for unification under one anti-conscription banner. He claimed that 'it took a century to give a home rule bill and it took only two or three days to conscript the young men of Ireland'.[97] On 21 April 1918 a series of after-Mass meetings took place across the county, with clergy and political leaders again calling for a policy of passive resistance to conscription. At Bornacoola Fr Joseph Guinan took the pledge from over 1,000 people. Local Protestant home ruler, Robert Thompson, told the meeting that 'the people of my Church have in the past held aloof from the popular movements carried on by their Catholic fellow countrymen. This, we must say, is not a dignified position to adopt for I believe there is not one of them who does not hate conscription'.[98] Praising the support of Thompson, John McDonald was 'pleased to say our Protestant neighbours are with us in the struggle against the latest blood tax'.[99] At Drumalease a large crowd heard local curate, Fr Francis Prior, call on the people to follow their spiritual and political leaders and urged that 'the Irish Volunteers, the chief hope of our country, must obey all orders from their leaders and officers'.[100] The meeting ended with the crowd marching in military formation, led by Fr Prior, 'with drums beating and Sinn Féin and AOH flags waving'.[101]

Calls for political unity among nationalists were common themes at meetings across the county. At an anti-conscription meeting organized by SF in Dromahair on 5 May 1918, Frs Galligan and Prior made a plea that party politics should not destroy nationalist unity against conscription 'as it would be an act of the basest treachery that ever was committed towards Ireland'.[102] Bertie Anderson, a Protestant Sinn Féiner from Calry in Sligo, advised the Volunteers to get properly disciplined and organized, and do nothing that would discredit the cause, stating that 'the enemy would like nothing better than see disunion and dissension in our ranks at this most critical time in our country's history'.[103] The CI reported that the presence of clergy at anti-conscription meetings ensured that gatherings were peaceful and 'conducted in an orderly manner'.[104] Nevertheless, the conscription scare resulted in ranks of SF and the Volunteers being filled with new members. Membership of SF in Leitrim increased from 2,470 to 3,340 between January and May of 1918.[105] Following an address by Paul Galligan, a Volunteer organizer, to a meeting at Aughnasheelin, the local company increased to over 200 men.[106] However, as happened in many other regions across Ireland, when the conscription crisis abated, Volunteer numbers decreased dramatically.[107]

As a result of the large-scale opposition to conscription, the British government relented and did not proceed with its enforcement. The conscription issue provided SF with renewed political impetus and inflamed anti-British sentiment among the Irish people. The conscription crisis produced an unequivocal challenge and threat to British authority in Ireland. It resulted in the further demise of constitutional nationalism and the triumph of SF over its nationalist rival.[108] Once more, the state's response to a concerted challenge followed a familiar pattern, with the arrest of seventy-three SF leaders on the night of 17–18 May 1918. The reason offered for the arrests were alleged collusion between SF and the German government. Prominent SF leaders throughout Ireland, including Leitrim's James Dolan, were arrested and deported to jails in England. While the police believed that Dolan's arrest and that of the other SF leaders would have a pacifying effect, Carrick board of guardians called for the immediate release of the prisoners.[109] Although many people were angry at the arrests, it was noticeable in Leitrim that meetings organized to protest against the arrests attracted much smaller numbers than the earlier anti-conscription gatherings. The RIC reported that most meetings lasted between ten and fifteen minutes, and noted that 'they won't have much effect'.[110] Nonetheless, condemnations of the arrests were widespread. The Breffni O'Rourke SF club viewed the action 'as this latest piece of trickery of the Freemason government of England'.[111]

An important element of SF's political strategy was to wrest control across Ireland of IPP-dominated local councils. In June 1918 the Edward Daly SF club in Mohill requested all councillors to vote for their party's candidates. This resulted in SF's James Teague being unanimously elected chairman of Mohill RDC. Despite a similar request from the Carrick SF club, UIL veteran Patrick Flynn defeated SF's Michael McGrath at the RDC and board of guardian elections. At his accession speech in Carrick, Flynn called for unity among nationalists and claimed that there were many aspects of SF policy that he supported. McGrath immediately questioned Flynn's overtures claiming that 'no man could carry two flags'.[112] At county council level SF emerged victorious on 15 June 1918 when Michael Murphy defeated his former UIL colleague, Thomas Fallon, by one vote to secure the chairmanship. During the meeting, reference was made to Fallon's previous support for the war effort and his recent vote at the Irish Convention against Ireland controlling customs and excise in a home rule parliament. At Aughawillan the Thomas Ashe SF club congratulated Murphy and his fellow Leitrim councillors for removing Fallon, 'whose action in the recent Convention misrepresented and degraded the people of Leitrim'.[113]

While political change was taking place at council level across Leitrim, police reports consistently referred to a relatively peaceful county. White gloves, the symbol of an absence of indictable offences, were presented to Judge Brown at both Manorhamilton and Carrick courts in June 1918. He claimed

> It is something to cause gratification and pleasure in the minds of all thinking men that in these times of sorrow and stress and tension of wars and rumour of wars of transition and unsettlement, there is at least one county in Connaught where indictable and organised crime do not exist at these Trinity Quarter Sessions.[114]

According to Justice Pim in his report to the Leitrim summer assizes, the only serious cases were a small number of arms raids and the cutting of telegraph wires which were 'attacks, not so much on the individual, as on the district and body politic'.[115] The quietude of the county was acknowledged by the authorities with Leitrim being one of only six counties in Ireland where the Crimes Act of 1887 was not operational in summer 1918.[116]

Despite this relatively peaceful environment, a number of political trials involving local republican activists took place in the summer of 1918. In Manorhamilton on 3 July 1918, Charles Timoney was sentenced to six months' hard labour and John O'Connell received a one-month sentence for unlawful assembly and illegal drilling. After the court was cleared following scuffles, Timoney declared: 'it is all a farce, and as a soldier of the Irish Republic I refuse to recognize this court and deny the right of the Resident Magistrate to try me'.[117] At Carrick on 12 July 1918, despite pleas for leniency from local parish priest, Fr Matthew McCabe, seven Drumshanbo Volunteers were sentenced to one month in jail for unlawful assembly in their local town on the night of Arthur Griffith's by-election victory in East Cavan.[118] On their release from jail on 10 August, the *Leitrim Observer* reported that the prisoners 'received a tremendous ovation and were escorted by a large number of friends to their respective houses'.[119] Similar scenes took place at the trial of Michael Mulligan at Carrick on 23 July 1918 for unlawful drilling at Ballinamore. The *Leitrim Observer* recounted how Mulligan questioned the court's right to try him and 'took the whole proceedings in an indifferent way, wearing a smile during the evidence'.[120]

Continuing a policy of repression, Dublin Castle introduced regulations that required organizers of public meetings and assemblies to acquire a permit from the authorities. As an act of defiance, Gaelic games were organized nationwide without any application for a permit on 4 August 1918 when over 54,000 members of the GAA played football and hurling across the country. One game was played in Leitrim at Gortlettragh between the local team and Johnstonsbridge.[121] Acts of defiance by republicans continued on 15 August 1918 with the reading of a SF manifesto by party activists at public meetings across the county. At Ballinamore, Carrick and Aughnasheelin, large forces of police did not interfere with proceedings.[122] The only arrest took place at Mohill, where Tim Ward, secretary of Mohill SF club, was detained.[123] Police reported that apart from Ward no other arrests took place across Leitrim because 'the evidence in these cases was not considered strong enough to warrant any proceedings being taken'.[124]

The launch of a renewed recruitment campaign in August 1918 proved to be more successful nationally than previous campaigns with 9,845 men joining between August and November 1918, compared to 5,812 recruits in the preceding six months.[125] In Leitrim the campaign provided advanced nationalists with a further opportunity to defy government policy. At Dromahair on 4 September 1918, prior to a fair day recruitment meeting organized by John O'Donel, posters were erected warning young men not to join the army. The *Sligo Champion* reported that the majority of young men rushed home before the arrival of the recruiting party. O'Donel told the small crowd that he was ashamed of the young men who had not remained and accused them of being 'afraid to come and listen to God's truth, but he supposed they would rather listen to a lot of lies told them by some rebel or other'.[126] At Ballinamore on 1 October 1918, a meeting was interrupted by locals and the police baton-charged a group of forty young men who continued to cheer and sing after the meeting ended. The interruptions resulted in the arrest and subsequent imprisonment of three local men: Con Gallogly, Patrick McAviney and Michael McHugh. At their trial on 5 October 1918 Judge Browne condemned the defendants, declaring that 'If these young men have a stomach for fighting or drilling, there are a hundred opportunities for them in the army or flying corps, and if they joined up and faced the real enemies of Ireland they would be of some service to their native land'.[127]

The triumph of Sinn Féin, 1917–18

Despite Canon O'Reilly warning people not to interfere with recruitment meetings at Carrick, interruptions took place at fair day meetings in the town on both 11 and 21 October 1918. Prior to the 11 October meeting, the front of the local recruiting office was covered with tar. On the following day Captain Phillips condemned the act and accused SF leaders of treason. Phillips told the crowd that 'the Irish people had turned down the IPP, who got them all that they enjoyed, in favour of a Spaniard'.[128] While recruiting was successful in some regions, little changed in Leitrim with police reporting in October 1918 that 'voluntary recruitment for the army is still very poor'.[129]

Leitrim's limited engagement with the war was reflected in the county's reaction to the cessation of hostilities on 11 November 1918. Only in Carrick was there any level of public celebration with a hoisting of a union jack at the main post office and a parade through the town by soldiers and supporters of the war effort. Later that night a crowd assembled at a bonfire at the town clock, singing and cheering. In a changing political environment, SF supporters also gathered singing republican songs and refused to disperse when ordered to do so by the RIC.[130] Welcoming the end of the war, the *Sligo Champion* observed that

> it cannot be forgotten that during most of the war period, owing to the perversity of British statesmen, the minds of Irishmen were busily occupied in combating militarism and tyranny in their own land. Their fight was for humanity and freedom on every front. To a large extent they succeeded. By sheer determination and unity they nullified the tyrannical threat of conscription.[131]

Throughout 1918 SF prepared assiduously for the expected general election. The nature of its mobilization process revolved around passive resistance, political education and preparedness. *Nationality* advised SF members that 'the chief work of every club is to educate public opinion into the conviction of the hopelessness of the Westminster policy. Public meetings, debates, social re-unions, with short addresses, will do much to spread the light'.[132] Alongside the establishment of an effective political organization at local level, the party ensured that every eligible voter was registered by undertaking a plebiscite in each parish. Police reported that 'the referendum or plebiscite is being used as an opportunity to make a house to house collection for funds, and it will also serve as a register for election purposes'.[133] The importance of effective preparation was emphasized by the South Leitrim SF executive at its meeting in Cloone on 3 February 1918: 'Leitrim Sinn Féiners must need to wake up in time and have all preparations made for the General Election so that when it comes, Leitrim will strike a blow – this time the final blow in the cause it advocated ten years ago'.[134]

At Kiltubrid the Seán Mac Diarmada SF club reported that by the end of February 1918 the majority of people in the parish had signed the plebiscite, 'with the exception of a very limited number of blue bloods'.[135] The SF executive urged every branch that 'the services of the women members should be availed of as much as possible, especially as a very large number of the new voters will be women'.[136] Whereas the previous by-election campaigns across the country were strongly backed by outside supporters who campaigned alongside local election workers, the party realized that this would not be possible at a general election campaign. SF headquarters advised local constituency organizations to ensure that proper local structures were in place, and warned local party organizations to leave 'nothing to chance, and by seeing that the election work in every constituency is organised down to the smallest detail'.[137]

While the 1918 general election was eagerly awaited by advanced nationalists, an important feature of the contest was the effects of the Representation of People Act, which became law in April 1918. The legislation extended the vote to all men aged twenty-one and to women over thirty who were householders or married to householders. Nationally, the electorate increased from 698,000 to 1,931,000. In Leitrim eligible voters increased from 12,209 to 30,079.[138] Consequently, the electorate had a more diverse social and gender composition, with increased numbers of younger voters, women and working-class males. Another consequence of the new legislation for Leitrim was the merging of the county's two constituencies into a single unit. Local representatives on Carrick RDC were unhappy. They passed a motion condemning 'the proposed redistribution scheme, under which the large and important county of Leitrim will be deprived of one of its two representatives'.[139] The official announcement of James Dolan's candidature for the 1918 general election was made in September 1918. Like many prospective election candidates, Dolan was a prisoner in Gloucester Jail. The *Leitrim Observer* noted that 'it is fitting then that another brother of the Dolan family should once more carry the flag of Irish independence and in placing it in the hand of the brother of Charles Dolan, Leitrim has acted wisely and honourably'.[140]

The IPP was in a state of disarray and hastily convened a selection convention at Drumkeeran.[141] Having previously informed John Dillon in September 1918 of his intention not to stand in the election, Smyth pledged his support to Meehan.[142] Following a protracted meeting, Thomas Fallon was selected. He subsequently withdrew but not before the *Leitrim Observer* expressed surprise

> that a nationalist of long standing [Fallon] who stood the stress of Forster's Coercion Acts, and always took a manly part in Ireland's

cause, should allow himself to be made a shield of, with the apparent object of saving the credit of those who are afraid to face the music.[143]

Following Fallon's withdrawal, Dillon was forced to request that Gerald Farrell, a Longford barrister, contest the Leitrim seat.[144] He was the son of J.P. Farrell, an IPP stalwart, and had family connections with Leitrim but his main residence and business interests were in Longford.[145] The *Leitrim Advertiser* suggested

> Mr Farrell has not the ghost of a chance and most of the Party supporters in Leitrim are sorry to see him now forcing a contest with all its bitterness when any of the former members or other county men could not see their way to go forward in the Irish Party interest.[146]

At a meeting of Leitrim County Council to discuss numbers of presiding officers at local polling booths, Councillor Thomas McGivney claimed that the discussion was a waste of time 'because the Sinn Féiners will have a walk over; there will be no necessity to fix the booths at all'.[147]

Dolan's campaign opened with a large rally in Ballinamore on Sunday 24 November 1918. Ben Maguire, Dolan's director of elections, claimed that a victory would ensure 'the death-knell of parliamentarianism in Leitrim and the end of corruption'.[148] A series of after-Mass meetings took place on 1 December, including one at Rantogue addressed by Rice O'Beirne from Ballinamore, who, as the *Leitrim Observer* reported, was 'in the past identified with the AOH but who has for a considerable time thrown in his able lot with the cause of Sinn Féin'.[149] A large SF rally in Drumshanbo heard a letter from Fr Anthony McGaver from Drumcong calling for support for Dolan and welcoming 'any movement that may help to dislodge from parliament the present parliamentary MPs and their idiotic leader, and I wish it every success'.[150]

Throughout the campaign, SF's well-organized political machine campaigned in every part of the county. Fr Michael O'Flanagan told a meeting in Drumkeeran on 9 December that he was delighted 'with the state of political feeling in Leitrim and emphatically declared that the constituency was thoroughly sound for the principle of self-determination'.[151] At an election rally in Mohill on 12 December the IPP was condemned for forcing a contest in Leitrim and putting unnecessary expense on taxpayers. Referring to Farrell's candidature, F.J. McCabe advised the electorate to 'give him such a thrashing that he will be afraid and ashamed to be seen in Leitrim again'.[152] SF framed the election debate as a referendum for self-government and a place at the post-war Paris Peace Conference.[153] There was no evidence of any radical social or economic policies being espoused by speakers, nor were there any women speakers on election platforms.[154]

The political health of the IPP in the county was demonstrated by the absence of any concerted election campaign in support of Farrell. At election nomination day, on 4 December, the *Roscommon Herald* reported that 'Mr Farrell was left practically alone in Carrick on Wednesday having no one with him except Mr Meehan and his brother Matt Farrell, Solicitor, Ballaghadereen'.[155] Farrell and Meehan were said to have received a very hostile reception from SF supporters in the town and sought refuge in the nearby Bush Hotel. The only meeting in support of Farrell was held in Killenumery.

On election day, 14 December 1918, the *Leitrim Observer* stated that 'no doubts are entertained of Mr Dolan's return by a substantial majority as reports from all parts of the county go to show that the majority of the people favour the principle for which he stands – Ireland's independence'.[156] Apart from a small number of minor incidents between AOH and SF supporters in Drumshanbo and Aughawillan, the election was conducted in an orderly manner across the county.[157] No IPP personation agents were at most of the polling booths in the county.[158] While the presence of personation agents would not have changed the result, the need for them was quite evident. According to Volunteer Patrick J. Hargaden, 'personation was indulged in on a large scale and our men voted for absentee or dead voters. There was no trouble and the election went off quietly enough'.[159] Not only were Cumann na mBan involved in political campaigning and the provision of hospitality to SF election workers, Margaret Brady recalled that they also voted for 'dead and absentee voters'.[160]

In preparation for the election count on 28 December, extra contingents of soldiers and police were drafted into Carrick. The previous evening soldiers removed republican flags around the town but these were soon replaced by local Volunteers. The result of the election nationally was a resounding victory for SF. It won 73 of the 105 seats in Ireland, while the IPP was successful in only six. Leitrim followed the national trend: Dolan got 17,711 votes compared to Farrell's 3,096, and seventy per cent of the county's electorate turned out. Dolan's share of the vote was eighty-five per cent, the largest recorded in the country. Following the election count, a large rally took place in Carrick with Canon Thomas O'Reilly presiding. Calling for unity among all nationalists, O'Reilly declared that different views should always be tolerated and that 'they should stand shoulder to shoulder, and they had an example of what unity did in killing the cursed Act of Conscription'.[161] Across Leitrim, Dolan's success was celebrated with torchlight processions, marching bands and bonfires.[162]

Dolan's victory, like that of fellow SF candidates, can be attributed to a range of factors, most notably the comprehensive transfer of political loyalty from the IPP to SF during the preceding two years. The IPP's inability to find a candidate from Leitrim to run in the election reflected the weakness of local party structures by late 1918. In contrast, the SF machine was efficient and organized, and the conscription crisis of 1918 merely consolidated an ever-increasing level of support for advanced nationalism. SF's electoral success was driven by events between 1916 and 1918 leading to a change of political allegiance in the wider electorate, rather than a change in its composition.[163] Such a comprehensive political mandate from nationalist Ireland provided the platform for a new and radical political initiative for advanced nationalism.

6 'On the last lap of the race for Liberty's goal': the Dáil counter-state, 1919–21

When the First World War ended on 11 November 1918, a wide range of nationalist groups across Europe quickly emerged to place their demands for national independence at the conference of allied nations that was scheduled to meet at Versailles, Paris, in January 1919. Unlike Finland, the Baltic states, Czechoslovakia and Poland – regions that were ruled by some of the defeated belligerents – Ireland's claim for self-government was from one of the victorious allied powers, the United Kingdom. However, Ireland's claim was bolstered by SF's overwhelming victory at the 1918 general election and the establishment of an alternative parliament, Dáil Éireann, in Dublin. The Dáil immediately set about establishing an alternative government and civil administration to that of the British. Over the next three years, it successfully implemented separate systems of local government and judicial administration in Ireland.

When the first Dáil assembled at the Mansion House in January 1919 only twenty-seven of the elected members were present. Thirty-four of its members, including Leitrim's James Dolan, were in jail. The *Sligo Champion* reported that Ireland's newly elected public representatives would now appeal to the Peace Conference and complimented the Dáil proceedings as 'conducted in a manner befitting the dignity of Irishmen'.[1] Calling for the immediate release of prisoners, the *Champion* condemned the government, declaring that 'its vacillation and indecision in regard to the Irish political prisoners may be justly characterized as contemptible from every point of view'.[2]

In Leitrim, having secured their political dominance, SF activity now turned to wresting control of the IPP-dominated local councils. The Robert Emmet SF club in Cloone declared: 'the present members of both county and district councils should be removed at the coming election, and their places taken by new earnest active workers for Irish freedom'.[3] Clooneagh SF called on its supporters to ensure victory at the local elections, urging that 'there can be no faltering now. We are on the last lap of the race for Liberty's goal, the goal for which untold generations of Irishmen have suffered and died'.[4]

Aside from the arrest of Hugh Turbett at Ballinamore in January 1919 for posting seditious literature, there was no evidence of political crime in Leitrim during the early months of 1919. Police reports consistently noted a peaceful county with only a small number of indictable offences. Addressing the grand jury of Leitrim on 6 March 1919, Justice Gordon complimented the people of Leitrim and noted that cases of drunkenness had decreased substantially from 357 in 1917 to 175 in 1918.⁵ At the quarter sessions at Carrick on 18 March 1919, white gloves were presented to Justice Brown, who observed that 'it speaks well for the peacefulness and orderliness of this county that up to the time of making up this Sessions calendar, now for two consecutive Quarter Sessions, I have now been presented by you with white gloves on four occasions, and it is a most creditable record'.⁶

While Leitrim was free from indictable crime and political violence, growing support for SF was evident. Following the government's decision to release Irish political prisoners in the spring of 1919, Dolan arrived in Dublin on 7 March 1919. When his sister, Mary, died the following day from pneumonia in the Meath Hospital, Dublin, celebration of his release was postponed.⁷ At the first welcome home rally for Dolan on 27 April 1919 at Ballinamore, the TD told a large crowd that 'the Great War has called into being the Peace Conference to establish the rights of the world, and Ireland has her representatives there knocking strongly, determinedly and persistently at the door; and Ireland means to see that Ireland's voice shall be heard there before there is any peace in the world'.⁸ A recurring theme of Dolan's public statements was a call for unity among nationalists in the county. For example, at an aeríocht in Drumshanbo he told supporters that 'they should welcome every man into their ranks so long as there was no malice against him'.⁹ The series of welcome home celebrations for Dolan continued throughout the late spring and early summer of 1919. At a meeting in Drumkeeran on 25 May 1919, described as 'the largest and most enthusiastic meeting ever held in the district', Dolan thanked the people for their support for SF. His conciliatory tone towards all shades of nationalism was proving a success as the *Leitrim Observer* reported:

> Sunday's platform contained all the opposing elements of former days and it is a pleasing sign of the times to note the friendly intercourses all day between politicians of different political views, all united in the one grand object of removing the shackles of slavery from our motherland.¹⁰

As SF's fortunes continued to flourish within the county, the sudden death in May 1919 of Patrick Flynn was a major blow to constitutional nationalism. Friend and foe alike praised Flynn's contribution to politics. At a meeting of Leitrim County Council, Eugene O'Neill Clarke, the county surveyor, stated that Flynn 'was an ornament to every Board with which he was associated'.¹¹

Reflecting the growing support for SF among elements of the clergy, a significant clerical presence was evident at party meetings in the county. At Sunday Mass in Drumshanbo in July 1919 Fr Matthew McCabe, the local parish priest, made his political views clear when advising his congregation to 'stand by Sinn Féin as it was now the only policy for them'.[12] Fr Edward Ryans, a curate at Aughavas, was a well known SF activist, and served as president of the South Leitrim SF comhairle ceantair. Addressing a meeting at Drumshanbo in July 1919, Ryans told the crowd that 'the young men were not content to have Sinn Féin a spark, but they fanned it into a flame that spread throughout the land'.[13]

The refusal by the major powers to accede to an official Irish presence at the Versailles Peace Conference received widespread condemnation from republicans. While police reports indicated that the decision at Versailles 'was taken very quietly in the county', at an aeríocht at Fahy in August Dolan reacted angrily. He declared that 'the majority of the men who sat at the Peace Conference had a mandate from their peoples to see that justice was done to every white race. The principle was adopted that there would be no peace in the world as long as there was a white race in slavery'.[14] The rejection of Ireland's claims for self-government meant that republicans became more resolute in their demands. At a meeting at Carrigallen, Dolan and Count Plunkett rejected all solutions to the national question other than complete independence. With discussion about forms of dominion home rule emanating from government, Dolan accused the British government of attempting to conscript the souls of the Irish people, having failed to conscript their bodies. He emphatically rejected any compromise and stated:

> the easiest way to settle the Irish question was for foreigners to clear out altogether and let the Irish people govern themselves. They would not be satisfied with any other solution of the Irish question and he stood up to the demands made by the people in December 1918, and they would have that and nothing else.[15]

The authorities finally reacted to Dolan's acts of public defiance by arresting him at his home in November 1919 for promoting the Dáil loan. Launched in the autumn of 1919, the initiation of the loan scheme was one of the most significant undertakings by Dáil Éireann in its attempts to run a *de facto* government and administration. The main aim of the scheme was to obtain financial support both at home and abroad for the fledgling administration. Over £5,000 was collected in Leitrim as part of the campaign. A novel scheme by local Volunteers in south Leitrim of levying a fee of 2s. per cow on each farm holding ensured a steady flow of funds to support the loan.[16] At Dolan's trial in Drumshanbo on 21 November 1919 large crowds gathered in support of their local TD with the result that the court was cleared. Before his sentence of two months' imprisonment was passed, Dolan refused to recognize the court, declaring that 'men, swords and bayonets will never still the heart of the Irish people'.[17]

In an increasingly unstable and defiant political environment, the authorities initiated a countrywide suppression of SF, Cumann na mBan, the Irish Volunteers and the Gaelic League on 26 November 1919. Following the government crackdown, the inactivity of SF locally and nationally was reflected in the lack of press reports from branches. Even before the ban, apathy and inactivity were evident in the ranks of Cumann na mBan. The Gorvagh branch condemned absences from meetings, stating that 'it is hoped that the members of each branch will organize their own districts and work in a good spirit, and not in the uninterested way in which they have worked in the past months'.[18]

Despite political turmoil enveloping the nation, Leitrim remained in a relatively peaceful and crime free state in late 1919. At the opening of Manorhamilton quarter sessions on 24 September 1919, Judge Brown, on accepting white gloves, congratulated the people of Leitrim and declared that

> it was all the more a matter of pride when they saw what had occurred in other parts where even contrary to the laws of humanity and the teachings of common Christianity men had not scrupled to send suddenly into the next world by the assassin's bullet brother Irishmen who were nurtured on Irish homesteads and were instructed, like themselves, in Christian doctrine. Leitrim was happily free from such an unenviable reputation. Long might it remain law abiding with each man helping his neighbour and all pulling together for the general good.[19]

Following Dolan's imprisonment and the nationwide suppression of SF, the CI reported in November 1919 that 'Sinn Féin is inactive and now that it has been suppressed no meeting has attempted to be held'.[20]

An important element in the establishment of a successful counter-state was control of local government structures throughout the country. Unlike in the pre-war years when local elected bodies were dominated by the IPP, competition emerged as early as 1919 among various local factions for the positions of chairman and vice-chairman on such bodies. At Carrick board of guardians Thomas Flynn was elected on the toss of a coin. Recalling his work with Seán Mac Diarmada during the 1908 North Leitrim by-election, Flynn doubted the sincerity of many of his fellow councillors' adherence to the ideals of SF. He wondered if Mac Diarmada 'turned in his clay when he saw the men who were today shouting about Sinn Féin – men who tried to kick him through the streets'.[21] At a meeting of Leitrim County Council on 18 June 1919, the outgoing chairman, Michael Murphy, was elected on his own casting vote, after being questioned about his SF credentials and the fact that he was a justice of the peace.[22]

With the suppression of many branches of advanced nationalism, renewed attempts at home rule were on the government's political agenda in early 1920.[23] Reflecting the mood of many nationalists, the moderate *Sligo Champion* was adamant that 'any lowering of the flag at the present time, or any compromise or trucking with the half measures of British statesmen would be rightly regarded as a betrayal of the living and an outrage on the dead'.[24] Despite ongoing suppression of SF, locally elected bodies continued to operate.[25]

By late 1919 increasing levels of political violence were condemned by the Catholic hierarchy and in the press. A number of local authorities, including Westmeath, Meath, and Dublin and Cork city councils, passed resolutions condemning the campaign. Leitrim County Council passed a similar resolution at its November 1919 meeting.[26] At the request of the South Leitrim SF executive, the November 1919 resolution was raised by Councillor Michael McGrath, who proposed in February 1920 that the council rescind it. Despite protracted debate, the original motion of condemnation stood on a vote of ten to five.[27]

An opportunity to test the extent of SF electoral support in the county came about at the 1920 local elections. No local elections had taken place since 1914 and the composition of the electorate had changed radically with the passing into law of the Representation of the People Act of 1918. A feature of the 1920 elections was the introduction of proportional representation, with the primary aim of ensuring a fairer representation for minority parties in the poll. Nationally, the elections were held in two stages: the urban area elections in January 1920 and the rural areas in June 1920. Both consolidated SF's hold on political power. The January elections saw SF, Labour and other nationalists winning control of 172 of the 206 borough and urban district councils. The RDC elections in June showed a much greater level of support for SF, which took control of 338 of the 393 county and rural councils, with many areas uncontested. All of Leitrim's district and county council electoral areas were uncontested, except Manorhamilton. There, IPP stalwarts Bernard Connolly and Thomas McGovern were comprehensively defeated; Patrick MacDermott, brother of Seán Mac Diarmada, was elected to the county council.

At Mohill RDC, which had witnessed the early transfer of loyalty to SF in 1917, 'all the candidates returned in the whole of the Mohill district were representative of the Sinn Féin principles'.[28] In both district councils in the Carrick area, the elections were uncontested, with twenty-three SF and two Labour candidates returned unopposed. Prior to the Carrick district council nominations being received, tension was evident between the Labour and SF factions. At a meeting of the Carrick branch of the ITGWU before the election, William Reilly, district organizer of the union, was insistent that Labour would contest the seat and called for support for the Labour nominee Joe McCormack, declaring that 'no trade unionist could support anyone standing in the name of Labour but Mr McCormack, and in the past they had too many hypocrites pleading to labour at election times and forgetting them when their ambitions were attained'.[29] With the withdrawal of Edward Doyle, an independent candidate, an election contest was avoided as six nominations were received for the six seats on the council. Unlike the urban municipal elections, when Labour won 324 seats to SF's 422, Labour only received eleven per cent of the vote in contested county council and RDC elections in June, demonstrating the difference of appeal for the party in many rural areas.[30] Even at a time when the ITGWU had reached its peak in terms of membership, union solidarity did not translate into votes at the ballot box.[31]

The *Leitrim Observer*'s post-election analysis maintained that despite the suppression of SF, 'the determination to be free has in the intervening period increased rather than diminished, and it is obvious that the various parties which tried to carry the country in favour of a home rule settlement have almost completely lost their followers'.[32] The newspaper advised the newly elected councils that 'the primary duty of Republicans is to see that the old and evil system is completely swept away and instead is established a system clean in its every detail'.[33] The political message to government was that the people supported SF in large numbers and the transfer of political power that was demonstrated nationally in December 1918 was replicated at local council level. Politically, the doctrine of constitutional nationalism was a spent force in Leitrim, as elsewhere, and while the voice of organized labour was present in the county, it had to take a back seat to advanced nationalism. Republicans had now received a comprehensive mandate from the Irish people. The Dáil, with the assistance of local government, could now advance the establishment of the counter-state.

The alternative government of Dáil Éireann grew steadily throughout the summer of 1920. Its implementation of a separate system of civil administration in areas such as local government and justice firmly established it as the *de facto* government of Ireland. The Dáil and its leaders, both nationally and locally, became fully preoccupied with asserting their authority across nationalist Ireland. Despite widespread violence, by mid-1920 the local elections had consolidated SF support in local government.[34]

In a spirit of conciliation, the first act of Ben Maguire, the newly elected SF chairman of Manorhamilton RDC, was to pay tribute to the work of the outgoing council, which 'might not be perfect in every detail, but at the same time they appreciated all the good work that they had done'.[35] At the town's local board of guardians, one of the first acts of the new body was a resolution which expunged from the record of the board a previous resolution condemning the 1916 Rising.[36] Leitrim County Council's first post-election meeting on 16 June 1920 elected Peadar Keaney, a Gaelic League activist, and Tim Ward, a former prisoner, as chairman and vice-chairman respectively. In his acceptance speech, Keaney stated:

> Where they had contests in the county they made the issue one of the Irish Republic versus the British Empire, and they were elected on the Irish Republic issue and came here to act in accordance with their pledge at the election. The responsibility was great, but he hoped to have the co-operation of the young and old men on the Council. The farming and business interests were represented on the Council, and when he spoke of the farmers he might say they were labourers, not big ranchers, and they had therefore the farming and business and labour interests represented.[37]

Assertions of their republican credentials were widespread among the newly elected councils. Leitrim County Council pledged allegiance to Dáil Éireann and declared that 'the First Republican Council of Leitrim ostentatiously congratulated the forces of the IRA on their many successes during the past year, and the many fortresses and seats of oppression destroyed, and we earnestly hope that they may continue their successes until victory crowns their arms'.[38] Actions ranging from replacement of the RIC by Volunteers in the escort of mentally ill patients to flying the tricolour over buildings were early manifestations of the regime change within local bodies in the county. Both Leitrim County Council and Mohill RDC refused to repair roads, claiming that in doing so, they were only aiding Ireland's enemies.

Relations with the Local Government Board (LGB) provided the new councils with a serious dilemma. The Dáil, fearing the loss of British revenue that accounted for nearly a fifth of local authority funding, was happy for councils to pledge allegiance to it while continuing to receive revenue from the LGB.[39] Despite the Dáil initially requesting local councils to correspond with the LGB, both Carrick and Mohill councils refused to co-operate with either the LGB or the surveyor of taxes. Both councils ordered the burning of all correspondence received from both bodies.[40] As a result of the widespread non-submission of accounts for audit, the British government issued an ultimatum on 29 July 1920 that any council refusing to co-operate with audits would no longer receive funds from the LGB. The Dáil responded by ordering councils to replace banks with trustees in order to conduct their financial affairs.[41]

In its attempts to hamper the rival civil administration, both police and military often raided council meetings and confiscated minute books.[42] One of the most serious incidents took place on 21 July 1920 in Carrick, where a joint meeting of Roscommon and Leitrim County Councils was hosting a delegation from the Dáil Commission of Inquiry into the Resources and Industries of Ireland led by Maurice Moore and Darrell Figgis. During the course of the meeting, an army raiding party, led by a Lieutenant Crowther, entered the council room and arrested Peadar Keaney and Figgis, and ordered that a rope be procured to hang them.[43] Figgis recalled that following the discovery of SF documentation in his possession, he was 'sentenced to be hanged, the sentence to be executed at once without delay'.[44] The intervention of the local Crown clerk, Robert Londsdale, ensured that Figgis was taken from the military and conveyed to the local RIC station and released. Crowther was subsequently detained in military custody and relieved of his duties on grounds of mental instability.[45]

One of the most remarkable achievements of the Dáil was the establishment of republican arbitration courts, which were organized by the party's branches and local executives in a three-tiered structure of parish, district and circuit courts.[46] Despite the presentation of white gloves at Manorhamilton quarter sessions in late May 1920, this symbolic gesture was even questioned by members of the judiciary. At the Leitrim summer assizes at Carrick in July 1920, Justice Pim described the presentation of white gloves as a 'mockery'. According to Pim, the reason why there was so little court business was because of intimidation by third parties of jurors not to attend and pressure being exerted on the public not to bring cases.[47] As a result, Crown court activity during this period was minimal and confined to malicious damage claims and public house licence transfers. Throughout the summer of 1920 a steady stream of Dáil court activity operated across the county; it dealt with a range of cases including minor land disputes, assault, and theft.[48]

As part of the administration of justice, local Volunteers took an active part in the enforcement of court decisions. Volunteers throughout the county were also involved in a range of activities, notably area patrols, recovery of stolen property, public house licencing enforcement and traffic duties.[49] At Kiltoghert parish court, the court chairman advised that a number of public order offences, including abusive language and drunkenness, would be dealt with severely by the court 'as the present time demanded a spirit of sobriety and friendship amongst the people, who are engaged in the resurrection of their national ideals and the regeneration of their country'.[50] The wide range of policing activity was demonstrated when, following a request from a local priest, the local Volunteers 'rounded up a number of people who were standing outside the church during the sermon and ordered them to go inside and listen'.[51]

By the summer of 1920 republican courts were well established and operated unhindered with the support of the general public and the legal profession.[52] Although court personnel changed, the majority of cases before the republican courts still revolved around land and property disputes. Among a sample of cases in the court registrar returns in 1921 were possession of a house, rights of way, and possession of a byre.[53] There was an initial toleration of these courts but British government policy changed in late August 1920. Attempts to hinder the development of republican local administration were boosted by the Restoration of Order in Ireland Act, which altered government policy from tolerance to repression. This resulted in court sittings being raided on an ongoing basis across the county.[54] While republican courts gained the support of much of the public, their success was circumscribed by the weakness of central direction, undue local influences, and disruption by both the police and military.[55] The operation of the courts was significant, as it demonstrated that civil disobedience was an alternate mode of resistance. Their capacity to function in relatively peaceful counties such as Leitrim, Galway and Laois demonstrated that British rule in Ireland was also threatened by one of the more potent aspects of non-violent republicanism.[56] Not only did republicans defy the government, they ensured through a combination of persuasion and intimidation that the institutions of government were boycotted.[57]

As repression continued across Ireland, the passing of the Government of Ireland Act on 23 December 1920 was the British cabinet's attempt finally to introduce home rule. The *Sligo Champion* observed that 'the English government gives a Christmas box to Ireland, a Partition Bill [*sic*] jocously called "home rule for Ireland". No one wants it, and no one is bothering about its provisions'.[58]

At local level, councils were preoccupied with the minutiae of gulley filling and sheep dipping in the face of mounting disruption and raids from the authorities. At Manorhamilton in April 1921 a meeting of the local board of guardians was raided and, following an inspection of the minute book, Ben Maguire was arrested and subsequently imprisoned.[59] The arrest of many councillors and travel disruption across the county also hampered the administration of local government. By July 1921 the Dáil had refused a request from Mohill RDC to operate a quorum of three people for council meetings. The background to the Mohill request was that the council had to disqualify seven members for non-attendance. Five of those were either in jail or on the run.[60]

Another operational issue for local councils was a lack of finance due to a cessation of grant aid and non-payment of rates. In January 1921 Leitrim County Council announced that owing to its financial position, it was unable to clean or repair public roads.[61] The decision to sell the dispensaries and board of guardian houses in Dromahair and Manorhamilton due to financial constraints generated much local opposition from both within and outside the council chamber. James McGorrin, president of the local guardians, observed that 'if we are to sell those houses, and next year we are again in financial difficulties and sell something else, we will soon have nothing to sell, and when things are settled down we will have to build and get into some property again'.[62]

While agrarian unrest swept across Galway, Mayo and Roscommon in early 1920, Leitrim, with the exception of the Gowel and Carrick areas, did not witness any largescale agitation during the period. The main reasons were the comparative absence of large grazier farms in the county and the fact that the rate of land purchase by tenant farmers was higher than in neighbouring counties. At Gowel, the arrival home from America of Jim Gralton in June 1921 heralded increased social unrest in the area. Gralton, a Volunteer and former member of the American Communist Party, advocated widespread land distribution. His activities stirred suspicion among many locals and SF leaders who feared the land issue would distract attention from the national question. The foundation of the National Land Bank by the Dáil in December 1919 resulted in loans being made available to the landless and to owners of uneconomic holdings with a view to enabling them to acquire additional land.[63] Consequently, co-operative societies were formed in many areas to facilitate the purchase of untenanted land. By 1921 the bank had lent a total of £316,590 to thirty-five societies with a membership of eight hundred, for the purchase of nearly 16,000 acres.[64] In Leitrim one society was formed in the Carrick district which facilitated the purchase of the Jamestown estate for £6,730. The campaign to redistribute the Jamestown land was led by Fr O'Farrell, the local curate, who was adamant that the campaign to redistribute the land would be peaceful and conducted on the basis of social justice and the common agreed principle of 'Ireland for the Irish, and the land for the people'.[65] At nearby Carrick Canon O'Reilly led a campaign that resulted in the purchase of a seventy-five acre farm for distribution amongst the landless and uneconomic landowners of the area. While the operations of the Land Bank were relatively modest, it prevented widespread violent land agitation and was an expression of the Dáil's commitment to tackling the question of landownership.[66]

Political agitation was not the sole preserve of SF; Leitrim's farmers were actively involved in late 1919 in the formation of the Irish Farmers' Union (IFU). This period coincided with the suppression of SF and many SF members in Leitrim were active in the union. A branch and executive network was established throughout the county in late 1919 and early 1920. At a meeting in Fenagh in November 1919 with Michael Murphy, SF chairman of Leitrim County Council, presiding, a large crowd was told that

> the farmers need no longer remain the only disorganised and inarticulate portion of the community. They had now their Union and their newspaper to ventilate their grievances and to keep them informed of those happenings that most concern them. They in Leitrim should now march on with the farmers all over the country in this Union of brotherhood and progress.[67]

Tensions were evident between the IFU and labour unions across Ireland, with a strike embargo by organized labour preventing the export of pork and butter products. According to Larry Hayden, IFU county secretary, the embargo was a very serious issue for farmers. He claimed that

> if labour called for arbitration before wielding the strike weapon he would venture to say that the farmers through the medium of their organisation would go half way to meet their demands, and in all probability both parties would come to a satisfactory settlement for both consumer and producer.[68]

While police reports highlighted the national growth of the ITGWU, this was marginal in Leitrim during the period.[69] By early 1920 the ITWU had six branches and nearly 400 members in the county, primarily composed of shop assistants and labourers in local councils. Unlike other counties, where farm labourers formed large segments of the union, the lack of large farms in Leitrim meant that there was an absence of this cohort from the county's union branches. Despite a relatively narrow base of union membership, as early as 1919 May Day was observed as a general holiday for shop workers in both Carrick and Ballinamore. In the absence of industrial unrest, trade union activity revolved around issues of increased wages for council labourers and the implementation of the Shop Hours Act which gave shop workers a weekly half-day holiday.[70] In pay negotiations on behalf of shop assistants, the Ballinamore branch of the ITGWU reported that local employers were friendly and acceded to their demands 'without any trouble'.[71]

Other union activity involved the local trades and labour council in Carrick campaigning for a reduction of food prices and condemning alleged profiteering by local shopkeepers.[72] In May 1920 agreement was reached between the union and employers on wage increases for outdoor labourers from 32s. to 40s. and for their indoor counterparts from 16s. to £1. The only serious industrial unrest that occurred was the seizure of a coal pit by miners on the Leitrim side of the county bounds with Roscommon in June 1921. In what has often described as 'the Arigna Soviet', nine miners took control of a local mine and sold coal directly to the public following the breakdown of wage talks with the ITGWU. After court action was instituted by the mine owners, the *Freeman's Journal* compared the Arigna incident to the workers' takeover of Knocklong creamery in Limerick.[73] The agitation in Arigna and at Knocklong and Bruree in Limerick was only short term and order was restored after negotiations.[74] Following the widespread dismissal of nationalist workers in Belfast, the union also supported a boycott of Belfast goods initiated by Dáil Éireann. At an ITGWU meeting in Carrick, William Reilly declared that no union member would handle Belfast goods in opposition to attempts by 'the capitalist class of Orangemen to break up the trade union movement in that city which has done much to elevate the position of the workers of all creeds and classes and further the cause of Irish nationality'.[75]

While the backing for Labour was marginal in a small-farm dominated rural economy, support for striking railway workers was demonstrated in Carrick in June 1920. At an after-Mass collection in Carrick to raise funds for the railwaymen who had been dismissed from employment because they refused to facilitate the movement of munitions for the British army, over £60 was collected.[76] Labour gatherings were also subject to suppression by the military, and following a military raid on a union meeting at Dromahair in April 1920, the local branch asserted the long established right of labour to hold meetings for the benefit of members, declaring that 'we do not think it is necessary to ask any permit from military or other forces'.[77]

Following the 1920 local elections, the Dáil and its local SF party machine exerted their authority across Ireland. Not only did they acquire a mandate from the people, but republican administrators successfully exercised their authority in a wide range of areas, including local government and courts administration. Their success was based on achieving both the support of and respect from the general public for efficient and fair governance. Despite a wide range of attempts by government to stymie the operation of the counter-state, republican administrators, not unlike their military comrades, ensured that Ireland was lost to Britain.

7 'Vengeance was swift and very destructive': War of Independence, 1919-21

Less than a month after SF's resounding victory at the 1918 general election, the first shots of Ireland's War of Independence were fired on 21 January 1919 by members of the South Tipperary Brigade, IRA, who killed two policemen and stole a consignment of explosives destined for a local stone quarry. For the next two-and-a-half years, as republican politicians and administrators built a parallel government to the British one across Ireland, their military counterparts fought a bitter and often brutal war against the Crown forces. Unlike the republican counter-state, which made consistent if modest inroads across nationalist Ireland, levels of political violence varied from negligible in many areas, including Leitrim, to intense and highly concentrated in other counties. Nevertheless, despite low levels of IRA violence in many counties, the administration of British rule was rendered impossible by campaigns of boycott, intimidation and civil disobedience.

The first signs of outward Volunteer activity took place in Leitrim at Ballinamore in July 1918 when police observed between sixty and seventy young men, under the direction of Michael Mulligan, drilling in a field near the town. Mulligan was subsequently arrested and sentenced to twelve months' imprisonment for unlawful assembly. While police reports give no indication of an active Volunteer organization, the first meeting of Volunteer units countywide was held at Gorvagh in August 1918. At this meeting, the South Leitrim Brigade was formed with three battalions covering Cloone/Carrigallen (1st Battalion), Ballinamore/Drumshanbo (2nd Battalion), and Mohill/Carrick (3rd Battalion).[1] Because of the geography of the county, the adoption of a north–south divide in the formation of Volunteer structures was both necessary and practical. North Leitrim Volunteer companies joined the brigade areas of south Donegal and north Sligo. The term IRA was used from 1919 onwards and in that year new companies at Dromahair, Newtownmanor, Killavoggy and Killargue became part of the 8th Battalion, Sligo Brigade, while companies in the villages of Tullaghan and Kinlough near the Donegal border joined the South Donegal Brigade. Martin Bernard McGowan from Kinlough became the commanding officer of the 2nd Battalion of the Sligo Brigade which was active in engagements with Crown forces in the north Sligo region in 1920–1. Branches of Fianna Éireann, the republican boy scout movement, were established in 1921 in the south of the county at Carrick, Gorvagh, Cloone, Dromod, Drumsna and Mohill.[2]

In Leitrim the only strike against the Crown forces during the first year of the War of Independence was an attempted assault by Charles Timoney on

Sergeant Hugh Devanny at Fivemilebourne in June 1919. Timoney, captain of the Drumalease company and president of the local SF club, had received a six-month prison sentence in 1918 for illegal drilling and unlawful assembly. At the subsequent trial in 1919 Devanny described the altercation with Timoney, who allegedly told the policeman 'I will shoot you like the officer in Tipperary'.[3] The defendant was bound to the peace for twelve months for the assault on the RIC sergeant. Aside from the Timoney incident, police reports described a peaceful county with an active SF party and little or no IRA activity. Peter Hart recognized the relative inactivity of many regions and argued that SF party organizers, as opposed to their IRA comrades, were more active and successful in the midlands and north Connacht.[4]

By early 1920 the political environment in Leitrim was showing signs of change. Although police reports indicated that in January 1920 recruitment to the RIC was in a healthy state, a change was evident a month later when the CI recorded that the 'general condition of the county was peaceable, but not as peaceable as it was. Several attempts have been made to intimidate prospective recruits for the RIC, and also some raids for arms and threatening letters'.[5] One such attempt at intimidation at Ballinamore resulted in the shooting of Patrick McCabe, a railway porter, on 24 March 1920. McCabe was stopped by a group of men near his home and, after indicating his intention of joining the RIC, was shot; his leg was subsequently amputated. Boycott and intimidation were not only directed at policemen and their families but in many instances at members of the local community who appeared to be friendly with the RIC.[6] No neighbour would transport McCabe to his compensation hearing at the Carrick quarter sessions: he had to walk the ten-mile journey on crutches.[7]

Having virtually no munitions, the IRA conducted an increased number of raids for arms during the spring and summer of 1920. Hugh Brady described a process whereby 'every house where it was known, or suspected, that there were arms of any sort, was visited by our men. In most cases, it was only a matter of calling for the arms'.[8] Similarly, Bernard Sweeney recalled little or no resistance being offered to Volunteers calling to households looking for arms. However, the IRA did encounter resistance at a small number of unionist households. At Kiltubrid in April 1920 Richard Taylor initially resisted the raiders by firing shots at them. After an exchange of gunfire and a threat to burn the house, Taylor surrendered his gun and ammunition.[9] At Ardrum on 21 May 1920, John O'Rourke, Michael McGoldrick and brothers Frank and Michael Sweeney arrived at the home of William Johnston to demand the surrender of arms and ammunition. Having been requested to return a short time later by the householder, the four men were arrested by a waiting RIC patrol. The following day train driver John Gaffney refused to take the men and a police escort to Sligo. Attempts to move the prisoners by road were thwarted by local IRA Volunteers who felled trees and blocked roads around the town. An intervention by the local clergy calmed the large crowd and the prisoners were returned to the local barracks.[10] After the police cleared the roadblocks, the prisoners were eventually transported to Sligo by road. At their subsequent trial in Carrick, all four men were acquitted, claiming that they went undisguised and unarmed with the sole intention of borrowing a gun. Dan Gallogly suggests 'that the reason they got off so lightly was due to the influence of the local postmaster, who wanted the boycott imposed on Johnson [sic], his brother-in-law lifted'.[11]

As in the south of the county, when arms raids began the only resistance that the north Leitrim IRA encountered were at the homes of unionist families. At those of both William Vanston and William McNasser, near Manorhamilton, shots were fired by the householders before they surrendered their arms.[12] A number of novel schemes were adopted in the search for arms. Eugene Kilkenny recalled dressing up in a British army uniform and collecting arms in the Cloone and Aughavas areas.[13] A rather unusual addition to the local arsenal occurred in September 1920 when Drumshanbo Volunteers rowed to Inisfallen Island on Lough Allen, the home of British army veteran Major Maurice O'Conor, and demanded two small cannon. Both were handed over and the *Anglo-Celt* reported that 'the raiders left a receipt for the cannon, apologized for intruding and assured Mrs O'Conor they would afford the island protection if needed'.[14] The home of Anne Godley at Killegar was raided when she and her steward were at church service. The police reported that the intruders 'helped themselves to brandy, cigarettes and cake on failing to find arms. Although some of the raiders have been identified no one will attend to give evidence'.[15] At Ballinamore, the owner of Newell's hardware shop was held up at gunpoint and a consignment of gelignite was taken from the shop's storeroom.[16]

As a result of the increasing number of arms raids across the county, the RIC visited homes and collected arms in order to prevent them falling into the hands of the IRA. When Volunteers called to the home of retired CI Ross Rainsford at Carrick they were told that he had already handed his arms to the RIC. At the spring assizes in Carrick on 4 March 1920, Judge Moore commented that, although the county was not 'as bad as other counties', he was unhappy that arms raids and intimidation were increasing.[17] Some local clergy, including Fr John Pinkman, curate in Mohill, 'warned young men against the danger and sin of taking part in raids for arms'.[18] By mid-1920 the CI reported that although

> no companies of Irish Volunteers are known to the police as existing officially in the county, every young Sinn Féiner is practically a 'Volunteer', and a member of some Sinn Féin club. It is not believed

that many arms are in the hands of these young fellows, nor much ammunition, but they must have a good many shotguns and old revolvers seized in raids.[19]

In spring 1920, in its attempt to hamper British civil administration, republicans initiated a campaign of intimidation which targeted state officials, including local rate collectors. The killing of Francis Curran, a 64-year-old rate collector, at Aughavas on 12 April 1920 was linked to the rate collection issue. Curran, a local farmer and father of eight children, worked for county councillor Michael Curran, and was an unpopular rate collector and an ardent critic of SF. Francis Curran was killed by two masked men, armed with shotguns, after returning from work at Michael Curran's. Although there was a general pattern of intimidating state officials during the spring of 1920, the reason for Curran's death was unclear.[20] Denouncing the killing, Bishop Hoare of Ardagh and Clonmacnoise proclaimed that

> they were told they were at war against the enemy. That was not so. War was declared by the head of the State. And all sides given an opportunity to prepare. This man was shot from behind a wall. It was all nonsense to talk of being at war with the enemy. If they did not make up for this, the scourge of God would fall on them.[21]

While many of Leitrim's clergy did not support militant republicanism, some of the county's Roman Catholic priests were active supporters. Like their parishioners, clergy transferred their political allegiance from home rule to SF's republican philosophy with relative ease. The involvement of clergy in the broader republican movement ensured that priests could exercise an element of control over republicans.[22] Condemnation of republican violence was a natural response for many priests, but as a state campaign of coercion ensued, clerical condemnation of IRA violence became more muted for fear of losing the respect of their congregations.[23]

As a result of the RIC's decision in late 1919 and early 1920 to abandon many rural police barracks and move to more fortified central locations, IRA GHQ initiated a centrally co-ordinated campaign to burn many vacant barracks to prevent re-occupation. The withdrawal of the police from many parts of rural Ireland further alienated the force from the local population and surrendered large areas of the countryside to republican courts and police. In Leitrim, as shown in map 4, despite the relative quietude of the county, the RIC vacated twenty-five rural barracks and moved officers to the main towns of Carrick, Mohill, Ballinamore, Drumshanbo, and Manorhamilton.

On Easter Saturday night, 3 April 1920, Leitrim IRA engaged in the widespread burning of vacated barracks at Rantogue, Drumsna, Garadice,

Farnaught and Fenagh. At Rantogue the raiders informed the wife of the local RIC sergeant of their intention to burn the building and assisted her in moving her possessions to nearby alternative accommodation. At Fenagh Volunteers also moved family possessions, including turf, to the local hall before burning the building.[24] Reporting on the burning of Farnaught barracks, the *Leitrim Observer* noted that the raiding party 'removed Mrs Gilroy and her family to a neighbour's house for shelter and safety, the men then removed the furniture and other belongings and piled them safely outside some distance away'.[25] This pattern of behaviour contrasted sharply with that of many other IRA units throughout the country, with policemen's families often being turned out of their dwellings without any recourse to aid from neighbours.[26] The AOH in north Kiltubrid condemned the destruction of property and warned that the actions of the raiders was 'no advancement to the interests of the country, but will bring a taxation on the already over taxed rate payers of the country'.[27] Burnings and raids on government offices continued throughout the spring and summer of 1920 at Keshcarrigan, Glenade, Gorvagh, Kiltyclogher, Cloone and Dowra. The only daylight burning of a police barracks took place at Cloone in July 1920 when the IRA blocked off the village before burning the local barracks.[28]

The release of republican prisoners from Mountjoy Jail was the background to the burning of the Masonic hall in Ballinamore during the early hours of 17 April 1920. Following a hunger strike in the pursuit of political status and to protest against detention without trial, the prisoners had been finally freed. Prior to the release, a nationwide general strike was called on 13 April 1920 by the Irish Labour Party and Trades Union Congress in support of the prisoners.[29] In Leitrim the strike was supported in all the main towns of the county. At Ballinamore, three hundred workers of the Cavan and Leitrim Railway Company stopped work in support of the strike.[30] When news of the government's concession to the prisoners' demands reached Leitrim, celebrations began across the county. At Ballinamore sections of the crowd broke a number of shop windows of boycotted unionist businesses that had refused to close on the day of the general strike. This boycott was eventually lifted following the intervention of a SF arbitration court and the issuing of a public apology by the business owners in the local newspaper.[31] Later that evening the RIC barracks was attacked by stone throwers and a group of men burned the Masonic hall.

The increase in violent activity in the Ballinamore district was raised in the House of Commons on 27 April 1920 by Colonel Wilfred Ashley, Conservative MP for Flyde, who listed a range of outrages, including arson, murder, boycott and intimidation. Ashley's demand for the immediate protection of the inhabitants was acceded to with the arrival of twenty-five soldiers in Ballinamore in early May 1920.[32] Despite the arrival of soldiers of the East Yorkshire Regiment in the county, IRA activity continued throughout May and June of 1920. This involved the derailment of a train outside Mohill and raids at Carrick's revenue and customs office. The Carrick raiders left a note, claiming that 'only documents harmful to the Irish Republic were taken'.[33] As a result of the intense period of barrack burnings, public bodies were well aware of the impending malicious damages claims on the ratepayers of the county. Noting that the Manorhamilton sub-district in north Leitrim was relatively free of violence and barrack burnings and that most claims originated in the south of the county, Councillor Irwin at Manorhamilton RDC expressed the belief that 'each end should bury their own dead'.[34]

By June 1920 the CI was demanding more reinforcements. He reported that existing troops were confined to guarding barracks and courthouses. Claiming that intimidation and boycott were widespread and contributing to low morale among the RIC, he advised that 'patrols should be sent out at night to assert the law and show the Sinn Féin party that they have not things all their own way as they practically have at present'.[35] In response, additional detachments of the East Yorkshires were drafted into Mohill and Carrick to assist the police. Both the *Irish Bulletin*, the official newspaper of the Irish Republic, and the *Sligo Independent* reported the planned enlargement of the military presence in Carrick and noted that 'a gun has been placed on the roof and sand bags and wire entanglements have been set up'.[36]

In early 1920 the introduction of British army veterans to bolster the ranks of the RIC as a response to increased levels of political violence and intimidation introduced a new phase of brutality to the conflict. The new recruits' mixed mode of dress, necessitated by a shortage of RIC bottle green uniforms, gave the group their infamous nickname – the 'Black and Tans'. Although officially classed as temporary RIC constables, they established themselves as a unique group with a different wage level, code of discipline and group culture.[37] Throughout the summer of 1920 Black and Tans and soldiers were drafted into Mohill, Ballinamore and Carrick. The *Leitrim Observer* reported in March 1920 that 'ex-soldiers partially attired in the uniform of the RIC and in khaki are doing duty at Carrick-on-Shannon, and the different towns throughout the whole county at the present time'.[38] In addition to the Black and Tans, the Auxiliary Division of the RIC was formed in July 1920 and consisted of former army officers who were recruited with the rank of police officer. During the War of Independence, Leitrim was under the control of the 13th Infantry Brigade of the British army's 5th Division with the Royal Sussex, East Yorkshire and Bedfordshire and Hertfordshire Regiments serving in the county. During the early autumn of 1920 two detachments of Auxiliaries were based at Longford and Boyle to police Longford, south Leitrim and north Roscommon. Although Boyle in County Roscommon was the area headquarters, military detach-

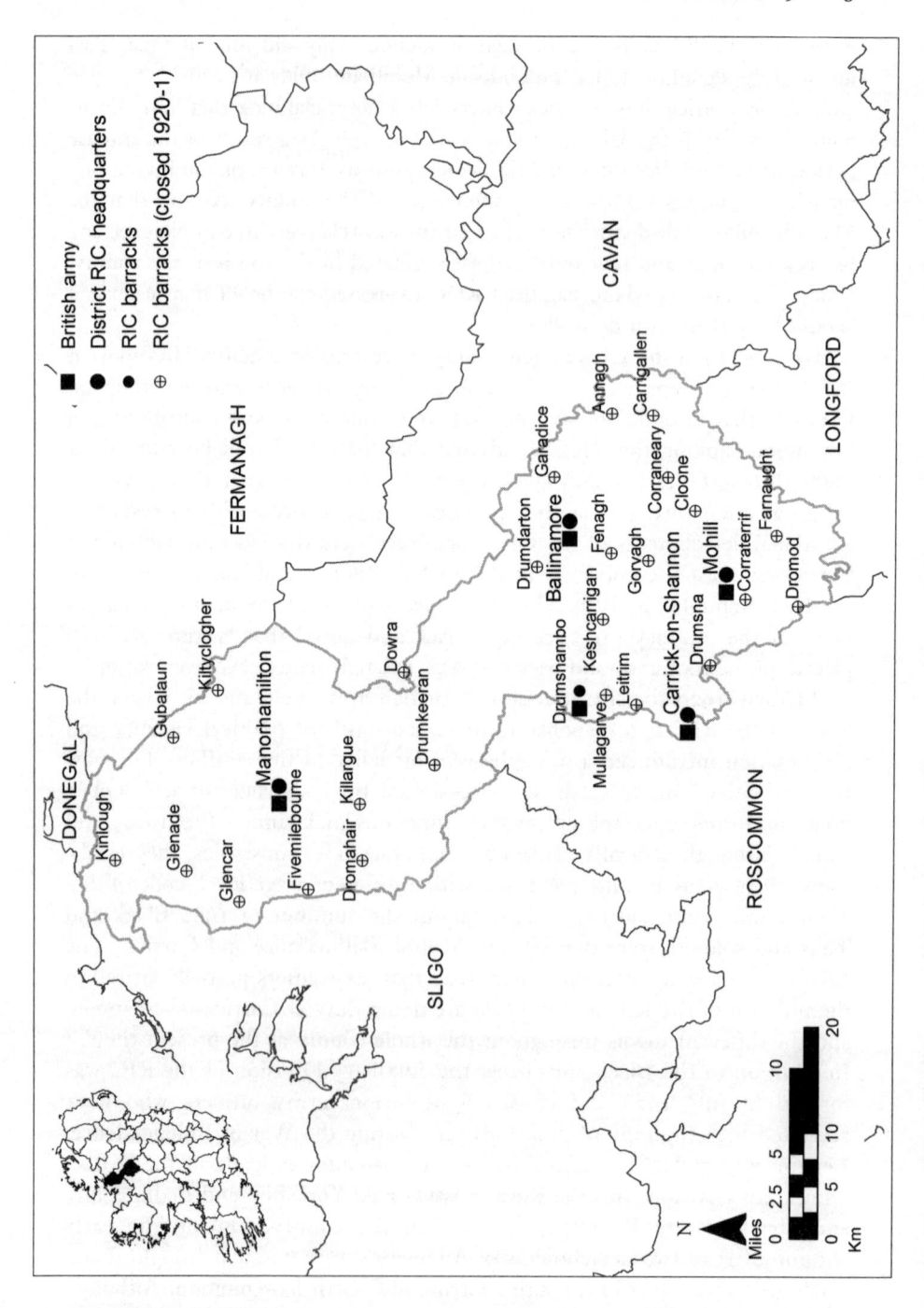

4 Distribution of Crown forces

1 Leitrim Rifles Militia at Carrick in the 1880s. This is the earliest photo of Crown forces in Leitrim.
2 (*below, left*), Charles Dolan, Sinn Féin candidate in the 1908 North Leitrim by-election.
3 Thomas Smyth, Irish Parliamentary Party MP for South Leitrim from 1906 to 1918.

4 Mohill, *c.*1912.
5 Drumshanbo Fife and Drum band, 1912.

6 Irish Volunteers at Manorhamilton in 1914.
7 National Volunteers at Ballinamore in 1914.

8 Poster advertising Bornacoola parade of Irish Volunteers, August 1914.
9 Locals with RIC officer at Drumshanbo, $c.$1915.

10 (*above, left*) Fr Patrick Clancy, British army chaplain and curate in Drumshanbo, 1908–16.
11 (*above, right*) Captain Thomas Gordon, Mohill, Royal Army Veterinary Corps.
12 Capt. John O'Donel, recruiter for the British army, 1914–18.

13 Seán Mac Diarmada, native of Kiltyclogher and executed 1916 leader.
14 Paul Galligan, Volunteer organizer in Leitrim.

15 Labour activist Jimmy Gralton with his sister, Mary Anne, in America, 1915.
16 Jimmy Gralton in later life.
17 Leitrim's first TD, James N. Dolan.

18 The aftermath of the burning of Dowra barracks by the IRA on the Cavan/Leitrim border in 1920.
19 Graffiti left by the Crown forces on Meehan's shop in Mohill.

20 (*above, left*) Cumann na mBan activist Margaret Sweeney.
21 (*above, right*) Joe Nangle, a member of the IRA ambush party at Sheemore in March 1921.
22 Michael Geoghegan, a member of the IRA ambush party at Sheemore in March 1921.

23 Volunteer Tom Beirne, killed at Selton Hill, March 1921.
24 (*below, left*), Volunteer Paddy Guckian, a survivor of the Selton Hill ambush at Gorvagh.
25 (*below, right*), William Latimer, shot as an alleged informer at Gorvagh in 1921.

26 Dr Charles Pentland in his Royal Army Medical Corps uniform, 1915.
27 North Leitrim IRA leader Martin Bernard McGowan.

28 Volunteer James McGlynn who was accidentally shot dead while enforcing the Belfast boycott at Drumshanbo in April 1921.
29 RIC District Inspector Thomas Gore Hickman.

30 Memorial card of Commandant Phil Gilgunn, killed in November 1922 during an attack on Manorhamilton.
31 Charles McGoohan in ceremonial National army uniform. McGoohan was a prominent member of the IRA's South Leitrim Brigade and later served in the National army.
32 British troops departing Carrick for the last time, January 1922.

33 Dr Patrick Muldoon, killed in Mohill in March 1922.
34 Commandant Harry McKeon, National army commander in south Leitrim in 1922.

35 Seán Mitchell, IRA O/C of IRA's South Leitrim Brigade on his wedding day.
36 Members of the February 1922 Northern Command raiding party on Enniskillen, following their release from prison. *Back row (left to right)*: Frank Reilly (Ballinamuck, Co. Longford), Charlie Reynolds (Gortlettragh, Co. Leitrim), John Kiernan (Newtowngore, Co. Leitrim), Bernie Sweeney (Ballinamore, Co. Leitrim), Seán Flood (Dublin). *Front row*: William Reilly (Longford), John Joe Griffin (Gortlettragh, Co. Leitrim), J. Lee (Longford), Joe Reynolds (Aghacashel, Co. Leitrim), Jim Davis (Derry).

37 Commandant Seán Mitchell (foreground) with National Army troops at Finner Camp, County Donegal.

ments were posted in Carrick, Mohill, Drumshanbo, Ballinamore and Manorhamilton throughout the period.[39] While the Auxiliaries were under the administrative structure of the RIC, for operational reasons they were under the command structures of the military. The old workhouse in Boyle was the base for 'E' Company under Lieutenant-Colonel S.F. Sharp, and 'M' Company was based at the county infirmary in Longford. Both auxiliary groups were formed as counter insurgency forces that operated independently of other RIC units and were primarily responsible for reprisal attacks and burnings in Leitrim.[40] Although both the Black and Tans and Auxiliaries were separate and distinct with different command structures, they were inseparable in the public mind.[41]

Despite the relative quietude of the north of the county, the only attack on an occupied barracks took place at Fivemilebourne in the early hours of 2 June 1920. While the barracks was in Leitrim, the attack was led by the North Sligo Brigade under Séamus Devins. Leitrim IRA companies, part of the the Sligo Brigade, blocked roads in the immediate area. Despite making a hole in the roof of the barracks and a protracted engagement with the six-man RIC contingent, the raiders were thwarted and eventually withdrew. The barracks was subsequently evacuated by the RIC and the local IRA burned the building on 16 June 1920. The vacated barracks at neighbouring Killargue was burned a week later.[42]

The first direct confrontation between police and the IRA took place at Mohill on 30 May 1920 with an attempted raid on the local railway station where a recently arrived consignment of steel shutters destined for the local RIC barracks were stored. A police patrol noticed the attempted break-in and a gun battle ensued but the raiders escaped. Unable to procure any local transport as a result of the police boycott, the *Sligo Independent* reported that 'the police then dragged cartloads of the window shutters to the barracks and barricaded the building'.[43] One of the more daring challenges by the local IRA to Crown forces took place early on Sunday morning 4 July when four soldiers of the East Yorkshire Regiment were overpowered while guarding a broken down military lorry at Drumreilly. The soldiers had been transporting furniture from an evacuated barracks at Carrigallen to Ballinamore when the truck got stuck on soft ground; a party was left to guard the vehicle overnight. Word of the military presence quickly spread, and the following morning ten Volunteers mingled with parishoners from Drumlea church. While passing the military lorry, they quickly overcame the troops, confiscated their arms and ammunition and burned the lorry before escaping. Mohill RDC immediately passed a resolution congratulating 'the soldiers of the Irish Republican Army on the victory they achieved at Drumreilly.'[44]

Given how poorly armed the IRA was, it generally engaged in less risky activities such as burning barracks and robbing post offices and local postmen.[45] From May 1920 raids on postmen in Leitrim were a regular occurrence.[46] Part of the reason for minimal military engagement by the IRA was an increased British military presence in the county.[47] Nevertheless, the first ambush in Leitrim took place outside Ballinamore on 2 September 1920, when a four-man bicycle police patrol was attacked at Crimlin. The ambush proved a failure because the eight-man IRA unit opened fire with shotguns when the police were out of effective range. After a brief exchange of fire, the police retreated. There were no casualties.[48] Later that night an IRA unit led by Bernard Sweeney burned Ballinamore courthouse.[49]

While little direct physical confrontation took place in 1920, the more covert activity of boycott and intimidation was used extensively by republicans. Part of this strategy was the deliberate isolation of policemen and their families from the communities that they considered themselves to be part of. The rationale for boycott made sense as RIC intelligence sources were used frequently in the war against republicans. Recalling a disturbed county with low morale among the RIC, the CI described the situation at Mohill in June 1920, 'where police officer's [sic] families are severally boycotted and where persons who befriend the police are threatened with serious trouble on that account'.[50] In June the newly appointed CI Charles O'Hara had to vacate his accommodation at the Bush Hotel because the proprietor had been intimidated for providing him with lodgings. By August 1920 the *Roscommon Herald* reported that 'throughout County Leitrim the boycotting of police is carried on and there is no outside intercourse with or assistance in any way rendered to members of that body'.[51] According to Patrick J. Hargaden, the RIC were 'treated as outcasts and everyone, or almost everyone shunned them'.[52] In order to acquire goods from traders, the police adopted a policy of entering premises, forcibly taking goods and leaving money. The *Irish Bulletin* reported that 'British police armed with revolvers raided several shops in Mohill, Co. Leitrim, and commandeered supplies. Payment was left for what was taken'.[53] The police stated that the traders appeared willing enough to do business on these terms and 'only pretended a reluctance to supply the police through fear'.[54] When informed that Crown forces were doing this in Leitrim, Michael Collins advised that no action be taken because 'when we have driven them to this position our boycott is a success'.[55]

Police reports in the summer of 1920 indicated low numbers of RIC recruits 'due to the consequence on their families'.[56] Threats against policemen and their immediate families, in addition to members of the wider community who were thought to be friendly or sympathetic to the RIC, were deeply rooted traditions in Ireland.[57] The historic weapons of boycott and intimidation forced the RIC and their families into an isolated and dangerous existence. Among its more common features were sending anonymous threatening letters, posting proclamations, administering oaths by force, raiding homes and damaging property.[58] At Carrick on 10 June 1920 a notice was placed at the post office and the office of inland revenue. It warned that 'notice is hereby given that all intercourses of any kind whatsoever between citizens of the Irish Republic and that portion of the Army of Occupation known as the RIC, is forbidden and that a general boycott of the said force is ordered: and that all persons infringing this order will be included in this boycott'.[59] At Drumshanbo and Kinlough, warnings were issued that anyone trading with or talking to the police would be deemed to be assisting the enemy and would 'be severally dealt with'.[60] While these everyday acts of harm and threat did not operate in isolation from political violence, they combined to create a fearful environment in the local community.[61]

Policemen were often targeted through intimidation of their families. An effective campaign of intimidation against police families in Leitrim resulted in eleven officers resigning from the force, the second-highest number in Ireland outside of Cork.[62] At Glenfarne creamery, manager Denis Sheelan refused to take milk from a local farmer until his son resigned from the RIC.[63] The *Roscommon Herald* reported that 'resignations from the RIC are being announced daily throughout Co. Leitrim, and a big proportion of those resigning are men of long service'.[64] Patrick J. Hargaden believed that, while a number of good young men resigned from the force in Leitrim, many who remained became more bitter towards republicans.[65]

As a response to increasing levels of IRA violence, a more brutal phase in the conflict was initiated by the authorities in the late summer of 1920. The change in character of the conflict from erratic and limited action to more widespread and ruthless conflict was facilitated by the passing of the Restoration of Order in Ireland Act in August 1920.[66] Despite low levels of violence in many areas countrywide, the new legislation and the arrival of the Auxiliaries in the autumn of 1920 was the beginning of a new phase in the conflict.[67] The threat to law and order led the authorities to resort to a range of coercive measures. These included internment, the use of courts martial, military tribunals and the imposition of curfews.

The first IRA fatality in a confrontation with Crown forces took place in Drumsna on the night of 11 September 1920 when Pat Gill, a local Volunteer, was shot dead while travelling to the wake of his cousin, Bernard O'Beirne, who was also a member of the IRA. The *Roscommon Herald* declared that 'what can only be described as a reign of terror existed in the peaceful Leitrim village, Drumsna for about an hour on Saturday night last'.[68] After passing a parked military lorry containing a party of soldiers, a shot was fired at Gill. At the subsequent inquest into Gill's death, Lieutenant Wallace of the East Yorkshire Regiment stated that Gill was requested to stop three times before being shot. Condemning the killing and returning a verdict of murder, the jury foreman stated: 'we draw the attention of the civilized world to the necessity of ridding our country from the tyrannical rule at the hands of a foreign government'.[69] The funerals of both O'Beirne and Gill attracted large crowds and their coffins were accompanied by IRA guards of honour.[70]

Controversy also surrounded the killing of 70-year-old James Connolly during a military and police raid at his home at Kinlough on 14 September. The Connolly family were known republicans. James (Junior) was a member of Leitrim County Council and served as an officer in the Kinlough company which was attached to the South Donegal Brigade IRA. Liam Ó Duibhir suggests that the raid was part of a reprisal for the burning of Dunkineely RIC barracks in south Donegal.[71] The police claimed that Connolly was shot when he rushed towards a nearby room, having refused to put his hands up when ordered to do so.[72] During the raid, Connolly's son was discovered in the house and arrested. The military authorities did not co-operate with Connolly's inquest and no military witnesses attended.[73] The jury found that the military were 'guilty of wilfull murder of a revolting and brutal character'. In response to a range of jury verdicts condemning the actions of Crown forces, inquests linked to deaths as a result of political violence were replaced by military courts of enquiry during the autumn of 1920.

On the night of 21 September 1920, while Crown forces were involved in the infamous sacking of the town of Balbriggan in Dublin, their comrades in Leitrim rampaged through Carrick. The attack on Carrick was a reprisal for the presence of armed IRA men patrolling the local fair on the previous day. Men with blackened faces fired shots and threw grenades into a number of buildings. The *Roscommom Herald* reported that

> a number of houses were entered by the raiders and young men taken out of their sleeping attire and marched some distance from their houses, had shots fired around them and were then forced to go down on their knees under threats of being instantly shot and forced to swear the police boycott in the town would be removed.[74]

Two shop assistants at Barrett's hardware, John Quinn and J.J. Higgins, who were local IRA members, escaped from the building but two of their colleagues were marched through the streets, placed against a wall and threatened that they would be shot.[75] Joe McCormack, the SF chairman of Carrick RDC, suffered a similar fate, when marched down the main street of the town. Shots were fired around him and he was forced to swear an oath that the boycott against Crown forces in the town would be lifted. The *Anglo-Celt* reported that 'large numbers of families left the town for the country, fearing a repetition'.[76] On the following day, the local RIC district inspector, having being refused service at Barrett's, returned with reinforcements and commandeered supplies.[77] Reporting on the Carrick raids, the *Sligo Independent* noted that 'the whole affair has caused much excitement in the town and hundreds of people from the country viewed the wreckage done in the short time by the disguised men, who are alleged to have been much excited'.[78]

A meeting was immediately called by local businesses and town residents to discuss the raids. This meeting was also raided by the military, though the intervention of Canon O'Reilly and Revd Beresford, the local Church of Ireland rector, resulted in the withdrawal of the raiding party. In Carrick both clergymen were part of a delegation that met the RIC CI and DI to discuss the recent actions of the Crown forces in the town. The *Anglo-Celt* reported that, following the meeting, all parties 'advocated peace and the forgetting of the past, denounced all crimes and appealed to all present to use influence to see that nothing occurs to life or property'.[79] Despite the assurances of the police, a heavy military and police presence continued in Carrick with ongoing searches of the general public. The printing works of the *Leitrim Observer* and the adjoining home of editor Patrick Dunne were raided by police and military.[80] Raids continued on 22 September at Drumshanbo when shots were fired and grenades thrown into the home of District Councillor John McPartlin. During the attack on the town, the home and business premises of Pat Conefrey, a local republican, were burned.[81]

Attacks and provocation by Crown forces continued across south Leitrim throughout September 1920 with a large police and military presence in the area. On 24 September, according to the *Roscommon Herald*, Ballinamore witnessed scenes of terrorism, 'now common across many towns in Ireland', as 'several groups of police invaded the town and at every point possible used every endeavour to goad the public into anger'.[82] The *Leitrim Observer* reported that Crown forces fired shots into the town hall and a young local man 'received a serious bayonet thrust and is now lying in a rather serious condition as a result'.[83] Raids and searches were becoming a common feature of daily life in the county. In October, on the eve of Carrick's annual agricultural show, the police imposed a curfew from 10.30 p.m. and raided the town's three hotels. At McLoughlin's Hotel, shop assistant Michael McTierney was arrested and when his lodgings nearby were searched, a SF membership card was found in a suitcase. McTierney subsequently received twelve months' imprisonment for the offence at a court martial in Athlone.[84] A large police and military presence was in place on the day of the agricultural show with widespread searches of people and vehicles.[85]

This pattern of activity continued throughout October with raids and searches across the county. Bernard Magee and his employer Patrick Briody were arrested at Carrigallen on 19 October for the possession of the republican newspaper, *An tÓglach*. Magee received twelve months' imprisonment for possession of seditious literature, but Briody was acquitted as Magee claimed that the newspaper belonged to him. James Gavin was sentenced to eighteen months' hard labour for possession of one round of ammunition that was found in his hat when searched in Carrick. At his court martial, Gavin claimed that he found the cartridge on the street outside the courthouse. Brigadier General C.S. Lambert recommended that an example would have to be made of Gavin, claiming that he 'may have to suffer in person for the greater sins of others'.[86]

The intensive military and police presence in the region ensured that IRA activity was virtually non-existent in the autumn of 1920. The only serious political crime was the attempted murder of rate collector, Michael Curran, at Aughavas on 6 October. Curran received minor injuries in an exchange of gunfire with a group of men who attacked his home. According to the *Roscommon Herald*, Curran was an unpopular man and a strong opponent of SF and 'many stories were told of his jibes at the expense of those who were in any way identified with the movement'.[87]

Throughout October and November 1920 troops regularly interfered with life in towns and villages across the county.[88] At Leitrim fair on 13 October 1920 plain-clothes police carried out extensive searches of young men in the village.[89] At Mohill the officer board of the town's GAA club abandoned a dance because of the fear of violence from a large military presence in the town.[90] Indiscriminate shooting by police and soldiers also took place at Drumsna, Dromod, Mohill and Johnstonsbridge.[91] According to Hugh Brady, the policy of coercion was counterproductive as the practice 'in many cases turned people who, if not openly hostile to, had no sympathy with Sinn Féin, or who were lukewarm, into enthusiastic Sinn Féiners'.[92]

Community facilities such as local halls and creameries were regular targets for reprisals by the Crown forces.[93] Aughavas hall was the first to be burned in the county on 22 October 1920 and in the weeks that followed halls were burned at Annaduff, Fenagh, Gorvagh, Gowel and Ballinamore. At the subsequent compensation hearing at Carrick quarter sessions on 13 January 1921, James Cox, the caretaker of Fenagh hall, described men arriving in lorries with police caps as the arsonists.[94] At Ballinamore the local Catholic hall was full of young people attending Irish classes. In his subsequent testimony at the Carrick quarter sessions, Hugh McKiernan, hall caretaker, described shots being fired, the young people being abused and the destruction of property, including a billiard table. The hall was then burned by the attackers. Local solicitor, J.A. Kiernan, described the attack as a 'piece of malicious and wanton destruction'. In awarding £704 to the plaintiffs, Judge Brown declared that the attack and burning of the hall was

> an act of brigandage pure and simple. It was impossible to conceive that uniformed men should descend upon a hall and proceed to destroy

it when people were playing innocent games and attending an Irish class, and he could not imagine how people in a Christian land could be guilty of such savagery.[95]

Following the death of Terence MacSwiney, the lord mayor of Cork, in Brixton Prison after a seventy-four day hunger strike on 25 October 1920, businesses across Leitrim closed as a mark of respect during MacSwiney's funeral. The CI reported that 'the death of the Lord Mayor of Cork occasioned no little excitement and little comment, and business was resumed as usual after Mass'.[96] While the majority of people still supported SF, he noted that 'the feeling towards the police appeared, however, to be changing for the better and the boycott of police has been removed from the entire county. Police patrols were able to move about more freely and this produced a good effect'.[97]

The first Leitrim-based police fatality did not take place in the county but near the village of Glasson in County Westmeath. Constable Sydney Larkin, a 22-year-old Londoner based in Carrick, was killed on 2 November 1920 in an ambush while en route to Athlone. Larkin was the driver of an RIC party from Carrick that was due to give evidence at the court martial of Carrick shop assistant, Michael McTierney. Larkin was killed along with Volunteer James Finn from Streamstown, County Westmeath.[98] In Leitrim Carrick's businesses were ordered to close by Crown forces to accord the same respect to Larkin as they had to MacSwiney.[99] During the days after Larkin's killing, following the imposition of a curfew at Carrick, sixty armed men raided the offices of the *Leitrim Observer* and destroyed the printing presses. Before leaving the raiders set fire to the building but through the efforts of the Dunne family and their neighbours the building was saved from total destruction.[100] The raiding party proceeded across the town and attacked the jeweller shop of John Dunne, brother of the editor of the *Leitrim Observer*. Outside the shop, the raiders drew a skull and crossbones, and wrote: 'Three lives for one of ours. Take heed. Up the Black and Tans.'[101] Noting attacks on a number of local newspapers, the *Irish Bulletin* observed that 'the natural consequence has been that the provincial press now avoids the publication of any but the baldest details of the military and constabulary excesses'.[102]

Coercion by the police and military continued in Carrick when soldiers ordered the removal of the tricolour from the Carrick workhouse. They subsequently removed the flagpoles from the building and threw them into the River Shannon.[103] Despite, or because of, such behaviour, Leitrim County Council acceded to a request from the local military garrison that Carrick residents would observe a two-minute silence on Armistice Day on 11 November. The council claimed that it met the request because of 'the courteous tone of the suggestion'. A demand that all shops close from 10.45 a.m. to 11.15 a.m. on 11 November was also accepted by local businesses after visits by police.[104]

The Cloone and Aughavas districts were attacked on 17 November 1920. After destroying the home of John Harte, a SF member of Leitrim County Council, the raiders took Harte from his home and fired shots over his head before he escaped by jumping into a river. At Annaghacoolan, brothers Bernard and Frank Ryan were placed on a hastily erected scaffold in their kitchen and threatened with hanging unless they gave information on IRA activities in the area. The *Roscommon Herald* reported that 'they were subjected to a half hanging process until their faces were nearly black and their tongues lolled forth. They were then forced to stand for an hour and a half in their bare feet and half naked in icy cold water while they were at the same time beaten with whips all over their bodies'.[105] According to the *Freeman's Journal*, the raids 'created a feeling of horror among all classes of the community'.[106] Fr Edward Ryans, curate at Aughavas, attracted the attention of a raiding party in early December 1920. As president of the South Leitrim SF executive, the priest was a familiar figure at republican gatherings. On 5 December Ryans was visited by two armed and masked men at his home and was ordered to surrender his shotgun to the RIC. Furthermore, the curate was threatened that if he did not refund £110 taken in a fine at a SF court, at which he had presided, that there would be serious consequences.[107]

In Leitrim, Longford and Sligo reprisals by Crown forces were significantly out of proportion with the extent of IRA activity.[108] Compared to both Sligo and Longford, republican military activity in Leitrim had been at an extremely low level.[109] Nevertheless, an unrelenting policy of coercion was carried out across the county. In many instances, this pattern of state violence can be explained as a response to the very effective system of boycott and intimidation carried out by republicans against Crown forces, state officials and their families. The RIC claimed that the intense nature of Crown forces' activity during the autumn and winter of 1920 had positive effects. They reported that the boycott of the force was lifted and that 'the terrorist element was defeated due to the firm and determined action of the police in holding up and searching Irish Volunteers'.[110] According to the CI, with the police once again able to move freely around the county without fear of ambush 'they were now receiving information from sources hitherto dried up'.[111] Nevertheless, increased violence convinced the authorities in November 1920 to sanction widespread internment. Camps were opened at Ballykinlar, County Down, the Curragh in County Kildare, Collinstown in County Dublin, and Spike and Bere Islands in County Cork.[112] In late January 1921, after a series of large-scale arrests in the Cloone and Aughavas districts, the *Roscommon Herald* reported that 'it was to the amazement of the people of these districts that so many arrests were made, especially of men who have taken no prominent part in politics at any time'.[113] With the exception of Frank Sweeney, quartermaster of the South Leitrim Brigade, who was interned in December 1920, the main IRA leaders in the county escaped arrest. Two prominent republican politicians, Sam Holt from Carrick and Drumshanbo's Andrew Mooney, were interned at Ballykinlar where republican prisoners appointed a camp council and staff to run the camp along prisoner-of-war lines. Both Holt and Mooney served as camp postmasters for no. 1 compound at Ballykinlar.[114]

In December 1920 the CI reported for the first time that 'information as to the formation of the south Leitrim Battalion IRA has come to hand and it is believed that some five or six companies have been formed'.[115] The concept of IRA active service units (ASUs) or flying columns was initially devised in mid-1920 when the column was to consist of twenty-six men divided into four squads.[116] Each ASU was to be a mobile force that worked independently and also as an aid to local units in initiating action in their respective brigade areas. In essence, in many areas, including Leitrim, part-time untrained Volunteers with meagre resources were attempting to take on a highly trained well-resourced army and police force. The ASUs offered safety and companionship for many men on the run, and, 'even if only a small minority of columns ever managed a successful ambush, the transition to active service was a game changing move for the Army of the Republic'.[117] Bernard Sweeney recalled the transition, stating that

> in December 1920, the active service unit, or flying column could be said to have come into existence. A number of the lads who were on the 'run' had come together for companionship and also for safety reasons and were staying in the one district. I suppose that it was the herd instinct or that we felt safer in numbers that drove us together.[118]

Despite their formation, IRA GHQ needed to ensure that the ASUs would become militarily active in the quieter counties. The relationship between GHQ and inactive areas remained tenuous, with GHQ having two means of influencing the action of local forces: it could send organizers or send arms.[119] By late 1920 GHQ regarded the neighbouring counties of Roscommon and Leitrim as too inactive militarily.[120] This assessment influenced the decision to send Seán Connolly, a GHQ staff officer and former leader of the North Longford Brigade, to Leitrim and north Roscommon to organize their ASUs. Prior to Connolly's arrival, Frank Davis, a member of the North Longford Brigade, was sent to Leitrim and reported that 'he found south Leitrim terrible'.[121] The proximity of both areas ensured close contact with the South Leitrim and North Longford Brigades. Ongoing meetings took place to share ideas and information on enemy movements. Both Séamus Wrynne and John Joe O'Reilly from Leitrim travelled to Longford for explosives training and while there they took part in the attack on Arvagh RIC barracks in County Cavan in February 1921.[122] Prior to the Arvagh raid, a co-ordinated assault involving both brigades in simultaneous attacks on Arvagh, Ballinamore, Roosky and Mohill barracks had to be abandoned because of an increased military presence in the region.[123] Before Connolly's arrival in Leitrim, IRA activity had increased and, according to police, local Volunteers were being urged by GHQ 'to commit outrages and they are doing their best to comply with their instructions'.[124] Increasing IRA activity led police and military to force civilians to travel with them on patrols. According to the *Anglo-Celt*, the presence of Murtagh Dowd, a SF court judge, travelling with a police patrol at Carrick, while holding a union jack flag, 'caused a sensation'.[125]

Very often the lack of central co-ordination from IRA GHQ meant that the impetus for a military campaign was dependent solely on the initiative of local activists.[126] The standard excuse of a lack of arms proferred by inactive areas was often an indication of lethargy on the part of IRA units that also affected their performance during the conflict.[127] Effective local leadership and organization rather than guns often dictated whether a region was active against Crown forces.[128] The absence of both effective leadership and arms hindered IRA activity in Leitrim. Ernie O'Malley, a GHQ organizer in Roscommon and Leitrim, described the South Leitrim Brigade's commander Seán Mitchell as 'neither active in mind or in intention, nor would he normally go out of his way to look for a fight' – a rather harsh judgement as Mitchell had led the Sheemore ambush.[129]

Hugh Brady, Bernard Sweeney and Patrick J. Hargaden claimed that the brigade possessed only a few service rifles and shotguns.[130] When questioned by Seán Mac Eoin on the levels of ammunition in the South Leitrim Brigade area, Tom O'Reilly, a local IRA man, replied that they possessed 'as much as would frighten sparrows out of a haggard'.[131]

The first attempt at a large-scale operation against Crown forces was planned for 16 January 1921. As part of a co-ordinated attack, Volunteers fired shots at Ballinamore RIC barracks in the expectation that Crown forces would travel from Mohill to aid their comrades. At Edentenny an ambush party had cut down trees and trenched the Ballinamore to Mohill road while waiting for Crown forces reinforcements. The immediate reaction to the Ballinamore and Edentenny incidents was one of outrage by some residents of the area. The *Roscommon Herald* reported that 'the people of Ballinamore, it is understood, signed a paper disassociating themselves from the recent attack on the police, or from having any connection with the alleged conspiracy on the lives of the police'.[132] In late January 1921 Thomas Early, a member of the Royal Air Force, who was home on leave, was shot and seriously injured near Leitrim village. Condemning the attack on Early, Canon O'Reilly warned that 'people who were guilty of murder had their blood spilt, and he knew of instances where they died in asylums or other places which brought disgrace on themselves and their families'.[133]

After a brief period of time in north Roscommon, Connolly arrived in Leitrim in February 1921. His first action was to divide the ASU into two units, one led by himself and the other by Seán Mitchell from Mohill. Describing Connolly's arrival, Bernard Sweeney stated that 'we also got some more rifles but never had more than ten or twelve at any time, and ammunition for the rifles was very low at all times, about ten or twelve rounds per rifle'.[134] Connolly was immediately involved in a number of failed ambush attempts at Annaduff, Fenagh and Ballinamore.[135] According to Sweeney, 'on several occasions, Connolly and I and some other members of the column came into Ballinamore to try and ambush a street patrol of the Tans and RIC. We put a mine, smaller portable type in the street but we never had any luck as the enemy never obliged us by turning up'.[136] At Drumshanbo on 2 March 1921 members of Connolly's ASU were lying in wait for a passing RIC patrol but abandoned the operation when detonators failed to fire. The ASU also planned to kill former CI Ross Rainsford while he played golf at Carrick but he failed to appear.[137]

Despite these setbacks, the Leitrim ASU's first successful engagement with Crown forces took place at Ballinawig, Sheemore, between Gowel and Carrick, on the morning of 4 March 1921. False information that local Volunteers would be attending Mass was passed to police, who, along with a detachment of soldiers from the Bedfordshire and Hertfordshire Regiment, raided the church at Gowel.[138] The regiment had recently arrived in Leitrim from Donegal and observed that 'the district is considerably more disturbed than that which we have vacated in Donegal, and though our hopes are high we have not yet been able to get the gunmen of the district under hand'.[139] On their return to Carrick, the raiding party was ambushed at Sheemore by Mitchell's unit. Charles McGoohan recalled that 'several people said "fire" at the same time and as soon as fire was opened the figures started to jump and tumble out of the lorries. It was difficult to say how effective this first volley was but afterwards it was some time before any fire was returned'.[140] In an attempt to outflank the ambushers, the party's commanding officer Lieutenant C.E. Wilson was fatally wounded.[141] During the short engagement Sergeant Healy and Constable Costello of the RIC were wounded. With a limited supply of ammunition and fearing the arrival of reinforcements, Mitchell withdrew his ASU (which comprised of McGoohan, Michael Geoghegan, Joe Nangle, Matthew Boylan, Thomas O'Reilly, Michael Martin and Harry McKeon), to safety after an engagement of less than thirty minutes.[142] With the departure of the ambushers, the police and military re-grouped and forced a young local boy to guide them by back roads into Carrick.[143] Reflecting on the ambush McGoohan suggested that 'Sheemore proved that Leitrim could produce good fighting men'.[144] Sergeant A.M. Austin of the Bedfordshire and Hertfordshire Regiment recalled

> a subsequent examination of the position revealed six rifle pits dug in behind a low wall at the edge of the wood, and on the crest of the hill. The ambushers were echeloned in the wood to account for the flanking parties. No doubt exists that the information as to the wanted men being in the chapel was false, and a trap for troops and police.[145]

Sheemore was significant because it was the first time that Crown forces suffered fatalities in Leitrim. The ambush was well planned, but the short nature of the engagement resulted in low casualty figures. For her bravery at Sheemore, Alice Gray was awarded the Order of the British Empire medal. Gray, a 55-year-old Dubliner and qualified nurse, was employed by the police as a woman searcher. When Wilson was shot, she immediately went to his assistance and administered first aid. Reports of the ambush noted her 'magnificent courage under fire. During the action she re-distributed the rifles of the wounded men among those who were only carrying revolvers'.[146] In his correspondence with the War Office in relation to Gray's action, Commander of British forces in Ireland Nevil Macready advised his colleagues to 'make a story of this but do not use name or description. Call this heroine "a loyal Irish lady of 55"'. Macready also recommended that Gray be awarded the Order of the British Empire, which was presented to her on 30 January 1922 in a private ceremony by the lord lieutenant at the Vice Regal Lodge. At Gray's request, the ceremony was private as she was 'hoping to proceed to Canada as quickly and quietly as possible'.[147]

While the ambush was deemed a success by the IRA, Volunteer Eugene Kilkenny described a heavy police and military presence in the south Leitrim area in the aftermath that hindered further IRA activity.[148] A planned attack in Mohill on a police patrol was abandoned because of the heavy military presence in the town.[149] Following the ambush, raids and reprisals were carried out in the local area and Gowel Temperance hall was destroyed by fire. At nearby Kiltoghert, Crown forces destroyed machinery at the local creamery before burning the building.[150] Ernie O'Malley described the scene:

> the concentration of troops, Auxiliaries and RIC, surprised at this activity in a quiet spot, were aggressive and overbearing in their raids, interrogations and destruction. Houses were burned close to Carrick, and a creamery near the chapel of Gowel, while the people left empty houses behind as if a famine had again struck this quiet countryside.[151]

While attempting to establish a site for an ambush near Gorvagh, Connolly's unit arrived at the home of James Flynn, local national school teacher, at Selton Hill, Gorvagh, in the early hours of 11 March 1921. Flynn was a republican sympathiser and a relative was a member of Connolly's ASU. On arrival, the ASU also occupied a nearby house owned by a local Protestant family, the McCulloughs.[152] As the ASU settled down to rest at Flynn's, their presence in the area became known and was spoken about openly in the local shop. Delia Mannion, the shop assistant and a member of Cumann na mBan, alerted the ASU and advised that they leave the area immediately. However, the IRA remained at Flynn's.[153]

In the late afternoon of 11 March 1921 the alarm was raised that a military convoy was on the Mohill to Ballinamore road nearby. Observing the military stopping at the top of the laneway to the Flynn and McCullough homes, James Flynn immediately alerted the ASU. The raiding party placed two Lewis machine-guns on gate piers overlooking both homes before approaching the two houses. The military claimed that they were immediately fired on by hidden gunmen.[154] Bernard Sweeney described what transpired at Selton Hill:

> I looked through the shrubs where I had taken up position and could see the enemy with machine-guns set in position. Each of our sections concentrated on the direction of where the machine-gun fire was coming and opened fire in that direction. The enemy were well informed of the position of the place and they had a force of military on the south side of us also, and they opened up with rifle fire and we had not a chance from the start.[155]

When the shooting had ceased, five members of the ASU – John J. O'Reilly (Miskawn), Séamus Wrynne, Michael Baxter, Joe Beirne and John J. O'Reilly (Derrinkeher) – were dead. Both Seán Connolly and Jack Hunt were wounded and captured. Connolly died later that night in Carrick Jail. Sweeney was also wounded but evaded capture by hiding in a drain from where he was rescued later that night by locals. Only three of the ASU – Paddy Guckian, Andy McPartland and Pee McDermott – escaped unhurt.

Recalling the shock of losing Lieutenant Wilson at Sheemore, regimental sources reported that 'vengeance was swift and very destructive, for a week later to the very day, the "brave boys" of the IRA lost six of their ablest and most experienced leaders in the South Leitrim Brigade'.[156] On the basis that officers involved in the Selton Hill shootings should not be identified, members of the press were not admitted to the court of inquiry at Carrick.[157] It found that no blame could be attributed to Crown forces for the deaths of any of the six men and concluded that 'these persons were killed by the

Crown forces in the execution of their duty and that blame for their deaths attaches to those who have encouraged them and others to take up arms against the Crown'.[158]

DI Thomas Gore Hickman was praised by his superiors for acting on information received and arranging the encounter.[159] Press reports indicated that an ambush party engaged with Crown forces, resulting in the shooting and capture of the ambushers with no casualties inflicted on the police or military.[160] The CI reported his belief that the 'gang had assembled to carry out an ambush near Mohill. The ground where they were caught was most unsuitable for an ambush'.[161] At the subsequent field court martial of Jack Hunt in Boyle, defending solicitor John A. Pettit questioned the military witnesses on the nature of the ambush. He enquired how could an ambush party be in a house seventy-five yards from the main road and suggested that 'it was curious out of all this firing done there was no one killed on the military side, and six were killed on the other side'.[162] Despite character references from the local priest, doctor and a Protestant merchant, Hunt was sentenced to ten years' penal servitude for possession of a revolver and ammunition.[163]

Following the court of inquiry, the bodies were removed from military custody to St Mary's church in Carrick before proceeding to their home areas. The *Anglo-Celt* reported that

> there was a great manifestation of grief in the town when the remains were removed from the military barracks. All houses were shuttered and blinds drawn as the cortège went through the town, and at the military headquarters, soldiers stood at the salute and guards presented arms as the dead were borne out on the shoulders of relatives.[164]

At Longford all businesses were closed during Connolly's funeral. The *Longford Leader* reported that 'as the funeral procession passed from the cathedral, an armoured car and two lorries containing police and Auxiliaries passed by and proceeded in the direction in which the funeral was going. Each man saluted the remains as they passed'.[165] Despite a large IRA presence at the funerals, Crown forces did not intervene. Sympathizing with the relatives, Bishop Finegan explained that had the men been killed in an ambush, he would have prevented a Christian burial, but the circumstances of their deaths were that 'they were shot escaping, not ambushing'.[166] Finegan was an ardent critic of both state and IRA violence. In his Lenten pastoral of February 1921, the bishop proclaimed: 'I condemn, abhor and detest violence from whatever side or source it comes, and I earnestly appeal to all, especially our young men, to be very mindful of the teaching of our Catholic faith and to conform their conduct in all matters to the requirement of God's law'.[167]

An IRA investigation was immediately conducted to discover how the authorities received the information of the ASU's presence in the area. The guilty party was identified as William Latimer, a local Protestant farmer, who had learned of the ASU's presence through his young son who had visited McCullough's early on the morning of 11 March. Latimer's mother had died and his son was sent to McCullough's for some items to prepare for her wake. The boy returned with news of the presence of armed men. Later, Latimer prepared to go to Mohill to make funeral arrangements and on the way he met local doctor, Charles Pentland. It was speculated that Latimer relayed the ASU's location to Pentland, who subsequently informed DI Gore Hickman in Mohill. Charles Pinkman, IRA brigade intelligence officer, concluded that

> whatever Latimer told Pentland, the doctor only stayed for a brief period at the dispensary and then returned to Mohill, and contacted District Inspector of the R.I.C. DI Gore Hickman personally. Immediately a mobilisation of police and Tans took place in Mohill, and as soon as Latimer arrived in the town he was contacted by both police and military officers, who then proceeded to Gorvagh.[168]

Latimer was shot dead at his home on 30 March 1921 by Michael Geoghegan and Matthew Boylan, members of the second ASU. Local Volunteers were initially tasked with the responsibility for killing Latimer but refused to do so.[169]

According to Pinkman, after the Selton Hill shootings typewritten circulars were posted to all republicans in Gorvagh, warning them that if anything happened in the area, lives would be lost and property destroyed. Notices were then posted by republicans to all Protestant families in Mohill and Gorvagh that if reprisals by Crown forces occurred in the wake of the Latimer killing 'so many lives would be forfeited and that every Protestant house in the area would be burned'.[170] No reprisals occurred and the CI reported that 'information was coming in fairly freely, but the murder of Latimer will, I fear, have such a terrifying influence on the people that for the present at least very little can be expected'.[171] Fearing for his life, Pentland immediately went to England, while Latimer's widow, Isabella, was subsequently awarded £4,680 as compensation for the death of her husband.[172]

Immediately after the Selton Hill incident, 'Leitrim went from bad to worse'.[173] In order to reorganize the brigade area, Collins sent Captain Paddy Morrissey, a GHQ staff officer, to the county. At his first battalion council meeting Morrissey stated that 'the South Leitrim Brigade was the worst brigade in Ireland and that the Third Battalion was the worst battalion in the brigade'. His comments were not well received and resulted in the resignation of the entire battalion staff.[174] Morrissey claimed that 'Collins was very sore over Connolly. He blamed the Leitrim people and Mitchell, the brigadier. Be careful he said to me, you are going into the most treacherous county in Ireland, but after a month I wrote back to him to say that the people were marvellous'.[175] Not only had Selton Hill resulted in the capture of a limited arms supply but the deaths of six active ASU members was detrimental to any hope of increased military activity in the area. Connolly's death had a serious effect on IRA activity in both south Leitrim and north Longford. According to Davis, following the jailing of Seán Mac Eoin and the death of Connolly, IRA action was minimal and 'harassing tactics were the only things we were capable of'.[176] By May 1921 the North Longford ASU had become so ineffective that the possibility of joining with their south Leitrim comrades was being considered.[177]

Bernard Sweeney believed that ongoing raids by Crown forces and disorganization in the ranks of the brigade made it 'harder every day to stay alive'.[178] The lack of an effective intelligence network to support the military campaign was also evident in Leitrim.[179] Sweeney admitted that the intelligence service was 'never highly organized in the area'. This was highlighted by several abandoned ambushes due to the non-appearance of Crown forces.[180] In one of the few intelligence reports forwarded to GHQ in August 1921, Pinkman stated that he could not furnish a complete set of information as he still had to enquire about the rank of the local British army commanding officer and the name of the army regiment stationed at Mohill. Neither could he supply the name of the Crown prosecutor in the county.[181]

Volunteer ranks were further depleted by the death of James McGlynn, a local Volunteer, in Drumshanbo on 12 April 1921 while enforcing the Belfast boycott. The boycott was instituted by Dáil Éireann as a protest against partition and sectarian attacks on the nationalist community across Ulster. When posting notices against non-compliant businesses, McGlynn's shotgun accidently discharged and killed him. The military enquiry heard that McGlynn's body was found with a shotgun by his side and boycott notices on his person. It found that his death was accidental 'when taking part with other person's [sic] unknown in an act of violence against certain residents of Drumshanbo'.[182]

Although direct military engagement was not a consistent feature of the 1919–21 period in Leitrim, enforcement by the local IRA and Cumann na mBan of the Belfast boycott was relentless. Whereas killing was the ultimate sanction for defying the IRA, defying a boycott was often punished by non-lethal, yet effective forms of violence.[183] Thomas McGovern, a Manorhamilton shopkeeper, was kidnapped by the IRA and was released only when he took an oath that he would no longer trade with the Ulster Bank.[184] In nearby Dromahair, James Kelly, a draper, was fined £40 by the local boycott co-ordinator for trading in Belfast goods. Hargaden recalled lists of Belfast firms who were on the blacklist were supplied to us and we raided the trains and vans for the goods of those firms. When we found such goods, which was nearly always we destroyed them or commandeered them. Bread vans were turned upside down and their contents spilled on the roadside and, in a short while, we had driven Belfast goods from the area.[185]

With the escalation of conflict, women played a major logistical role for the IRA by providing food, shelter and clothing for men who were on the run. Margaret Brady recalled that 'we provided clean shirts for the men, and knitted socks for them. We also organized billets for the column and cooked meals for them'.[186] The transportation of arms, administration of first aid and intelligence gathering was carried out by women.[187] Cumann na mBan members were also prominent in the enforcement of the Belfast boycott campaign in the county. Brady recalled that 'as well as going to the various shops and warning the owners not to stock Belfast goods supplied by the black-listed firms, the girls of Cumann na mBan did a big amount of intelligence work in this respect and were able to keep watch on all goods coming into the area'.[188] Despite the vital role played by women in the campaign, a Leitrim IRA commander told a Cumann na mBan organizer that he should not be expected to 'trust these girls with the secrets of the IRA'.[189] A core group of fifteen women worked closely with active Volunteers in Leitrim. Although many of their roles were classed as auxiliary, many women transported arms and were very active in scouting and intelligence gathering.[190] Throughout the early phase of the military campaign, women took advantage of gender stereotypes as in most instances police and military would not search them. However, the introduction of female searchers by British authorities restricted the role of Cumann na mBan. Bridget Doherty recalled a raid on her home in early 1921: 'I was put into a room in my house where I was undressed almost naked by two female searchers. I am positive that one of the searchers was a man dressed up as a woman'.[191]

In April 1921 two members of the Crown forces died at Ballinamore. Wilfred Jones, a Black and Tan, was shot on the outskirts of the town near the railway station while in the company of local girl, Margaret Sadlier. His killer was Charles McGoohan, a member of the No. 2 ASU and one of the Sheemore ambush party. McGoohan had received information that Black and Tans socialized freely in the town and that Jones was meeting a girl near the railway station. McGoohan recalled how he

> found him [Jones] standing on the roadside. I don't know if he had already drawn his gun at my approach, but a considerable gun battle ensued in which I got off seven shots and he got off three and the last

from the prone position. His companion I believe was injured also. I think I showed a fair turn of speed away from the scene for a couple of hundred yards when I slowed down and reloaded my guns. I had two: a Smith and Wesson 45 and a Colt automatic 45, so the enemy was out-gunned as well as surprised. Anyhow he lost.[192]

The wounded policeman was transported to the local barracks on a cart, and died a short time later.[193] That night Thomas Mugan, a member of the RIC from Mayo, was killed at Ballinamore barracks. Official reports claimed that he was killed when loading his rifle.[194] Hugh Brady claimed that Mugan was shot by Black and Tans, while preventing them from leaving the barracks to carry out reprisals in revenge for the killing of Jones.[195] According to Ernie O'Malley, Mugan's death 'saved a few houses and maybe some lives that night'.[196] Houses were raided in the Ballinamore area in the following days and Sweeney claimed 'the Tans were practically mad in the town of Ballinamore. They beat up every man they could lay their hands on'.[197]

The second killing of an alleged informer in the county took place at Garadice, near Ballinamore, on 22 April 1921 when 54-year-old John Harrison was beaten and shot dead near his home. A Protestant and father of twelve children, Harrison and his wife, Jane, lived five miles from Ballinamore on a forty-acre farm. According to Brady, suspicions that Harrison was a spy were confirmed in material taken in a mail raid at Garadice station.[198] In the early hours of 22 April, a group of men arrived at the Harrison home and ordered Harrison to come out. He refused and only complied when the IRA threatened to burn the house.[199] According to Head Constable Black from Ballinamore, Harrison was found 'dead and horribly mutilated'.[200] A piece of cardboard tied with Harrison's bootlace was placed around his neck with the warning: 'Informers and traitors beware'.[201] Jane Harrison was subsequently awarded £4,640 for the death of her husband.[202]

Two further killings of Black and Tans took place in Ballinamore and Carrick on 16 May 1921. At Carrick barracks, Constable Leonard Hart from London was shot dead by Constable Johnson when a firearm was accidently discharged.[203] At Ballinamore Constable Thomas Tasker was killed in a similar incident by Constable Colin Hay who was subsequently sentenced to two months' imprisonment for recklessly handling a firearm.[204] While travelling to Boyle to collect a military ambulance to convey Tasker to Dublin, DI Gore Hickman was ambushed at Drumsna but escaped uninjured.[205] According to Eunan O'Halpin, fourteen per cent of police casualties during the War of Independence were classed as accidental, having being inflicted by the victim or his comrades.[206]

With a limited arms supply and ongoing raids by Crown forces, road trenching was regularly undertaken by the IRA in Longford and Leitrim to impede the movement of Crown forces.[207] At Gorvagh on 26 May 1921 a group of between ten and fifteen young men were taken by surprise while trenching a road with the sudden arrival of soldiers and police. Five of the group – James Moran, James Doonan, Tom McGarty, Michael Moran and Michael Earley – were captured after a brief pursuit across fields. In a subsequent petition for the early release of Earley by DI Gore Hickman, the police officer claimed that Earley was 'a delicate boy' who had been forced at gunpoint to take part in the trenching.[208] Suspicion for alerting the RIC was directed at the local Church of Ireland rector Thomas Bayly, who had earlier passed through Gorvagh.[209] The clergyman subsequently left the area under police escort to England.[210]

Intensive Crown force activity continued unabated throughout May and June 1921 in the hunt for IRA activists. The authorities were conscious that the railway network was being used for carrying dispatches between the countryside and the city.[211] Train searches were frequent and intensive, including inspection of a train's coal supply for dispatches and arms.[212] Police reports identified the Slieve an Anerin mountains between Ballinamore and Drumshanbo as an IRA hiding place.[213] In early June an extensive search involving over four thousand men, aided by aeroplane support, was carried out.[214] Although six IRA men were captured, most of those on the run evaded capture by crossing the mountain to County Cavan, which was outside the search area.[215]

Widespread searches by Crown forces in May and June 1921 were part of a nationwide strategy by the authorities to round up wanted men and search for arms.[216] An incident at Ballinaglera church on 5 June 1921 caused controversy when it was alleged that Crown forces entered the church during Mass and dragged members of the congregation outside. Fr Michael Kelly, the parish priest, wrote formally to the lord lieutenant to complain. According to Kelly, he witnessed an officer dragging people off their knees and, having intervened, the priest was 'driven back by the church gate by the officer's subordinates with revolvers after which they entered the sacristy and church, where their conduct was most objectionable'.[217] Replying to a parliamentary question by T.P. O'Connor about the incident, Sir Hamar Greenwood, the Irish chief secretary, denied the priest's allegations. He claimed that two men were detained when they were observed transferring documents to a woman in the congregation and that Mass was not interrupted in any way.[218] The conflict ended as it started with the burning of RIC property, the force's motor stores at Mohill railway station in early July 1921.[219]

Despite attempts by IRA GHQ in Dublin to impose some sort of uniformity, the War of Independence was a series of small localized campaigns, rather than a nationwide struggle, with little co-ordination between brigades.[220] Such a campaign meant that there was considerable variations in patterns of violence between and also within counties. In Leitrim the limited action that took place was primarily concentrated in the south of the county. After their release from internment James Dolan and Ben Maguire focussed on political activity. Dolan's pacifism was noted by police who reported that 'the quietude of north Leitrim is due to the restraining influence of Dolan, who, although an ardent Sinn Féiner, in practice ... is strongly opposed to murder and methods of warfare adopted by the extremists'.[221]

Throughout the two-and-a-half year campaign from 1919 to 1921, only two members of the Crown forces were killed by the IRA in Leitrim; three policemen were killed by their colleagues in controversial circumstances. Six members of the IRA and two civilians were killed by Crown forces, and three civilians were killed by the IRA. While Seán Connolly died less than three weeks after his arrival in Leitrim, during that short period the South Leitrim Brigade was provided with effective leadership and organization. Ernie O'Malley believed that after the killings at Selton Hill 'the men were despondent and leaderless. The Leitrim brigade had lost some of its best officers and its new and real driving force, Seán Connolly'.[222] The lack of a centrally controlled and directed republican military campaign for most of the War of Independence meant that local initiative was crucial. A dearth of arms, an ineffective intelligence network and poor leadership confined the resistance in Leitrim to a limited number of activities such as road trenching, raids on mails and implementation of the Belfast boycott. Nevertheless, acts of civil disobedience and defiance were staged successfully by Leitrim republicans. In many instances, this terror was directed, not at Crown forces, but against members of the local population who were seen as not complying with republican directives. Where Leitrim differed from other regions was the extreme levels of state violence. These retaliatory acts were disproportionate to the levels of IRA military activity in the county and can best be explained by the widespread success of a campaign of boycott and intimidation against Crown forces, state officials and certain members of the local community. Although violence was cyclical in many regions, with both sides motivated by a desire to hit back at the enemy for the last attack, retaliatory violence in Leitrim was directed at the local population, who were seen as complicit by the authorities in boycott and intimidation campaigns.[223] The county passed through different phases of conflict that included arms raids, low level operational activity and an intense period of violence following the Restoration of Order in Ireland Act, yet boycott and intimidation remained an important and effective element of the republican campaign.[224] Unlike other areas, where the drift to violence was often explained as an overreaction by the IRA to violence by the Crown forces, this was not the case in Leitrim.[225] As the conflict was characterized by experiment, improvisation and self-discovery, Leitrim republicans learned that covert forms of resistance were often the most effective weapons in their armoury.

8 'The opportunity of being mistress in their own house': the transition to self-government, 1921–2

In welcoming the truce and cessation of hostilities in July 1921, the *Sligo Champion* noted that 'the feelings of joy and happiness which pervaded the atmosphere were evidenced no less in the Crown forces in the country than in the demeanour of the Irish people themselves'.[1] According to the *Roscommon Herald*, the truce was 'hailed in these districts with much delight by all shades of opinion and a hope is expressed that should the representatives meet, a happy and peaceful settlement of the present struggle will be brought about'.[2] However, the *Herald* warned that if any future settlement was not just 'the rivers of blood and tears, the terror and agony brought to hundreds of thousands of homes, all would rise up in judgement if there were a paltry surrender'.[3] Unlike many other regions, a broad acceptance of the terms of the Treaty meant a relatively seamless transfer of both military and political power taking place in Leitrim. While the 'high politics' of Dublin and London was pre-occupied with the terms of any future political settlement, Leitrim was consumed by a reactivated republican movement, widespread resistance to paying rates and continuing political patronage by the county's new rulers. British power was disappearing but age old habits prevailed.

As the terms of the truce ensured that the Dáil government operated alongside its British counterpart, republicans prepared for the formal establishment of new agencies of state. The most pressing issue facing republican administrators was the collection of rates. Since 1920 rate collection was proving to be one of the most serious challenges facing Leitrim County Council.[4] A politically unstable environment meant that many ratepayers took advantage of the situation to avoid or delay paying. By September 1921 only £1,000 of £50,000 due had been collected.[5] According to some councillors, the reasons for non-payment included poor economic conditions for ratepayers and a fear that people would have to pay twice to both Dáil and British authorities.[6] Large amounts of monies due, dating back to 1920, remained uncollected and by October 1921 the situation in Leitrim was desperate.[7] Reports of intimidation of rate collectors, the withholding of monies collected and council disputes with rate collectors added to the chaos. In late 1921 a Dáil inspector attending an anti-rates meeting to explain the need for payment had to fire shots over the heads of the unreceptive crowd to escape. The rates issue in Leitrim was so serious that it merited discussion by the Dáil cabinet, where William T. Cosgrave was persuaded not to resort to more drastic methods of rate collection for fear of alienating the public.[8] By November

1921 the county council threatened to sack some rate collectors for non-collection and requested the public 'to support them in the administration of the affairs of the county'.⁹ At a meeting in Drumsna, James Dolan admitted that the 7s. 3d. in the pound was a high rate and claimed that 'it was only a war rate and was but a small sacrifice the people of County Leitrim were asked to make'.¹⁰ An IRA public proclamation issued in December 1921 by General Seán Mac Eoin (now commandant of the IRA's Western Division) ordering all rate payers to pay within twenty-one days or be 'treated with the utmost vigour' had little effect.¹¹

Despite all the pleas and threats, the issue of non-payment continued into the following year, even though the rate of 3s. 2d. in the pound was the lowest on record.¹² A combination of poor economic conditions and political opportunism resulted in widespread non-payment of rates throughout the county.¹³ At a meeting of the county council on 15 April 1922, a deputation from Kinlough Farmers' Union pleaded inability to pay because 1921 'was the worst year for farmers since the famine'.¹⁴ The county secretary claimed that the collection record for all rate collectors was bad with only £36,782 collected and £49,544 still outstanding in April 1922.¹⁵ The impracticality of the county council's request that the IRA protect the local rate collectors was demonstrated by the IRA's refusal to enforce court decrees since they themselves were active in the anti-rates campaign.¹⁶ As a result of decreased revenue, there were little or no road repairs and road labourers' wages dropped from £1 16s. to £1 7s. a week. Despite criticism of the wage reductions, and attempts by the ITGWU to have the policy reversed, the council's position remained unchanged.

As financial pressure on local government finances increased, the Dáil administration initiated a policy of amalgamating the Poor Law unions. In Leitrim, Kinlough and Ballinamore Unions were to be abolished while Carrick, Mohill and Manorhamilton Unions would be retained. Predictably, the proposal occasioned widespread opposition from local factions in the affected areas. Myles Prior, relieving officer at Ballinamore Union, protested against closure and questioned 'how will a poor father or mother see their sick child if the child is in a hospital twenty or thirty miles away?'.¹⁷ Setting aside arguments relating to patient welfare, the main reasons for opposition to such amalgamations was the loss of local employment.¹⁸ Following union rationalization in the county, political tensions emerged between the three remaining unions. Opposition was strong across the county. Carrick, Mohill and Manorhamilton each asserted its claim to secure the county hospital or county home.¹⁹ On 2 November 1921 a conference of union delegates voted to adopt a report of the local government medical inspector recommending a county home and hospital in Manorhamilton, and a district hospital and county infirmary at Carrick. The decision angered Tim Ward, the chairman of Leitrim

County Council, who was from Mohill. He alleged that 'wire pulling had been carried on and he wished the public to know that'.[20]

While the issue of rates and union amalgamations were some of the more important issues facing local councils, the more mundane issues of supply contracts to local workhouses, education, road repairs, and wage rates also preoccupied local bodies. Despite widespread criticism from local councillors, strict adherence to Dáil procedures prevented the appointment of an assistant surveyor for the county in September 1921.[21] Furthermore, two tillage experts were not retained by the County Committee of Agriculture because of the budgetary situation in the county.[22]

Like their counterparts in Sligo and Longford, Leitrim's SF clubs and IRA units attempted to exert influence on council appointments.[23] In January 1922 Leitrim County Council decided that roads foremen would be chosen by local SF clubs, in consultation with the county surveyor, Eugene O'Neill Clarke.[24] Despite the Department of Local Government instructing Clarke not to cooperate with these clubs, Leitrim's local government inspector considered the county surveyor powerless, concluding that 'every Sinn Féin Club in County Leitrim is a County Council'.[25] Nevertheless, Dáil inspectors continued to attempt to prevent clientelism by the county's new power brokers. The process of appointment to three vacant posts as temporary rate collectors in August 1920 involved the Leitrim SF executive forwarding twelve names to the council, and the appointments were made in consultation with the Dáil local government inspector at a private council meeting.[26] Dáil inspectors were also present at a meeting of the council's finance committee when the issue of unvouched expenses for the IRA members taking patients to Sligo Asylum was raised. Admonishing the council for its policy, the inspector stated that 'the county council has no authority to make payment for a lunatic without vouchers'.[27] Increasing levels of maladministration, dissent and a deteriorating rate collection issue eventually led to the appointment of a commissioner from the Department of Local Government to replace the council in June 1923.[28]

After the truce Crown forces had observed an increasingly active republican movement reactivate parish courts and establish IRA training camps across the county. The police reported regular breaches of the terms of the truce by Leitrim republicans throughout the autumn of 1921, notably drilling, intimidation and SF collections. In October DI J.B. Hornell stated that three men, acting on a written order from three local district councillors, took bedding from Manorhamilton workhouse for a local IRA training camp occupied by sixty men. Camps near Ballinamore were also noted. Furthermore, police reported the erection of public notices at Carrick and Manorhamilton issuing orders to boycott local businesses that sold Belfast and English produce. Similarly, in Ballinamore police found public notices with the names of nineteen local girls listed as 'keeping company with the enemy forces of occupation and do not deserve to be recognized by any true Irish boy or girl'.[29]

While advanced nationalists had continuously criticized the old IPP for alleged patronage and clientism, the new power brokers in Leitrim continued in a similar fashion when appointing road foremen and labourers. Whereas the establishment of the Civil Service Commission and the Local Appointments Commission was an attempt by the government in the 1920s to introduce meritocracy to senior public appointments, local councillors could still make appointments to lesser grades and thereby continue the practice of dispensing patronage.[30] Tensions between the county council and Eugene O'Neill Clarke resulted in victory for the council as the surveyor was stripped of authority to make appointments to lesser grades. Patronage also extended to appointments at the new county home and infirmary. When a meeting of the Leitrim county home committee in April 1922 heard that a number of suitably qualified candidates from Leitrim, Antrim, Sligo and Sunderland, England had applied for two nursing posts, Ben Maguire declared that 'we need consider none but those from Leitrim' and advised that the posts be allocated between north and south Leitrim applicants. Consequently, a Miss Ward from Arigna and a Miss O'Rourke from Kiltyclogher were appointed.[31]

Following nearly five months of negotiations between British and Irish representatives, the Anglo-Irish Treaty was signed on 6 December 1921. British recognition of Irish autonomy and complete control of internal affairs within the twenty-six southern counties were among its benefits. Retaining the king as head of state, partition and a continuation of a constitutional link with the Empire ensured opposition to the Treaty from Éamon de Valera and his supporters. However, both public opinion and a large number of Dáil deputies supported the agreement on the basis of renewed peace and the view that the Treaty was a 'stepping stone' to eventual reunification and separation from the Crown.[32]

According to the *Roscommon Herald*, news of the signing of the Treaty was greeted with 'much public rejoicing throughout County Leitrim'.[33] An immediate consequence of the Treaty was the release of prisoners, who were welcomed home at a series of rallies throughout the county. Prisoner releases remained a major issue for republicans through the autumn and winter of 1921. A small number of prominent republican leaders were liberated following the truce but the majority remained incarcerated in overcrowded camps and jails. The *Sligo Champion* challenged the English government by declaring that if they were sincere in seeking lasting peace they should 'release the prisoners without further delay'.[34] At a meeting of the Manorhamilton board of guardians in October 1921, members passed a resolution advising the SF negotiators in London to suspend peace negotiations until 'all the internees and political prisoners are released'.[35] Although most were freed in December, some of their comrades remained in prison until early 1922.[36] At a welcome home rally for released prisoners at Carrick, Andrew Lavin advised those present that on this issue, they should 'keep cool and keep their powder dry until Dáil Éireann had given its decision on the Peace Treaty'.[37]

At Manorhamilton, Dolan praised Collins, Griffith and the Treaty negotiators. They had, he declared, 'achieved a magnificent victory and signed a treaty which would be the foundation stone of peace and friendship between the two countries'.[38] Explaining his reasons for supporting the Treaty, Dolan intimated that the threat by Lloyd George of a resumption of war was realistic. Yet, he reassured the crowd that 'we shall be a free people. Some say our freedom is limited, but if we look around and examine the small nations of the world, we will realise that we will have to bow in this wicked world to the forces of might'.[39]

While the public mood in the county was in favour of the Treaty, the *Roscommon Herald* reported that 'there are many in favour of Mr de Valera's attitude'. However, the *Herald* warned that 'the men who vote for rejection would find it as difficult as the members of Redmond's old Parliamentary Party to get re-elected in the next appeal for the verdict of the voters'.[40] On 30 December 1921 the South Leitrim comhairle ceantair met and instructed its councillors to vote for acceptance of the Treaty. At a specially convened meeting following the comhairle meeting, Leitrim County Council ratified the Treaty and instructed the four members of the newly constituted Leitrim–Roscommon North electoral area, James Dolan, Thomas Carter, Andrew Lavin and Count Plunkett, to vote in favour of acceptance. While Plunkett and Dolan were experienced politicians, Carter, a shopkeeper from Drumreilly, and Lavin, a farmer from Boyle, were political novices.

Arguing for ratification of the Treaty, recently released prisoner Ben Maguire stated that whereas the agreement did not yield the full measure of freedom for which Seán Mac Diarmada and Terence MacSwiney had died, 'it gives us certain things we never had before'.[41] During the Dáil Treaty debates, Dolan again praised the plenipotentiaries, declaring that 'he did not look upon the Treaty as final and everlasting. All countries were developing and this was only a step forward in the development of their country'.[42] The ratification of the Treaty by Dáil Éireann by a margin of seven votes on 7 January 1922 saw Dolan, Carter and Lavin taking the pro-Treaty side, with Count Plunkett supporting de Valera. News of the ratification was received in Carrick 'by a marked quietness and calm that can be better imagined than explained'.[43] No public celebrations or political gatherings took place and this atmosphere prevailed during the following months. The editorial of the *Roscommon Herald* reflected the view of many that the Treaty 'gives a good means to an end and affords the Irish people the opportunity of being mistress in their own house, with a control, despite all the fights made in the centuries past, that could never be obtained before'.[44]

As the SF ard fheis in February 1922 avoided a vote on the Treaty and a general election was postponed for several months, maintaining unity was the main priority for national leaders. The *Sligo Champion* observed that 'the tables are turned, Ireland, not England is on trial before the world now, and unless reason prevails, disaster will ensue'.[45] At Carrick Fr Edward Dalton, the local curate, advised that in the interests of peace, no public political meetings should be held and that people should be free to make up their own minds on how to vote in the upcoming election.[46] In Leitrim major conflict between both sides was avoided and preparations for the impending general election proceeded in a very low key fashion, with only one public meeting hosted by the pro-Treaty side taking place on 17 March 1922 at Carrick. Prior to that meeting, Andrew Lavin was kidnapped and held for a brief period by gunmen before being released. At the sparsely attended public assembly, Dolan was heckled by a group of IRA members who shouted: 'you were in your feather bed when the boys on the run had a thorn quick for a pillow'. Both Carter and Dolan emphasized that the Treaty ensured Ireland would finally take control of its own affairs.[47]

While candidate selection meetings were held by both sides, the only visit by a prominent national leader took place at Aughnasheelin on Easter Sunday night when General Seán Mac Eoin attended a concert in the local parish hall. Mac Eoin stated that his visit to Aughnasheelin was a social one and that irrespective of political differences people should be allowed to vote without any interference or intimidation.[48] With an agreement reached nationally on SF panel candidates, no Labour candidate emerged in the Leitrim–North Roscommon constituency and the four sitting TDs were selected. The only perceived opposition for the panel candidates was the selection of Roscommon-based Charles McCarthy by the Irish Farmers' Union. The withdrawal of McCarthy following a meeting with the panel prior to the submission of nominations on 6 June 1922 ensured that no contest would occur in Leitrim–North Roscommon. In response to the withdrawal, the panel candidates issued a statement stating that because 'the national battle is not yet won', they deemed the withdrawal of McCarthy 'as an act of patriotic duty which deserves the highest commendation'.[49] Farmers' representatives were following the path of Labour and acceding to the demands of separtists who insisted on the postponement of other issues until the national question was solved.

Early in 1922 Leitrim witnessed the withdrawal of Crown forces across the county. The *Roscommon Herald* reported that 'the IRA are vigilantly engaged in the protection of the people, and to their credit it may be said that everything is well conducted and law and order maintained'.[50] Attempted cattle drives and land seizures at Drumlion and Gowel resulted in the arrest and subsequent release of Jim Gralton.[51] While SF had feared that forced land redistribution would alienate cross-class support, the rulers of the new state

The transition to self-government, 1921–2

also wished to enforce the law and prevent land seizures. In Leitrim, in addition to issuing a proclamation prohibiting land seizures, Commandant Harry McKeon of the National army confiscated the cattle of trespassers.[52] Despite the prevalence of small farms in the county, land seizures were not a major issue among smallholders because of the absence of large grazier farms.

In Leitrim the transfer of power was conducted in an orderly fashion with the majority of people and their public representatives accepting the terms of the Treaty. The fact that there were no organized labour or farmers' representative candidates meant that no contest took place in the 1922 election which contributed to a relatively peaceful political environment in the county. Apart from the rates issue and minor land agitation, Leitrim did not witness the widespread political unrest experienced in other regions. Continuity rather that change dominated local politics as the new rulers were consumed with the same broad range of issues as their predecessors. Both locally and nationally, a culture of cautious conservatism, an emphasis on the fostering of nationalism and the absence of a social or economic vision for an independent Ireland bore a striking resemblance to the old regime.

9 'There is this particular type of madness amongst a section of the people': Civil War, 1922–3

With the signing of the Anglo-Irish Treaty on 6 December 1921, all parties to the agreement had different perceptions of what it entailed. Under its terms, a twenty-six county entity, the Irish Free State, was established that would have dominion status within the British Empire, and, consequently, recognize the British monarch as the formal head of state. To the Irish delegation, the terms ensured British recognition of Irish statehood, a native Irish administration and control of a wide range of governmental functions. While it offered less than the coveted Irish Republic, the Irish negotiators believed that full independence would, in time, be achieved. Opponents argued that under dominion status Britain would continue to exercise undue influence over Irish affairs. Furthermore, they objected to provisions such as the oath of fidelity that members of Dáil Éireann would have to swear to the British monarch. After an acrimonious series of debates, the Dáil approved the Treaty by 64 votes to 57 on 7 January 1922. Despite attempts to re-unify both factions at a political and military level, the country plunged into chaos as many influential IRA leaders led their men in opposition to the Treaty. While the pro-Treaty side were winning the political debate, the majority of prominent IRA leaders were opposed to the Treaty. Only Seán Mac Eoin in Longford, Eoin O'Duffy in Monaghan and Michael Brennan in Clare aligned with their IRA GHQ colleagues – Collins, Mulcahy and J.J. O'Connell – in support of the settlement. The IRA's South Leitrim Brigade backed Mac Eoin's support for the Treaty and a peaceful transfer of military bases and police barracks to local IRA units began in February 1922.[1] While the transfer of power in Leitrim was less acrimonious than in other regions, the local population witnessed a mixture of lawlessness and criminality hidden behind a concerted campaign of resistance by anti-Treaty forces based around the county's borders with neighbouring Roscommon and Sligo.

The *Freeman's Journal* reported the withdrawal of Crown forces from Leitrim in late January 1922, stating that 'all the Black and Tan members of the RIC in Leitrim have been notified that their services will no longer be required after February 1'.[2] In early February 1922 detachments of the Royal Sussex Regiment based across Leitrim withdrew from their barracks which were immediately occupied by the county's pro-Treaty IRA units. Before departing on 14 March the RIC dumped surplus ammunition and explosives in the River Shannon to prevent munitions falling into the hands of local IRA units. Local newspapers welcomed the departure of the RIC and reflected that 'it's a big change in twelve months when the paid bullies would not allow the people to walk the streets without insulting and abusing them'.[3]

While the South Leitrim Brigade supported the Treaty, IRA units in the north of the county joined the 3rd Western Division under the leadership of Sligo anti-Treatietes, Brian MacNeill, Séamus Devins and Billy Pilkington. Like many other families at the time, the MacNeills were divided over the Treaty. MacNeill's father, Eoin, was a Free State minister and his brother was a serving officer in the new National army. The strength of anti-Treaty sentiment among the Sligo IRA ensured that the border regions of Sligo and Leitrim formed part of the bulwark of opposition to the new state.[4]

As a result of increasing lawlessness nationwide, one of the first actions of the Provisional government was the formation of a civic guard on 21 February 1922. While deployment of the force was temporarily delayed until August 1922, due to internal divisions and an abortive mutiny, attempts were made to establish a police structure nationwide. In many areas of Leitrim, local IRA units that were occupying barracks and police stations acted as the enforcers of local law and order.[5] In a politically unstable environment it was often difficult to differentiate between political incidents involving anti-Treaty IRA units and ordinary criminals taking advantage of societal instability.[6] Robberies were a daily occurrence with 319 post office raids reported across Ireland between 23 March and 19 April 1922.[7] At Gorvagh on 31 January 1922 26-year-old Hugh Canning was killed in an altercation with neighbours.[8] At nearby Mohill, a local merchant, Patrick McKenna, was shot and seriously wounded in an incident linked to the sale of a public house. Three men were subsequently arrested by the local IRA and charged with the attempted murder of McKenna.[9] On 6 May 1922 raiders stole £200 from the Northern Bank at Drumshanbo and within three days the bank was again raided.[10] In the same week Carrick railway station was raided by armed and masked men and a large amount of money was stolen.[11]

The political division of Ireland into two separate states not only split nationalist Ireland, it also gave rise to renewed outbreaks of large-scale sectarian violence across Northern Ireland. During the six-month period between the signing of the Treaty on 6 December 1921 and 31 May 1922, 81 Protestants and 169 Catholics were killed in violent circumstances in the newly formed northern state.[12] Despite two Craig–Collins agreements in January and June 1922, part of whose terms ended the Belfast boycott in return for the re-instatement of sacked Catholic shipyard workers, Collins approved clandestine IRA violence against the new northern state. Collins's northern policy was based on a number of complex factors, including keeping the northern IRA pro-Treaty and his willingness to reunite with the anti-Treatyites against a common enemy.[13]

The establishment of an Ulster Council/Northern Command under the leadership of Frank Aiken, with Seán Mac Eoin as his deputy, resulted in a violent border campaign from January to June 1922 pursued against the Crown forces by both pro-Treaty and anti-Treaty IRA units. While a number of major confrontations between the IRA and Crown forces took place on the border, including at Clones, County Monaghan, in February 1922 and at Pettigo, County Donegal, in May 1922, few incidents erupted on the Leitrim border with Fermanagh.[14] Among the more serious was a co-ordinated kidnapping of prominent unionists organized by the Northern Command in response to the threatened execution of republican prisoners at Derry Jail. These raids on the night of 7-8 February were organized from a base at Blacklion on the Cavan/Leitrim/Fermanagh border and involved the deployment of IRA units from Longford, Leitrim, Armagh and Mayo into Fermanagh and Tyrone. While the raids proved successful in the Tyrone area, where the IRA kidnapped twenty-one local unionists, the IRA raiders in Fermanagh met strong resistance. A speedy deployment of Ulster Special Constabulary resulted in the capture of the IRA kidnappers outside Enniskillen.[15] Five Leitrim republicans – Bernard Sweeney, John Kiernan, Joe Reynolds, John Griffin and Charlie Reynolds – were among the fourteen-man raiding party.[16] At their trial in March 1922 the defendants refused to recognize the court and asserted that their actions were politically motivated. Rejecting these claims, Justice Wilson told the court that 'the group were taking peaceable subjects out of their beds in the dead of night and doing with them as they wished'.[17] Before sentencing the defendants to ten-year prison terms, the judge added that 'a crime was a crime whether it was committed by a politician, a saint or a butter merchant'.[18]

Only two further significant incidents took place in the Leitrim–Fermanagh border area during the campaign against the new northern state. On 28 March 1922 Charlie McGoohan led an attack on the Royal Ulster Constabulary (RUC) barracks at Belcoo, County Fermanagh, overpowered its occupants and seized a large quantity of arms and ammunition.[19] The sole fatality of the campaign in the region took place one week later on 5 April 1922, when a six-man RUC patrol was ambushed on the Fermanagh–Leitrim border at Garrison. The machine-gun attack resulted in the death of Constable Edwin Plumb and the wounding of two of his colleagues. Three of the patrol retreated to the local barracks but on their return with reinforcements, they could only recover two policemen. The following day Plumb's body was discovered on the Leitrim side of the border in a badly mutilated state and was taken back to Garrison RUC barracks by local clergymen.[20]

The lack of government authority in early 1922 contributed to the revival of land seizures and cattle drives across the country.[21] In Leitrim, agrarian agitation led by labour activist Jim Gralton was primarily confined to the south of the county near Carrick. Gralton, a former IRA member had returned to Leitrim from America in 1921 where he had been actively involved in the American labour movement. Within months, he built the Pearse-Connolly hall on his own land with the aid of local voluntary labour and used the venue for social functions and community education.[22] In late April 1922, Gralton and his followers seized land at Mong from Wilton Vaugh, sub-sherriff of Leitrim. The *Anglo-Celt* reported that Vaugh's land was 'now taken over by the Gowel Committee who state that they will use it, particularly for the grazing of cows of poor people resident in the district'.[23] In a similar incident, cattle were driven off John O'Donel's land near Carrick and onwards for over thirty miles to his home at Manorhamilton.[24] Further agitation took place at Dromod where a group of local men were charged with a land seizure and warned to desist from such activity. The court heard that the defendants 'took the law into their own hands and no civilized government could tolerate such an act, which was sheer Bolshevism'.[25] Such pronouncements were common as restraining forces of conservatism were present within the republican movement that prevented a radical distribution of grazing land for smallholders and the landless.[26]

Unlike many neighbouring counties, Leitrim did not have large numbers of estates and grazier farms, with only 21 farms in the county comprising more than 200 acres compared to 254 in Galway, and 108 in Roscommon.[27] The composition of land holdings in Leitrim (over 90 per cent were under 50 acres) and an above average rate of land purchase by tenant farmers contributed to a low level of agitation in the county.[28] Consequently, instances of land seizures were few. When Patrick and Bernard Gilhooley attempted to seize the land of a neighbour in May 1922, their defence at a republican court in Drumsna was that their father, who sold the land to a neighbour named Fox in 1897, was 'fond of a drop and he was not as cute as Mr Fox was'. Faced with the threat of imprisonment by the court, both men gave an undertaking to vacate the land.[29]

While SF had feared that forced land redistribution would alienate cross-class support for the party, the rulers of the new state also wished to prevent land seizures and enforce law and order.[30] Although the minister for agriculture, Patrick Hogan, believed that the solution to the land question lay in the completion of land purchase through new legislation, he was also convinced that the state should quell disorder by force if necessary.[31] Hogan, himself a substantial farmer, derided land agitators as having no genuine claim to land and being from 'the worst elements in the country districts with a pretty liberal sprinkling of wasters from the towns'.[32]

From the spring of 1922 the reaction of the authorities in Leitrim to attempted land seizures and cattle drives was swift. Commandant Harry McKeon, National army commanding officer in south Leitrim, issued a public proclamation in April 1922 prohibiting land seizures in his district. Part of

McKeon's policy was the seizure of trespassing cattle and transporting them to Dublin's cattle market for sale.[33] He publicly announced that Dáil Éireann would acquire large tracts of land for division 'and that persons requiring land will have loans advanced to them for purchase'.[34] Nevertheless, agitation by Gralton and his supporters continued. In their attempts to thwart Gralton, government troops occupied the Pearse-Connolly hall at Gowel. During a stand-off between locals and the National army, troops threatened to burn the building. On 30 May 1922 James McLoughlin, a National army officer, was killed in an accidental shooting when he failed to respond to a sentry's challenge while approaching the occupied hall.[35]

In a concerted land agitation campaign across Ireland, many 'big houses' were destroyed by a land hungry population intent on forcing land redistribution. While thirty-nine such houses were destroyed in Connacht during the Civil War period, only one incident occurred in Leitrim at Glenfarne.[36] As a result of the volatile political climate, the owners of Glenfarne hall, a Belfast timber harvesting company, had abandoned the property, which was subsequently looted by locals. The property was later occupied by National army forces in September 1922.[37]

By early 1923 the government had established the Special Infantry Corps (SIC) to prevent land seizures and quell land agitation and industrial unrest. Hogan and his cabinet colleague, Kevin O'Higgins, saw the new force as the protectors of the social and moral fabric of Irish society.[38] In Leitrim the activities of the SIC were minimal. When a detachment of the 2nd Infantry Battalion based at Carrick arrested a five-man gang at Kilmore on 21 May 1923, only Michael Duignan was associated with 'land trouble'. The remainder, described as 'active Irregulars', were handed over to Commandant Seán Mitchell and interned at Boyle.[39]

The most pressing issue for Leitrim farmers in 1922 was rates. While many farmers opportunistically refused to pay rates, many others faced genuine economic hardship. By 1922 economic conditions were so bad in parts of the west of Ireland that the Irish White Cross had set aside £25,000 for the relief of distress.[40] Leitrim County Council demanded intervention by the Provisional government to assist smallholders in economic distress within certain Congested District Board areas of north Leitrim.[41] Rate collection was also hampered by local IRA units who threatened rate collectors.[42]

Despite attempts to preserve unity within the ranks of the IRA, clashes between the two factions increased. The occupation of the Four Courts in Dublin on 13 April 1922 by republicans led by Rory O'Connor heightened tensions between the opposing sides. In March 1922 rival units in Limerick city contested the right to occupy vacant barracks.[43] In Sligo skirmishes took place during March 1922 between government troops and anti-Treaty factions which occupied the main barracks in the county.[44] By contrast, all barracks in

Leitrim were occupied by pro-Treaty forces. However, the fragility of the situation in the region was demonstrated at Boyle where the local barracks was taken over by Martin Fallon, leader of the North Roscommon Brigade, who initially declared that he was anti-Treaty. Following a meeting with Seán Mac Eoin and Eoin O'Duffy at the Bush Hotel in Carrick in late March 1922, Fallon changed to the pro-Treaty side. On hearing of Fallon's defection, Brian MacNeill, adjutant of the 3rd Western Division of the anti-Treaty IRA, immediately took over Boyle barracks and Fallon's pro-Treaty faction withdrew and occupied the local workhouse. As Carrick was under pro-Treaty control, the strategic importance of the town of Boyle as a gateway to Sligo and north Leitrim resulted in anti-Treaty reinforcements arriving in the town to protect the barracks. While tensions were building at Boyle, the early months of 1922 in Leitrim were characterized by an environment of relative peace. Only two political incidents took place, both in Carrick: Parke Masonic hall was burned down and shots were fired at soldiers near the town's barracks.[45]

Following six months of division, dissension and failed attempts at compromise at a national level, the Civil War began on 28 June 1922 with the bombardment of the Four Courts by government forces. Reporting on the outbreak of formal hostilities, the *Leitrim Advertiser* described how 'a feeling of despair and sadness has come over the population at seeing the country now enmeshed in the throes of civil war, with Irishmen fighting against other brave Irishmen'.[46] An equally despondent *Roscommon Herald* declared

> all the blood, misery, suffering and ruin endured in Ireland for the last six years goes for nothing, when just as much or even better might have been had for the ask under Redmond's old worthless Parliamentary Party. It is this reflection that makes the Civil War now raging in Dublin, so maddening and heart-depressing.[47]

In contrast to the War of Independence, there was no formal republican unit in Leitrim during the Civil War, which forced anti-Treaty IRA men to join units in north Roscommon and Sligo.[48] While all three Western Divisions of the IRA were anti-Treaty, the South Leitrim Brigade supported the December 1921 settlement. IRA veteran Jim Gallagher recalled that the few Leitrim anti-Treaty members of the IRA in south Leitrim went to Boyle barracks to join their north Roscommon comrades because in Leitrim the 'whole Brigade became pro-Treaty'.[49]

The causes of the Irish Civil War conflict were complex and not necessarily related to the Treaty settlement.[50] Unlike many conflicts, political divisions across class lines were not evident.[51] Nevertheless, support for the anti-Treaty side was more prevalent in poorer areas of the west and south, with militant republicanism sometimes portrayed as 'a lower-class rural phenomenon' aided by anti-Treatyites, fuelling agrarianism among uneconomic landowners and the landless.[52] Support for the Treaty in Leitrim was heavily influenced by the positions taken on the settlement by local leaders. Furthermore, although elements of all social classes supported the Treaty, the strongest support for the Provisional government came from the upper echelons of Irish society, and in areas of relative prosperity where there were more established links to the British economy.[53]

Support for the Treaty among all classes in Leitrim was reflected in a high level of enlistment into the National army during the early months of 1922.[54] An IRA review took place at Drumsna on 14 February and the *Roscommon Herald* reported that 'all the shop assistants and workers are enrolled in the ranks of the Army'.[55] In early March 1922 1,100 men presented themselves at Carrick barracks to join the army and the newly formed Civic Guard.[56] The experience of Leitrim, a county where over eight-five per cent of farmers possessed holdings of less than thirty acres, confirmed that neither poverty nor prosperity influenced participation in the conflict among the general population.[57]

With strong republican resistance prevailing across large areas of the west of Ireland, the National army was intent on taking control of the region by recapturing republican occupied towns. Within twenty-four hours of the Four Courts' bombardment, government forces recaptured Finner Camp in Donegal, adjacent to the Leitrim border. Two republicans were killed, including James Connolly, a SF member of Leitrim County Council and a captain in the 3rd Western Division. Connolly's father had been killed in controversial circumstances by Crown forces in 1920. John Connolly was the second Leitrim republican to die in the opening weeks of the Civil War. His family received a note informing them that his body was in a coffin in Tullaghan church and that his death was the result of an accidental shooting. Connolly's father told his inquest that his 18-year-old son was an apprentice shoemaker in Bundoran, but he had left his employment to fight with the republican forces. The jury found 'that the deceased died near Tullaghan on 11 July 1922, and the cause of death was shock and haemorrage as a result of a gunshot injury, but how inflicted there was no evidence to show'.[58]

By early July 1922, the *Freeman's Journal* reported that government forces controlled Carrick 'with no Irregulars in the whole of the south Leitrim area'.[59] In an attempt to stop the National army advancing westward towards Boyle, republicans unsuccessfully attempted to destroy the railway bridge crossing over the River Shannon at Drumsna.[60] Since April 1922 Boyle was jointly controlled by both pro- and anti-Treaty forces, and in the battle for control of the town in June 1922, National army commander and former leader of the North Roscommon Brigade, Michael Dockery, was killed. On 3 July 1922 pro-Treaty reinforcements arrived from Athlone, which decisively turned the battle in favour of the National army. After a protracted four-day battle, the National army captured the town and republicans retreated to the nearby Arigna mountains on the Roscommon–Leitrim border. As they retreated, a group of republicans ambushed a National army patrol at Ardcarne outside Carrick, killing one soldier, before the attacking party was captured by government forces. National army victories continued and with the re-capture of Sligo town in late July 1922 government forces were in control of all the main towns in Sligo, Leitrim and Roscommon. Despite losing control of the towns, the anti-Treaty IRA successfully transferred large supplies of arms and ammunition to remote hideaways in the surrounding countryside and mountains. Such resources ensured that the conflict would be protracted, and in spite of initial National army successes, large areas of Connacht, especially in Sligo, Leitrim, Mayo and the Connemara area of Galway, still caused major problems for government forces.[61]

With the National army in control of the major towns, republican strategy in the region revolved around a campaign of guerrilla warfare based in the mountains of Arigna and north Sligo. Republican resistance was concentrated around two groups, the Arigna column under the control of Edward (Ned) Bofin and a larger group under the command of Billy Pilkington and Brian MacNeill based at Rahelly House on the Gore-Booth estate on the Sligo–Leitrim border. National army intelligence reports identified Bofin as a leader 'known for his soldierly qualities', who compelled his men to go to bed at 8 p.m. each evening and rise at 2 a.m. in order to conduct operations under cover of darkness.[62] While good communications existed between both groups, no unified command structure, nor any co-ordinated military strategy, existed between them.[63]

Pilkington's group attacked the town of Manorhamilton on 9 July 1922 and were involved in a number of incidents in north Leitrim. During the course of the attack, the local curate, Fr John Brady, intervened and stood in front of the National army garrison. He informed the attackers that 'he would remain there, and if they attacked the barrack he would be the first to fall'.[64] The republicans acceded to the priest's request and withdrew. A week later, on 16 July 1922, Manorhamilton barracks was again attacked by republicans with rifle and machine-gun fire.[65] In addition to attacks on National army garrisons, republicans were also involved in road trenching and attacks on mails and trains. In July bridges were destroyed and roads blocked with fallen trees to hinder the movement of the National army.[66] Increasing levels of attacks on infrastructure forced William Cosgrave to request clergy and other public figures to direct and assist local populations to clear road and bridge obstructions. At Killargue in July Fr Daniel McManus, the local curate, organized local people to clear road obstructions put in place by anti-Treaty forces on the Drumkeeran to Manorhamilton road.[67] Pro-Treaty TD James Dolan had a narrow escape during an attack by Pilkington's unit on Glenfarne railway station in the same month. On 5 July Pilkington's column captured a National army outpost at Kinlough, and the fifteen-man garrison were disarmed.[68]

The months of August and September 1922 in the region were a period of military stalemate with both sides pre-occupied with maintaining control of their respective areas.[69] During this time a peace initiative proposed by Fr James Roddy from Geevagh failed, despite a three-day ceasefire bringing both sides to peace talks. On the mistaken assumption that a permanent truce had been negotiated, several members of the Arigna column arrived at Boyle barracks where they were arrested. The men were subsequently released, having been informed that the cessation in hostilities was only temporary.[70]

One of the few significant actions undertaken in Leitrim was the capture of Drumsna garrison on 24 August 1922 when a large quantity of arms and ammunition was captured by the anti-Treaty IRA. In the subsequent military inquiry, Private Philip Brady, who was on sentry duty at the time of the attack, claimed that he was taken by surprise and overpowered by the raiders who were in stocking feet when approaching the building. The raiders detonated a mine near the barracks door before overpowering the seven-man unit.[71]

During the first weeks of Civil War the conflict in the north-west followed the general pattern nationwide. The capture of large strategic military locations like Boyle and Sligo was mirrored across Munster, where government forces, possessing superior manpower and equipment, asserted state authority while anti-Treaty forces retreated to the surrounding countryside. Republican strategy reverted to a guerrilla campaign, capturing isolated army posts, disarming the occupants, and retreating to mountain strongholds with captured arms and ammunition. As such, the vast majority of Leitrim's countryside was peaceful and fighting was confined to the county's border areas with Sligo and Roscommon. Despite protracted fighting to control the region's major towns in the summer months of 1922, only three fatalities occurred. Following the death of Michael Collins in August 1922 the conflict entered a new and more brutal phase that was characterized by a low intensity, yet violent, guerrilla campaign.[72] The new leadership in government no longer felt the need to appease anti-Treaty opponents as Collins had attempted, and concentrated its resources on asserting its authority.[73]

Sniping along Leitrim's border with Fermanagh was now confined to occasional attacks by republicans, with the National army concentrating its efforts in the fight against their former comrades. Throughout September 1922 confrontations increased between anti-Treaty and government forces across Leitrim. At Dromod, government forces under the command of Commandants Harry McKeon and Tom Carter intercepted republicans on the estate of Ormbsy Gore. The group had earlier crossed the River Shannon from County Roscommon. During the gun battle, anti-Treatyites on the

Roscommon side of the river kept up concentrated machine-gun fire on McKeon's men in an attempt to aid their comrades. After an hour-long engagement, three republicans were captured and taken to Carrick.[74] An attack on 14 September 1922 on Drumshanbo barracks by the Arigna unit, led by Bofin, resulted in the overpowering of the garrison and the capture of rifles, ammunition and explosives. In the course of the attack Private James Dolan was killed; before departing the raiders set fire to the building. Despite protracted searches throughout the summer of 1922, the National army was unable to dislodge the Arigna republicans. During one search on 14 August 1922 a fourteen-bed republican field hospital, staffed by four nurses, was discovered in the mountains.[75]

Seán Mac Eoin, commander of National army forces in the midlands and north-west, faced a number of logistical and organizational issues. Within the Western Command area, which stretched from Athlone to Donegal, many of his units were located in dispersed and isolated posts. The presence of two well-armed republican columns in rough mountainous terrain on the Sligo, Roscommon and Leitrim borders ensured a prolonged conflict.[76] Morale among young National army soldiers was also low with many placed in isolated outposts across the region. At Dromahair in September 1922 the National army soldiers surrendered their barracks, a Lewis machine-gun, and twenty rifles and ammunition to republicans as a protest about lack of pay and supplies.[77]

Attempting to take control of the region, Mac Eoin deployed experienced and war-hardened troops to the north Sligo–Leitrim border.[78] In a co-ordinated military operation, troops from Manorhamilton, Boyle and Sligo, under the command of Mac Eoin, and troops from Finner Camp, under the command of Commandant Joe Sweeney, engaged in extensive searches which resulted in the capture of large numbers of anti-Treatyites. During Sweeney's advance south, the republican-controlled north Leitrim villages of Kinlough and Tullaghan were captured and thirty republicans surrendered at Kiltyclogher.[79] On the outskirts of Manorhamilton, fourteen republicans in possession of arms and explosives were arrested.[80] In their attempts to thwart National army advances, the anti-Treaty IRA derailed trains across the region. At Dromahair, they apologized to the train crew, informing them that they were compelled to take such action because 'their comrades had been surrounded by numbers of Free State troops and it was their duty as republicans to take every possible step to checkmate the movements of the Free State soldiers'.[81]

In reaction to the rapid advance of government forces, Pilkington's headquarters at Rahelly House was evacuated and republicans sought shelter in the nearby mountains. En route to a meeting with Pilkington at Glencar, Brian MacNeill, Séamus Devins, Paddy Carroll and James Banks were shot dead by the National army on the slopes of Benbulben. The nature of the killings proved controversial with claims that the four were taken away from the main body of troops and executed by machine-gun. While official sources reported that the men were retreating from an ambush site, Captain Charlie McGoohan was accused of directing the killings after the men had surrendered.[82] On the same day two republicans, Harry Benson and Tom Langan, were also intercepted by the National army. The bodies of both men were found eleven days later at the bottom of a ravine. Benson's body contained bullet wounds to the head and shins, while Langan's body had seven bullet wounds and a bayonet wound. MacNeill's body was taken to Dublin for a private family funeral; the other funerals at Sligo attracted large crowds. Votes of sympathy were passed by local organizations to the family of Devins, a local TD and county councillor, and his comrades who had died 'in a fight which they thought was right'.[83]

By the end of September 1922 Mac Eoin's operation in the area was deemed a success, yet isolated bands of republicans continued to operate in the area.[84] The RUC barracks at Belcoo on the Fermanagh/Leitrim border was attacked by gunfire on 15 October 1922, and the *Freeman's Journal* reported that the attackers were 'roving bands of Irregulars who have recently been seen in Glenfarne and Kiltyclogher districts of Co. Leitrim'.[85] One of the few anti-Treatyite successes in the autumn of 1922 was the destruction of the River Shannon railway bridge at Drumsna, which disrupted railway operations temporarily between Dublin and Sligo.[86]

The wounding of Fr John Casey, curate in Drumshanbo, on 25 October 1922 in a shooting incident outside the town brought renewed attention to the region. Casey was returning from a funeral in Ballyshannon on his motorcycle when he was shot at Galley bridge, on the outskirts of Drumshanbo. The *Roscommon Herald* described the priest's SF sympathies during the War of Independence, reporting that 'his service not alone to Leitrim but for the entire cause have been unequalled and there was scarcely a man, clerical or lay, to whom such attention was paid by the British government during the reign of terror'.[87] It was believed that the curate failed to stop when instructed to do so by republicans. Despite receiving a bullet wound, Casey continued to the parochial house in Drumshanbo, where he was treated by a local doctor, and afterwards transported to Dublin where he recovered.[88] The shooting took place two weeks after the Irish bishops issued a pastoral letter supporting the legitimacy of the Provisional government and proclaiming 'the guerrilla warfare now being carried out by the Irregulars is without moral sanction; and therefore the killing of National soldiers in the course of it is murder before God'.[89]

Within two days of the Casey shooting a large force of National army troops with armoured cars searched the Arigna mountains for republicans, but with little success.[90] Despite the presence of a National army garrison in Drumshanbo, the Arigna column continued to carry out raids on the town.[91]

One of the few chivalrous acts of the conflict took place at Drumsna when a car containing National army officer Captain McNabola was ambushed by republicans. Travelling with his sister and a friend to Carrick, McNabola was on medical leave from the army having been injured at Boyle in July 1922. After stopping the car, the ambushers discovered that their target was still recuperating from his wounds. Having informed the travelling party that they would not shoot an injured man, the republicans procured a horse and trap from a local farm and McNabola and his companions were transported to Carrick.[92]

At Manorhamilton on 17 November 1922 a republican unit arrived in the town with the intention of commandeering goods from shops, and raiding the local post office. Unknown to the them, soldiers were already patrolling the town and an exchange of fire took place which resulted in the shooting of republican leader, Philip Gilgunn. Although the raiding party succeeded in commandeering clothes and foodstuffs and tobacco, the badly injured Gilgunn had to be transported to St Vincent's Hospital in Dublin where he died the next day.[93]

The establishment of the reconstituted Civic Guard in September 1922 resulted in Sligo–Leitrim becoming a specific police division with two subdivisions headquartered in Carrick and Sligo. By early 1923 four barracks were established in the county at Carrick, Manorhamilton, Ballinamore and Carrigallen.[94] The Provisional government was very aware that a successful depiction of the new entity as a non-political police force was vital to it being accepted by local communities. At its inception, the commissioner of the new force, Eoin O'Duffy, announced that it was 'a police force for all the people, and not for any section of the people'.[95] Despite O'Duffy's hopes, the newly constituted force was regarded by republicans as a symbol of the new state. As a result, civic guards were only stationed in districts that were perceived to be under government control. In spite of these limitations, the establishment of a police presence in Leitrim was essential because of increasing levels of lawlessness. Whiskey, tobacco, boots and sides of bacon were stolen from Carrick railway stores in September 1922 by people 'not connected with any side in the present struggle, and who are only to be found when brigandage is the predominating factor'.[96] The arrival of police in the county resulted in a dramatic decrease in crime in towns with a police presence; yet, crime continued in areas where police were not stationed.[97] A police presence did not prevent a group of armed men cycling into Ballinamore and robbing the town's four banks.[98] Armed raiders also robbed post offices at Drumsna, Drumkeeran, Leitrim and Glenfarne.[99]

At Ballaghameehan on 17 October 1922 two men assaulted the barman at McGowan's public house and removed the till from the premises. Placing the till on a donkey cart outside, they emptied it and made their escape by bicycle towards the border. Locals immediately petitioned the Provisional government to have an army or Civic Guard presence in the area.[100] On 11

October the premises of Robert Gorby at Newtowngore was raided by armed and masked men. A ton of flour, bacon, sugar, boots and whiskey were taken to a waiting horse-drawn wagon. The raiders then robbed cash and clothes from Johnston's drapery store nearby.[101]

Whereas IRA chief of staff Liam Lynch specifically ordered that members of the police force were not to be physically harmed in any way, intimidation was permitted and carried out throughout the country.[102] On 17 November the first attack on police in the county took place at Ballinamore. Members of the Arigna column arrived by train from Drumshanbo, and placed roadblocks on the outskirts of the town. The intervention of the local curate prevented the burning of the Civic Guard barracks, but the raiders took police uniforms and equipment before proceeding to take goods from local shops. After transporting the proceeds of the raid to the railway station, the gang departed by train towards Arigna.[103] On 29 December a twenty-strong raiding party forced their way into the police barracks at Carrigallen. While the policemen were treated 'very courteously' by the raiders, the barracks' consignment of uniforms, raincoats, blankets and leggings were confiscated.[104] Two months later, on 23 February 1923, raiders returned to Carrigallen in a less courteous mood. A warning to leave the town was made to the police, and their bedding and equipment was burned.[105] Patrick Campbell, one of the six police stationed at Carrigallen, recalled that 'before leaving the leader of the gunmen warned us that if we didn't clear out immediately we would not be warned again'.[106] Between September 1922 and the summer of 1923, two of the county's four police barracks were attacked. Similar incidents were witnessed across Ireland where over 200 stations were attacked and one civic guard murdered in the same period.[107]

Ongoing raids on banks and post offices resulted in National army soldiers providing armed guards across the county on fair days when large sums of money were in circulation.[108] With increasing security at banks, mail cars and postmen again became an easy and regular target for thieves. Prior to Christmas 1922 three mail cars were held up at Leitrim village and the raiders ordered the drivers to accompany them to the Arigna mountains. The *Irish Independent* reported:

> there was a very valuable consignment, including Christmas parcels and registered letters. It was stated that letters and parcels to private individuals would be returned. The drivers were treated most hospitably, and got bumpers of whiskey on their arrival at the mountains, and also were given a substantial meal.[109]

Increasing numbers of raids on post offices and mail cars in the Drumsna, Drumshanbo and Leitrim districts resulted in all pension payments being transferred to the head office at Carrick.[110]

During December 1922 Leitrim witnessed three deaths in an increasingly lawless environment. An agrarian dispute was the cause of the death of Francis McCarron, a 57-year-old farmer, at Drumshanbo on 2 December.[111] Ten days later, three raiders shot 29-year-old Thomas and 74-year-old Carson Dennison during a raid on the family shop and bar at Drumkeeran. The Dennisons, a local Church of Ireland family who had traded in the town for decades, were sympathetic to republicans during the War of Independence.[112] Thomas died almost immediately, while his widowed father, Carson, died three days later in hospital. No arrests occurred after the killings but republicans from Arigna were suspected.[113]

The relationship between republicanism and the Protestant minority population in the years of the revolution is contested. Narrow definitions of Irishness often excluded non-Catholics and the Protestant experiences of the revolution included death, flight, boycott, intimidation, occasional inconvenience and indifference.[114] With the exception of one incident in the north of the county, where a number of Protestant families near Manorhamilton were subject to threats to leave their homes in May 1922, there was no evidence of widespread intimidation against Protestants in Leitrim. The background to the Manorhamilton incident involved a raid by armed men on seven Protestant homes, claiming that the properties were required for nationalist refugees from Belfast. When the families reported the incidents to troops in Manorhamilton and to James Dolan TD, a telegram reply was received. It read: 'Minister of Defence Dáil Éireann assured protection, Four Courts forces also assured protection. Orders to this effect sent to Dromahair and Manorhamilton. Advise people return home'.[115]

While Protestant businesses in Leitrim suffered as a result of the strict enforcement of the Belfast boycott, it affected all businesses. In many instances, attacks on Protestant businesses cannot be seen in isolation from the wider conflict over the Treaty as all sections of society were exposed to violent acts.[116] Between 1911 and 1926 the southern Irish Protestant population fell by one-third from 327,176 to 220,723. During that same fifteen-year period the Protestant population of Leitrim fell by 1,736, a drop of 32.21 per cent, greatly exceeding the decline of the Catholic population of the county, which experienced a 5.37 per cent drop.[117] A multiplicity of factors, including British military withdrawal, agrarianism, land reform, economic migration and marriage patterns, explain the decline in the minority population.[118]

Across Leitrim, intimidation against some Protestants took place but the victims were often targeted for their hostility towards republicanism or resentment over landownership.[119] Furthermore, the Protestant population had already contracted before the 1919–23 period. The Methodist population in the county declined from 524 in 1912 to 405 in 1916, more in anticipation of home rule rather than in response to the creation of the Irish Free State.[120] Declining numbers of births and baptisms were also identified in rural deans' reports in the wider Protestant community. Across ten Leitrim parishes, baptisms declined from 518 children in the years between 1910 and 1919 to 356 in the following decade.[121] While some clergymen identified economic reasons for migration and emigration in the years before 1919, in later reports they cited the changing political environment as reasons for population change.[122] In 1921 Revd Austin Sweetman at Fenagh attributed the increasing numbers of Protestant departures from his parish to 'anarchy'. Both Revd Matthew Porteus at Manorhamilton and Revd S.J. Haylett at Drumreilly reported 'unsettlement in [the] country' as reasons for the departure of some of their congregations.[123]

One of the preferred destinations for many Leitrim Protestants was nearby County Fermanagh. Census returns in 1925 indicated that of 2,117 Protestant Fermanagh residents who had left the Irish Free State in the preceding five years, 292 were from Leitrim, 51 were from Sligo, 55 from Galway, 34 from Mayo, and 6 from Roscommon.[124] In submissions to the Boundary Commission in 1925, both Revd Thomas Walmsley and Fermanagh councillor Thomas Scott stated that large numbers of Protestants had left the Manorhamilton area to settle in Fermanagh. Scott claimed that seventy percent of families in the Garrison-Manorhamilton district 'have transferred into Northern Ireland over the last five years'.[125] The proximity of Fermanagh may explain the extent of the exodus but such large numbers leaving Leitrim may demonstrate that, while there may not have been a concerted campaign of sectarianism, many Protestant families may have experienced intimidation. While few firm conclusions can be drawn regarding the departure, forced or otherwise, of such a large cohort of the population, the historical evidence suggests that Protestants were not randomly or routinely attacked; public hostility to republican ideals or long-standing resentments over landownership explain why certain Protestants were targetted.[126]

By January 1923 National army reports referred to anti-Treaty forces as an enemy with depleted numbers, lack of organization and unified control, and almost complete ineffectiveness from a military standpoint.[127] While open conflict with government forces was non-existent in the region, isolated shooting incidents and raids on shops and post offices continued. Arigna republicans were involved in raids at Ballyconnell in County Cavan on 6 January 1923, where Michael Cull was shot dead by Captain J.F. Kellegher, a National army officer, while raiding Owens and Richardson's hardware shop. The fearsome reputation of the Arigna column was demonstrated in a request for anonymity at Cull's inquest by the soldiers involved in the shooting. Writing to General Seán Mac Eoin, Colonel Pádraig Woods stated that Kellegher's home was located on the Cavan–Leitrim border and 'stands in grave danger from Bofin and his followers'.[128] At Dowra, on the same day as the Ballyconnell shooting, Michael McManus, a National army soldier, was killed in an attack by members of the Arigna column.[129] At Mohill in January 1923 the local barracks was fired on by attackers in nearby hills and gunmen fired shots at a passenger train near the town.[130]

Leitrim's first fatality of 1923 was Patrick O'Boyle, from Drumshanbo, who was shot dead near Arigna on 31 January 1923. The circumstances surrounding the death of O'Boyle, a World War One veteran and secretary of the Leitrim War Pensions Committee, were clouded in mystery. Because of O'Boyle's background, suspicion was immediately pointed at the Arigna column. His death was attributed to him not hearing a challenge to halt by republicans owing to heavy rain.[131] When the body was recovered in the aftermath of the shooting, the *Leitrim Observer* reported that 'there were indications that he received spiritual ministrations, as in one of his hands there was a crucifix, and the other bore traces of his having held a blessed candle'.[132] Both government and republican sources condemned the killing.[133]

In one of the more audacious attacks of the conflict, a 100-strong raiding party from Arigna entered Ballinamore in the early hours of 1 February and attacked the thirty-five man garrison. After a six-hour gun battle, the garrison surrendered when the roof collapsed following the detonation of a mine. The National army troops were taken to Drumshanbo on a seized train and later released. Before leaving the town, the post office and a local bank were raided. The *Freeman's Journal* reported that as a result of the incident, 'a large force of National troops has been poured into Leitrim and developments are expected to follow'.[134]

On 6 February 1922 fifty heavily armed men from the Arigna column attacked the town of Ballyconnell. During widespread looting and burning of business premises, Seán McGrath, an Irish teacher from Galway, and William Ryan, a shop assistant at Owens and Richardson's hardware shop, were shot dead by the raiders. The shop's owner, William Owens, was seriously wounded in the attack.[135] During the thirty-five minute raid the raiders informed local people that the attack was revenge for the death of Michael Cull. The *Roscommon Herald* reported that the attackers 'came from the direction of the mountains in County Leitrim and swooped down on the village when most of the inhabitants were at breakfast. The pillagers wrecked and looted at will, and generally behaved like an army of men run amok'.[136]

The viciousness of the Ballyconnell raid prompted an immediate response from the authorities. Richard Mulcahy, as minister of defence and chief of staff, admitted the problems that the government had with the Arigna column. In a speech to Dáil Éireann, he stated that

> some of our men in that area, not undertaking to believe that those men were as black as their present deeds have painted them, have contrary to

orders, and, contrary to the spirit of discipline in the Army, been carrying on a sort of negotiations with them. Anyone who knows the hinterland of mountains lying behind Ballinamore and Ballyconnell knows that for the work that we have to do in that area we have not sufficient troops to effectively control those mountains and to get that band of Irregulars that we know have been hiding there for some time.[137]

Describing the activities of the Arigna column, Mulcahy declared that

> there is this particular type of madness amongst a section of the people in the country who are armed, who are supported in their madness by feeling that they are following an ideal, and by gathering to themselves all the phrases and all the words that have supported our national struggle in the past.[138]

Despite differences in cabinet between Mulcahy and O'Higgins on aspects of the military campaign, the government presented a united and uncompromising policy of dealing with the anti-Treaty IRA.[139] Commenting on the attack on Ballyconnell, O'Higgins told the Dáil that

> I want to combat the view that it was a natural thing to expect that a body of Irishmen would descend upon this little town and proceed to murder their fellow citizens. It was not a natural thing. It is perhaps the most unnatural thing that has happened since this unnatural strife began.[140]

Throughout the early spring of 1923 National army strategy revolved around heavy concentrations of troops in searches for republicans.[141] In the northwest, reinforcements were transferred to the area from Cavan, Longford and Dublin in an attempt to capture the Arigna column. Despite over 600 troops and armoured vehicles searching the Arigna mountains, harsh weather conditions and prior warning of the impending raids resulted in the capture of only three men.[142] Notwithstanding the heavy military presence in the area, soldiers in four National army outposts on the Boyle–Carrick road were overpowered, and rifles and ammunition were taken. Private Andrew Callaghan died from wounds sustained in the attack. In a further raid on an isolated garrison at Drumsna on 19 February 1923, one republican was captured when the attackers were surpriseed by the arrival of reinforcements from Carrick and Drumshanbo.[143]

While attempting to evade military patrols, Séamus Cull and Paddy Tymon, two prominent members of the Arigna column, were killed on 27 February 1923 in an explosion on the Arigna mountains. Both had rowed across Lough Allen from a safe house at Cormongan, near Drumshanbo, and sought refuge in a cave. At the inquest into their deaths held at Drumshanbo, Captain Baxter, a National army officer, claimed that the military patrol that he was leading discovered a rifle, a revolver and some bedding at the mouth of the cave. Baxter stated that on further examination of the area, they discovered a small room in the dugout and a hole leading further into the cave. Having received no reply for over a two-hour period, and believing that the cave was empty, Baxter detonated an explosive in order that the cave could not be used again by republicans. An excavation commenced after the explosion, and the bodies of Cull and Tymon were discovered.[144] Counter-claims suggested that the troops knew the men were in the cave, and deliberately detonated the mine with the intention of killing them.[145] Baxter's testimony is contradicted by National army operations reports which stated that 'troops believed dug out was occupied, called on them to surrender which they refused to do'.[146] The inquest jury found that 'death was due in each case to shock caused by an explosion through military operations in Arigna Valley, and they considered no blame attested to anyone'.[147] A large National army force was present at the funerals of both men and all male mourners in attendance were searched.[148]

Within one month of the deaths of Cull and Tymon, similar state atrocities against republicans in Kerry, involving the use of mines, took place. An unwillingness to curb the excesses of its soldiers, including the murder of prisoners, characterized the government.[149] During the closing months of the Civil War the National army was involved in a series of organized massacres of republicans.[150] Within cabinet, O'Higgins and Hogan were adamant that the government would restore law and order and the adoption of executions as part of public policy from November 1922 demonstrated that intent.[151]

The content of Lenten pastorals in February 1923 referred to the need for law and order and gave continued support to the Provisional government. In his pastoral letter, the primate of All Ireland, Cardinal Michael Logue, was unequivocal in his condemnation of 'an orgy of crime and outrage' enveloping the country.[152] Denouncing republicans and their use of force, Bishop Hoare of Ardagh and Clonmacnoise proclaimed that 'there must be a government and that government must protect itself by making laws and executing them'.[153] Although noting that his diocese of Kilmore was comparatively free 'of these grave and terrible violations of the law of God', Bishop Patrick Finegan claimed that 'some crimes – deplorable crimes – have been committed within its boundary'.[154] Finegan exhorted 'young men and others in the diocese who may have become mixed up either from motives of mistaken patriotism, or of private loot in these terrible acts, to repent at once and approach the tribunal of penance'.[155] In addition to condemnation from the hierarchy, certain clergy criminalized the actions of the anti-Treaty side using terms such as 'murderer', 'bolshies' and 'riff-raff' in denunciations from the pulpit.[156]

By the spring of 1923 attacks by republicans on government forces became infrequent. While units of the Arigna column continued to operate, no large-scale operations were undertaken following the Ballyconnell attack. Trains continued to be a target for republicans in isolated attacks across the north of the county. At Glenfarne on 7 March 1923 passengers were ordered from the Sligo–Enniskillen train by a group of armed men, who burned carriages before sending it driverless towards Manorhamilton where it stopped outside of the town.[157] At Carrick on 13 March 1923 shots were fired over a two-hour period at both the military barracks, and the National army outpost at the local railway station.[158]

A heavy National army presence and ongoing searches resulted in the capture of a number of republicans during March 1923. On 12 March two republicans, Frank Slevin and James O'Donnell, dressed in women's clothing, were arrested on the outskirts of Manorhamilton. Reports suggested that both men had earlier entered the town, 'presumably to raid the banks, but finding an armed guard on the premises, they left'.[159] After a two-hour gun battle with soldiers on 13 March 1923, eight men, including local republican leader Philip Rooney, were captured at Kiltyclogher.[160] Paul Bofin, brother of the Arigna column leader, was also captured in early March.[161]

Widespread searches in the last remaining republican strongholds of Munster and north Connacht continued throughout March and April of 1923. In Waterford an attempted meeting of the IRA executive in the Nire Valley was moved to four different locations because of the threat of National army raids.[162] Despite IRA chief of staff Liam Lynch's calls for the fight to be continued, republican resistance decreased in the wake of imprisonments and executions by government forces. Although Lynch recognized a declining level of morale in the south, he believed (incorrectly) that republican forces were strong in other areas.[163] On 25 March 1923 Ned Bofin and three other men were arrested at Riverstown, County Sligo. Regarded as the identified leader, with Billy Pilkington, of republicans in the region, his arrest was a serious blow to the anti-Treaty side. Labelled by English newspapers as the 'De Wett of the West', the *Roscommon Herald* reported that the 'capture of the man with many exploits to his name was important and sensational'.[164] To many local people who supported and sheltered the Arigna column, their exploits were a form of social banditry, and the group were seen not as criminals but rather as champions of just causes.[165] Following Bofin's capture, organized republican resistance in the region almost immediately disappeared. By early April 1923 military intelligence reported the surrender of Owen Cull, one of the Arigna leaders, and an inactive local column.[166]

The final months of the conflict were characterized by isolated gun and arson attacks on the homes of government officials. The homes of both Commandant Seán Mitchell, and Eugene Kilkenny near Mohill, and Charles McGoohan at Ballinamore were burned in March and April of 1922.[167] Intimidating warning notices, a familiar weapon of Leitrim republicans, were posted outside churches in south Leitrim in March 1923, threatening members of the local population, including priests, doctors and farmers with sons in the National army.[168] Condemning the notices, the *Freeman's Journal* reported:

> the world has learned to expect nothing less from the Bolsheviks but merciless persecution of the teachers and professors of every Christian creed. But the last thing it expected was to find Irishmen borrowing a leaf from Soviet practice. Yet the proclamation posted on Catholic churches in south Leitrim, threatening expulsion or death to all doctors, priests, and ministers, might have been drafted at Moscow except for the fact that even Lenin and Trotsky would hesitate to show their hand so openly.[169]

Although the killing of Dr Paddy Muldoon in Mohill on 18 March 1923 had no direct political motive, an indirect political connection was suspected. Muldoon was shot dead at 11 p.m., having just parted company with Edward Geelan, clerk of the local district council. Geelan claimed that Muldoon was confronted by three men and was shot with a rifle from close range. Although Muldoon was identified as a SF supporter who had provided first aid classes to Cumann na mBan during the War of Independence, the *Roscommon Herald* claimed that 'since the split he took no sides in the Irish struggle, and an uncharitable word towards anybody was never heard from his mouth'.[170] Suspicion was immediately directed towards republican priest, Fr Edward Ryans from Aughavas, whom the authorities believed had Muldoon killed by a local IRA gang. Ryans, together with a local girl Mary Kate Gallogly, had appeared in court in Dublin in February 1923 on charges of attempted abandonment of a baby girl at a church in the city. At his trial, Ryans denied that he was in the process of abandoning the child and insisted that he was merely supporting the young unmarried mother who had worked as a housekeeper for him temporarily. While the state entered a *nolle prosequi* for Gallogly in May 1923, Ryans was remanded in custody.[171] The motive for the killing was linked to suspicions that Muldoon knew the priest was the father of Gallogly's child and that he would report this to his close friend, Canon Masterson.[172] While Ryans had an alibi on the night of the killing, reports indicated that he may have collected the gang following the shooting.[173] The Criminal Investigation Division report concluded that 'it appears to be very difficult to obtain any definite information locally regarding the affair'.[174] Although inconsistencies appear in statements made by witnesses for Ryans, nobody was ever charged with the killing of Muldoon and the case was closed. Following his subsequent release, Ryans was exiled to America by Bishop Hoare.[175]

By April 1923 the only reported activity by republicans in the north of the county was the derailing of a train at Glenfarne and the burning of Dromahair courthouse.[176] Fairs, church gatherings and any event that attracted large crowds also attracted interest from government forces. At Leitrim village on 1 April 1923 the local chapel was surrounded and all men in the congregation were searched.[177] In spite of the increased level of National army activity, isolated attacks against relatively easy targets characterized the closing weeks of the conflict. On 30 April an IRA gang shot 72-year-old farmer Michael Reynolds at Johnstonsbridge. Reynolds's son was a former member of the RIC who had resigned from the force. The *Roscommon Herald* reported that the home of another ex-RIC man nearby was also raided on the same night.[178] At Reynolds's inquest, the coroner Dr Arthur McGauran stated that 'as a Leitrim man born, bred and reared in the county, I regret exceedingly that such conduct can go on amongst the people'.[179]

A similar incident on 15 May 1923 at Cloone resulted in the wounding of Patrick and Philip McGuire. A group of men called at the McGuire home and requested Philip to accompany them outside. In an attempt to wrest a revolver from one of the gunmen, both McGuire brothers were injured before the gunmen made their escape. The *Freeman's Journal* reported that 'no reason is assigned for the attack, but it is generally assumed that it is attributable to the fact that one of the boys had been in the National army up to lately'.[180] On the night of 25 May 1923 former National army officer Patrick Keville was killed near his home. A group of men had earlier visited Keville's home, examined his army discharge papers and proceeded to a neighbour's house where Keville was visiting. The inquest jury found that Keville 'was foully murdered by a person or persons unknown'.[181] A subsequent pension application on behalf of Keville's family confirmed that he was gathering intelligence for government forces in the south Leitrim area at the time of his death.[182]

The killing of Liam Lynch in Tipperary on 10 April 1923 marked the beginning of the end of the Civil War. Six weeks later, on 24 May 1923, Lynch's successor Frank Aiken ordered republican forces nationwide to dump arms, heralding an end to nearly twelve months of bitter conflict.

Following the death of Collins, the Civil War entered a more protracted and vicious phase. Draconian legislation and increasing levels of state violence prompted similar levels of viciousness by republicans. In many instances, the nature of certain actions by the Arigna column blurred the thin lines distinguishing political agitation from ordinary crime.[183] While lawlessness prevailed in Leitrim following the cessation of hostilities, the surrender and capture of the main protagonists based at Arigna meant the end of anti-Treaty resistance in the county. Although political violence in the region resembled the national pattern, the activities of the Arigna republicans was unique, and very often resembled the actions of elements of the Crown forces during the War of Independence. Formal hostilities ended in May 1923 and republican arms were never surrendered. Yet, the conflict continued to leave an indelible mark on the Irish political landscape in the decades that followed.

10 Revolution?

Despite being one of the first regions where SF challenged the hegemony of John Redmond's IPP in the 1908 North Leitrim by-election, by 1912 any support accrued by SF had dissipated. The dominant political doctrine in the county was Redmondism and the IPP's widespread support base derived from an expectation of home rule and the continuing transfer of land from its hereditary owners to their tenants, which seemed assured. Ironically, the success of land reform had begun to erode political activisim by farmers that was previously mobilized through the United Irish League.[1] While minor acts of agrarianism took place, the absence of large grazier farms in the county ensured relative peace. Unionist opposition to home rule and the formation of the UVF consolidated the support of Leitrim's nationalists under the flag of the Irish Volunteers, but it is important to note that this only gathered significant momentum when the IPP moved to support the movement in the early summer of 1914. Although the intervention of the First World War in August 1914 may have averted a civil war in Ireland, it caused the division of the Irish Volunteer movement, with the vast majority of Leitrim's members firmly supporting Redmond.

The IPP's local support base was neither in a state of decay nor unrepresentative of local political opinion in 1914, but Redmond's support for the British war effort contributed to the ultimate decline of the IPP.[2] Whereas local UIL membership remained high, an absence of branch activity and no political opposition resulted in high levels of lethargy in party organization. Without doubt, the First World War helped to shape the Irish Revolution and over time the IPP's support for the war effort caused many nationalists to desert the party.[3] As recruiting and conscription became critical issues during a protracted war, the identification of the IPP with recruiting proved a crucial factor in its loss of support. What was distinctive about the IPP in Leitrim was the unwavering support of the county's two MPs in promoting recruitment. Unlike many of their parliamentary colleagues, both Leitrim MPs, as committed federal imperialists, firmly supported recruitment on platforms across the county, thus further weakening the cause of constitutional nationalism. Indeed, at the 1918 general election, SF specifically targeted Leitrim's MPs for their position on recruitment.[4]

The war in Europe and the 1916 Rising sealed the fate of John Redmond and the IPP. The effect of the Rising and the government's subsequent policy of executions, arrests and imprisonment changed the political landscape of the county and of the country in general during the months that followed. British government ineptitude in allowing the military to punish and pacify Ireland turned an indifferent population into a broadly hostile one. The *Sligo Nationalist* reported that 'the strong military measures taken to put down the "Rising" in Sligo and Leitrim are beginning to be regarded with amused contempt by the people of these counties'.[5] Such contempt manifested itself in changing public opinion, most notably among key influential figures.

While the time-honoured resolutions of support for Redmond were passed by the IPP-controlled organs of local government, the establishment of the Irish National Aid and Volunteer Dependants' Fund played an important role in channelling opposition to British policy towards a common cause. There is much evidence in post-Rising Leitrim to support Caoimhe Nic Dháibhéid's finding that the fund also provided a platform for many nationalists who were disillusioned with Redmond.[6] From the early summer of 1916 active and efficient republican groupings emerged throughout the county to create an alternative voice for Leitrim's nationalists.

Across Leitrim, the response to the war was one of enthusiasm and patriotic fervour among early enlistees and civic leaders, closely followed by a phase of indifference and opposition. A prolonged war and mounting casualties curbed much of the early enthusiasm and hindered recruitment, with the only beneficiaries being the county's farmers who profited from an increased demand for agricultural produce. Disproportionate numbers of recruits from the county's towns and lack of response from rural districts indicated that economic factors played a major part in the decision to enlist or remain at home.[7] Despite having one of the lowest levels of military recruitment, the county witnessed the mobilization of an active female non-combatant population in a range of charitable activity to assist the war effort. Like those promoting recruitment, these initiatives were organized and directed by members of the middle and upper classes. With the suspension of recruitment tours in the wake of the Rising, and negligible recruitment, the war became a peripheral event for most people in Leitrim. The passing of the Military Service Act in 1918, providing for conscription in Ireland, brought the war back to the centre stage of local politics. While a broad coalition including the Catholic Church, the IPP and SF campaigned successfully against conscription, the latter gained the most politically from the anti-conscription campaign with 43 branches totalling 3,466 members established in Leitrim by July 1918.[8]

In the post-Easter Rising environment, a series of by-elections in neighbouring North Roscommon and South Longford in 1917 demonstrated the attractiveness of republicanism and exposed the weakness of a declining IPP. The elections further politicized the people of Leitrim and contributed to the growth of SF within the county. Leitrim had one of the largest SF membership bases in Ireland. In many areas such as Cloone and Drumsna a relatively seamless transfer of political loyalty by supporters of constitutional nationalism to SF occurred.[9] Rather than witnessing a radical political transformation, the experience of Leitrim demonstrated that continuity rather than change marked the rise of SF. Although the latter represented a perceived new phenomenon, its members and supporters were broadly the same people who had supported and held membership of the IPP's local support organizations. The presence of such support meant that while SF embraced agrarianism when it suited its electoral needs, republicans would never disrupt the emerging economic and social status quo to the detriment of nationalist landholders.

Leitrim was not a major theatre of violent resistance. However, the establishment of a republican counter-state in the wake of the 1918 general election challenged the existing structures of state political power within the county.[10] Not only did this unprecedented and pioneering initiative defy the British goverment, it also provided a form of self-government before the formal establishment of the Irish Free State.[11] While Leitrim's republican administrators established efficient and alternative systems of local government and justice, they faced a number of difficulties from both the existing authorities and the local population. In addition to the financial challenges posed by the suspension of LGB funding, a protracted anti-rates campaign by Leitrim's farmers threatened the effective administration of local government. Nevertheless, this did not hinder the implementation of public policy decisions, many of which were, as in the past, influenced by local interests and political factions. A culture of cautious conservatism, and the upholding of the status quo, provides clear evidence that a pattern of continuity, rather than change, was emerging.

While Ireland witnessed unprecedented levels of conflict between 1919 and 1921, an over concentration on political violence ignores the less dramatic yet effective campaigns of boycott and intimidation, which were widespread in Leitrim.[12] The success of these methods provoked the ire of the state, and Leitrim suffered disproportionate levels of violence directed by the state against the local population. Such widespread levels of state violence in a region described as 'quiet' distorts somewhat the reality of the local environment, where non-violent resistance prevented the full and effective operation of civil society, and the state's forces responded with levels of violence that were intimidatory and destructive.

From the outset, given the high levels of emigration and relatively small population, the potential pool of 'revolutionaries' was limited. A number of factors, including the absence of an effective leadership and a lack of arms, hindered the development of a campaign in Leitrim. Arms raids, several attempted ambushes and barrack burnings marked the extent of direct military action against the state. Pressure from IRA GHQ, supplemented by outside leadership, led to a limited military campaign in south Leitrim in the early months of 1921. The topography of north Leitrim was as suited to guerrilla warfare as other parts of the county and perhaps even more so; yet the influence of SF's James Dolan, a noted pacifist, contributed to the lack of direct military engagement with Crown forces there. Nevertheless, boycott and intimidation were as widespread in the north of the county as in the south, which raises questions about the apparent 'quietude' of the region.

In a similar pattern to the War of Independence, political violence during the Civil War was confined to a small number of specific areas of the country.[13] Most of Leitrim did not witness widespread violence, but the conflict in the north-west traversed county boundaries with roving anti-Treaty IRA units battling against government forces across Leitrim, Roscommon and north Sligo. Despite the county sharing some of its border with the new northern state, little cross-border violence in the region occurred from the spring of 1922. The broad support of Leitrim's IRA units for the Treaty was influenced by the stance of General Seán Mac Eoin, whose North Longford Brigade had co-operated closely with their south Leitrim counterparts in the 1919–21 period. Following the capture of the region's main towns during the summer of 1922, the conflict developed into guerrilla warfare until the formal end of hostilities in May 1923.

A feature of the conflict was a series of extra-judicial killings and state violence. The activities of elements of republican groups contributed to increased levels of lawlessness and criminality against both the National army, the Civic Guard, and the local population. Although the Civil War in the north-west broadly followed national patterns, the republican unit based at Arigna was involved in a widespread campaign of terror against both government forces and the civilian population. The group's involvement in the killing of innocent civilians at Drumkeeran and Ballyconnell demonstrated that in certain instances, criminality and brutality were interspersed in the broader political conflict.[14] Such an environment provided the context for the eighteen criminal, agrarian and political killings in the region.

Although four Protestants were killed during the 1921–2 period, two as alleged informers and two in the course a robbery, there is no evidence of widespread sectarianism in the county. Agrarian violence was directed against Protestant landholders and Protestant businesses were intimidated during the Belfast boycott. While there is no evidence that a co-ordinated campaign against Protestants was carried out in Leitrim, with Catholic businesses also being targeted as part of the boycott campaign, nevertheless, high levels of migration of Protestants to nearby Fermanagh indicate that few Protestants remained unaffected by the pervasive sectarian atmosphere in some districts.[15] In Leitrim Protestants were assumed to be loyalists and therefore potential enemies of the emerging state. This could, and did, increase the vulnerability of individual Protestants in the aftermath of events such as those at Selton Hill. At the same time, the interdependence and mutual amity in a small rural environment where opinions were formed not by ideologues or a distant city-based revolutionary class explains the absence of sectarian and ethnic violence that was prevalent in the urban and industrialized north-east.

If the definition of revolution is significant and fundamental political change achieved through violence, then one can argue that in the case of Leitrim, the 1912–23 period was indeed revolutionary. However, a more detailed analysis reveals that little alteration in the structure of society took place in both Ireland as a whole and Leitrim during the period. Politics and society in the county of Leitrim did not witness any mass transformation due to the challenge to law and order by republicans from 1916 to 1923. A mostly satisfied small farmer class had already benefitted from the fruits of land reform, ensuring the presence of a conservative peasant culture across the county. While a combination of government ineptitude and underlying anglophobia saw the IPP replaced with SF, no radical transformation occurred in the political culture of Leitrim. The evidence of the Irish Revolution in the county shows that no gulf existed between constitutional and advanced nationalism. A larger, more efficient and determined organization emerged in the wake of the 1916 Rising, when 'the political culture of nationalist Ireland re-emerged, draped in a tricolour that barely obscured the outline of a golden harp'.[16] The common denominator for both advanced and constitutional nationalism was independence, with neither doctrine having a coherent or radical social and economic vision for an independent Ireland. Throughout the period, the public were willing to defy both Crown and republican administrations in a manner that was not based on politics, loyalty, or allegiance but rather self-interest. In so doing, the revolution in the county did not evolve in isolation from the forces of rural conservatism; it merely accommodated the many different strands of nationalism that were already present in Leitrim society. A continuation of parliamentary institutions, local government, common law and judicial structures leads to the conclusion that evolution, rather than revolution, took place across Leitrim and Ireland between 1912 and 1923.

While the Irish Revolution in this poor, thinly populated, rural county in north-west Ireland possessed some distinctive characteristics, events also demonstrated broad similarities with many of her near neighbours. Certainly land reform and the democratization of local and national government heralded a new era; yet the new state replaced many of the old patriarchal and deferential structures with alternative forms of authority. Thus the term 'revolution' has only limited application in Leitrim during this period. Because the goals of Irish nationalism were very narrowly focused under the IPP, its overthrow by SF did little to broaden that focus; in fact, it narrowed it even further.

Notes

CHAPTER ONE *Leitrim in 1912*

1 Margaret Dixon McDougall, *The letters of Norah on her tour through Ireland* (Montreal, 1882), p. 147.
2 David Fitzpatrick, 'The geography of Irish nationalism, 1910–1921', *Past & Present*, 78 (1987), 113–44.
3 CI Leitrim, Dec. 1920 (TNA, CO 904/113).
4 Census of Ireland 1911, *Area, Houses and Population*; HC 1912–13; also the *Ages, Civil or Conjugal Condition, Occupations, Birthplaces, Religion and Education of the People, Province of Connaught, County of Leitrim*.
5 Terence Dooley, *'The land for the people': the land question in independent Ireland* (Dublin, 2004), p. 235.
6 Fitzpatrick, 'Geography of Irish nationalism', 138–9.
7 David Seth Jones, *Graziers, land reform and political conflict in Ireland* (Washington, 1995), p. 221.
8 Fitzpatrick, 'Geography of Irish nationalism', 138–9.
9 Philip Bull, 'Land and politics, 1879–1903' in D.G. Boyce (ed.), *The revolution in Ireland, 1879–1923* (Dublin, 1998), p. 45.
10 UIL Quarterly Returns, RIC Annual County Inspectorate reports, 'Secret Societies and Nationalist Associations', Dec. 1900 (TNA, CO 904/20).
11 Jones, *Graziers*, p. 221.
12 Michael Wheatley, *Nationalism and the Irish Party: provincial Ireland, 1910–1916* (Oxford, 2005), p. 42.
13 CI Leitrim, Jan. 1910 (TNA, CO 904/80).
14 Inspector General's report, Crime Special Branch (hereafter CSB/IGCI report), May 1907 (NAI, 1552/SN).
15 CI Leitrim, May 1911 (TNA, CO 904/84).
16 Donal J. O'Sullivan, *The Irish constabularies, 1822–1922: a century of policing in Ireland* (Dingle, 1999), p. 185; Jim Herlihy, *Royal Irish Constabularly officers: a biographical dictionary and genealogical guide, 1816–1922* (Dublin, 2005), p. 262.
17 Wheatley, *Nationalism*, p. 50.
18 RIC Annual County Inspectorate report, 'Secret Societies: Register of Home Associations', 1890–93 (TNA, CO 904/16).
19 Inspector General's report, May 1908 (NAI, CSB/IGCI, 2055/s).
20 Ibid., Sept. 1908 (NAI, CSB/IGCI, 2172/s).
21 CI Leitrim, May 1910 (TNA, CO 904/81).
22 Mel Cousins, 'The creation of association: the National Insurance Act, 1911 and approved societies in Ireland' in Jennifer Kelly and R.V. Comerford (eds), *Associational culture in Ireland and abroad* (Dublin, 2010), p. 161.
23 CI Leitrim, Dec. 1916 (TNA, CO 904/101).
24 CI Leitrim, CI Longford, CI Roscommon, CI Sligo, Dec. 1916 (TNA, CO 904/101).
25 Patrick Maume, *The long gestation: Irish nationalist life, 1891–1918* (Dublin, 1999), p. 125.
26 *Leitrim Observer* (hereafter *LO*), 13 Apr. 1912.
27 Ibid., 23 Sept. 1916.
28 CI Leitrim, CI Longford, Dec. 1916 (TNA, CO 904/101).
29 *LO*, 22 Apr. 1916.

30 Conor McNamara, 'A Tenants' League or a Shopkeepers' League?: urban protest and the Town Tenants' Association in the west of Ireland, 1909–1918', *Studia Hibernica*, 36 (2009–10), 135–60.
31 RIC Annual County Inspectorate report, 'Secret Societies and Nationalist Associations', Dec. 1900 (NAI, CSS/26, 268 51891).
32 William Murphy, 'The GAA during the Irish Revolution' in Mike Cronin, William Murphy and Paul Rouse (eds), *The Gaelic Athletic Association, 1884–2009* (Dublin, 2009), pp 61–76; Seán Ó Súilleabháin (ed.), *Scéal Liatrioma: Leitrim GAA story, 1886–1984* (Carrick-on-Shannon, 1984), pp 11–12.
33 CI Leitrim, May 1911 (TNA, CO 904/84).
34 Wheatley, *Nationalism*, p. 63.
35 Pádraig Ó Fearaíl, *The story of Conradh na Gaelige* (Dublin, 1975), p. 17.
36 CI Leitrim, May 1911 (TNA, CO 904/84); CI Leitrim, Nov. 1912 (TNA, CO 904/88).
37 Timothy G. McMahon, *Grand opportunity: the Gaelic Revival and Irish society, 1893–1910* (Syracuse, 2008), p. 88.
38 *Leitrim Advertiser* (hereafter *LA*), 29 Jan. 1891.
39 *Sligo Champion* (hereafter *SC*), 13 June 1891.
40 Daniel Gallogly, *The diocese of Kilmore, 1800–1950* (Cavan, 1999), pp 224–6.
41 David W. Miller, *Church, state and nation in Ireland, 1898–1921* (Dublin, 1973), p. 211.
42 Jennifer Kelly, 'Popular attitudes to formal medical care in early-nineteenth-century County Leitrim', *Breifne*, 10:44 (2008), 573–86.
43 Inspector General's report, May 1907 (NAI, CSB/IGCI, 1552/SN).
44 Ciaran Ó Duibhir, *Sinn Féin: the first election 1908* (Manorhamilton, 1993), p. 40.
45 Ibid., p. 54.
46 Inspector General's report, May 1907 (NAI, CSB/IGCI, 1552/SN).
47 Marnie Hay, *Bulmer Hobson and the nationalist movement in twentieth-century Ireland* (Manchester, 2009), p. 73.
48 Ó Duibhir, *First election*, pp 73–4.
49 Michael Laffan, *The resurrection of Ireland: the Sinn Féin party, 1916–1923* (Cambridge, 1999), pp 29–30.
50 Gallogly, *Kilmore*, p. 235.   51 Laffan, *Resurrection*, pp 29–30.
52 *SC*, 6 June 1908.
53 Michael Farry, *Sligo: the Irish Revolution, 1912–23* (Dublin, 2012), p. 6.
54 Wheatley, *Nationalism*, p. 43.   55 CI Leitrim, Jan. 1910 (TNA, CO 904/80).
56 Ó Duibhir, *First election*, p. 86.
57 A.C. Hepburn, *A past apart: studies in the history of Catholic Belfast, 1850–1950* (Belfast, 1996), p. 161.
58 Wheatley, *Nationalism*, p. 252.   59 *SC*, 6 June 1908.
60 *LO*, 13 May 1911.   61 Ibid., 17 June 1911.

CHAPTER TWO 'We stand solidly and united behind John Redmond': Leitrim and home rule, 1912–14

1 *LO*, 13 Jan. 1912.
2 Paul Bew, *Ideology and the Irish question: Ulster unionism and Irish nationalism, 1912–1916* (Oxford, 1994), p. 71.
3 F.S.L. Lyons, 'The two faces of home rule' in Kevin B. Nowlan (ed.), *The making of 1916* (Dublin, 1969), p. 120.
4 James McConnel, *The Irish Parliamentary Party and the third home rule crisis* (Dublin, 2013), p. 223.
5 Bew, *Ideology*, p. 80.

6 CI Leitrim, Dec. 1912 (TNA, CO 904/88).
7 Canon Patrick Sheehan, 'The blindness of Dr Gray', quoted in Wheatley, *Nationalism*, p. 42.
8 *Anglo-Celt* (hereafter *AC*), 14 Sept. 1912.   9 *LO*, 13 Feb. 1915.
10 Ibid., 17 Feb. 1916.   11 McNamara, 'Tenants' League', 158.
12 *LO*, 20 Dec. 1913.   13 McNamara, 'Tenants' League', 159.
14 *LO*, 13 Dec. 1913.   15 CI Leitrim, Dec. 1913 (TNA, CO 904/91).
16 McConnel, *Irish Parliamentary Party*, pp 218–19.   17 *LO*, 17 Jan. 1912.
18 Ibid., 28 Sept. 1912.   19 Ibid., 16 Nov. 1912.
20 Ibid., 20 June 1913.   21 Ibid., 10 Jan. 1914.   22 Ibid.
23 Quincey Dougan, *Leitrim: a county at war* (Carrick-on-Shannon, 2015), pp 11–12.
24 Matthew Kelly, *The Fenian ideal and Irish nationalism, 1882–1916* (Woodbridge, 2006), p. 225.
25 *LO*, 27 June 1914.
26 CI Leitrim, June 1914 (TNA, CO 904/93); Farry, *Sligo*, p. 19.
27 CI Leitrim, July 1914 (TNA, CO 904/94).   28 *LO*, 29 June 1912.
29 Cormac Ó Súilleabháin, *Leitrim's republican story, 1900–2000* (Ballinamore, 2014), p. 33; Dougan, *Leitrim*, pp 6–8.
30 *Sligo Independent*, 16 June 1912.
31 Miriam Moffitt, 'The Protestant experience of revolution in County Leitrim, 1911–1928', *Breifne*, 12:46 (2011), 307.
32 Dougan, *Leitrim*, pp 11–12.   33 *LO*, 26 Sept. 1914.   34 *LO*, 14 Mar. 1914.
35 Ronan Fanning, *Fatal path: British government and Irish Revolution, 1910–1922* (London, 2013), p. 130.

CHAPTER THREE *'People of the county unanimously in favour of the British': Leitrim and the First World War, 1914–16*

1 *LA*, 6 Aug. 1914.
2 Philip Orr, '200,000 Volunteer soldiers' in John Horne (ed.), *Our war: Ireland and the Great War* (Dublin, 2008), p. 65.
3 *LA*, 6 Aug. 1914.   4 *AC*, 22 Aug. 1914.
5 *Roscommon Herald* (hereafter *RH*), 8 Aug. 1914.   6 *LO*, 15 Aug. 1914.
7 Catriona Pennell, *A kingdom united: popular responses to the outbreak of the First World War in Ireland and Britain* (Oxford, 2012), p. 51.
8 *LA*, 13 Aug. 1914.   9 CI Leitrim, Aug. 1914 (TNA, CO 904/94).
10 *LA*, 6 Aug. 1914.
11 Redmond note, n.d. [1914] (National Library of Ireland (NLI), John Redmond papers, MS 15,258/9/93).
12 *AC*, 22 Aug. 1914.   13 *LO*, 26 Sept. 1914.
14 *Fermanagh Herald* (hereafter *FH*), 26 Sept. 1914.   15 *LO*, 19 Sept. 1914.
16 James McConnel, '"Après la guerre": John Redmond, the Irish Volunteers and armed constitutionalism, 1913–1915', *English Historical Review*, 131:553 (2016), 1445–70.
17 *LO*, 3 Oct. 1914.   18 Ibid., 31 Oct. 1914.   19 Ibid., 7 Nov. 1914.
20 Ibid., 10 Oct. 1914.   21 Kelly, *Fenian ideal*, p. 233.
22 *RH*, 24 Oct. 1914.   23 *Longford Leader*, 24 Oct. 1914.
24 *LA*, 22 Oct. 1914.   25 *LO*, 24 Oct. 1914.   26 Ibid., 19 Sept. 1914.
27 Ibid., 10 Oct. 1914.   28 Ibid., 12 Sept. 1914.   29 *LA*, 8 Oct. 1914.
30 Ibid., 12 Nov. 1914.   31 CI Leitrim, Aug. 1914 (TNA, CO 904/94).
32 *LA*, 26 Sept. 1914.

33 D.G. Boyce, '"That party politics should divide our tents": nationalism, unionism and the First World War' in Adrian Gregory and Senia Pašeta (eds), *Ireland and the Great War: 'A war to unite us all?'* (Manchester, 2002), p. 193.
34 Patrick Callan, 'Recruiting for the British army in Ireland during the First World War', *Irish Sword*, 17:66 (1987), 42–56; David Fitzpatrick, 'The logic of collective sacrifice: Ireland and the British army, 1914–1918', *Historical Journal*, 38:49 (1995), 1017–30.
35 *LA*, 22 Oct. 1914.   36 Ibid., 31 Dec. 1914.
37 Memorial records (Leitrim County Library).
38 Brendan Mac Giolla Choille (ed.), *Intelligence notes, 1913–1916* (Dublin, 1966), pp 181–2.
39 *LO*, 31 Oct. 1914.   40 Ibid., 7 Nov. 1914.   41 Ibid.
42 CI Leitrim, Dec. 1915 (TNA, CO 904/98).   43 *LO*, 16 Jan. 1915.
44 Ibid., Nov. 1914–Jan. 1915 (TNA, CO 904/95–6).
45 CI Leitrim, Mar. 1915 (TNA, CO 904/96).
46 James McConnel, 'Recruiting sergeants for John Bull?: Irish Nationalist MPs and enlistment during the early months of the Great War', *War in History*, 14:4 (2007), 424.
47 Colin Reid, 'The Irish Party and the Volunteers: politics and home rule army, 1913–1916' in Caoimhe Nic Dháibhéid and Colin Reid (eds), *From Parnell to Paisley: constitutional and revolutionary politics in modern Ireland* (Dublin, 2010), p. 47.
48 *LO*, 19 Sept. 1914.   49 *LA*, 27 Aug. 1914.   50 *LO*, 5 Dec. 1914.
51 *LA*, 10 Dec. 1914.   52 *LO*, 23 Jan. 1915.   53 Ibid., 21 Aug. 1915.
54 Miller, *Church*, p. 311; RIC Inspector General's report, Oct. 1914 (TNA, CO 904/96).
55 *LA*, 11 Mar. 1915.   56 *LO*, 18 Mar. 1916.
57 Mac Giolla Choille, *Intelligence notes*, p. 171.
58 John M. Osbourne, *The voluntary recruiting movement in Britain, 1914–1918* (London, 1982), p. 13.
59 *LO*, 23 Jan. 1915; *AC*, 10 Apr. 1915; *FH*, 28 Aug. 1915.
60 *AC*, 10 Apr. 1915.   61 Ibid.   62 *RH*, 10 Apr. 1915.
63 *AC*, 10 Apr. 1915.   64 *LO*, 24 Apr. 1915.   65 Ibid.
66 Ibid., 15 May 1915.   67 *LO*, 13 Apr. 1915.
68 CI Cavan, Sept. 1915 (TNA, CO 904/98).
69 *Weekly Freeman's Journal*, 23 Jan. 1915.   70 *LO*, 19 June 1915.
71 Ibid., 27 Feb. 1915.   72 Ibid., 8 Apr. 1916.   73 *AC*, 23 Oct. 1915.
74 *LO*, 23 Oct. 1915.   75 Ibid., 22 Apr. 1916.   76 Ibid., 20 Sept. 1915.
77 Ibid., 9 Oct. 1915.   78 Ibid., 19 June 1915.
79 Ben Novick, *Conceiving revolution: Irish nationalist propaganda during the First World War* (Dublin, 2001), p. 21.
80 Osbourne, *Voluntary recruiting*, p. 132.
81 CI Leitrim, Oct. 1915 (TNA, CO 904/98).   82 *RH*, 20 Nov. 1915.
83 *LO*, 27 Nov. 1915.   84 *LA*, 25 Nov. 1915.   85 *SC*, 27 Nov. 1915.
86 Pennell, *A kingdom united*, p. 39.
87 CI Leitrim, Nov. 1915 (TNA, CO 904/98).   88 *FH*, 1 Jan. 1916.
89 *RH*, 1 Jan. 1916.   90 Ibid., 20 Nov. 1915.
91 Mac Giolla Choille, *Intelligence notes*, p. 181.   92 *LO*, 23 Oct. 1915.
93 Ibid.
94 William Doris to John Redmond, 8 Mar. 1916 (NLI, Redmond papers, MS 15262/3).
95 McConnel, 'Recruiting sergeants', 424.   96 *LO*, 11 Mar. 1916.
97 *LA*, 4 Feb. 1915.   98 *LO*, 14 Oct. 1914.
99 P.J. Casey, K.T. Cullen and J.P. Duignan, *Irish doctors in the First World War* (Sallins, 2015), p. 1.
100 *LA*, 9 Dec. 1915.   101 *FH*, 2 Oct. 1915.

102 E.A. Aston to Maurice Moore, 11 Aug. 1915 (NLI, Maurice Moore papers, MS 10561/1).
103 Dominic Rooney, 'Manorhamilton's Irish Volunteers 1914', *Leitrim Guardian* (2001), p. 47.
104 *SC*, 3 Apr. 1915.
105 Pauline Codd, 'Recruiting and responses to the war in Wexford' in David Fitzpatrick (ed.), *Ireland and the First World War* (Dublin, 1986), p. 26.
106 This list was published by the county registrar indicating eligible voters for the forthcoming 1918 General Election who were absent from their homes and serving abroad in the armed forces.
107 Absent voters' register, Oct. 1918 (Leitrim County Library). 108 *LA*, 10 Aug. 1914.
109 Ibid., 20 Aug. 1914. 110 Ibid., 17 Dec. 1914.
111 Peter Whearity, '"Come and find sanctuary in Éire": the experiences of Ireland's Belgian refugees during the First World War', *Historical Studies in Ethnicity, Migration and Diaspora*, 34:2 (2016), 192–209.
112 *LO*, 27 Mar. 1915. 113 *AC*, 3 Oct. 1914. 114 *LO*, 27 Feb. 1915.
115 Ibid., 15 May 1915. 116 Ibid., 19 Sept. 1914. 117 Ibid., 26 Dec. 1914.
118 Ibid., 4 Dec. 1915. 119 Ibid., 29 Jan. 1916.
120 Margaret Downes, 'The civilian voluntary aid effort' in David Fitzpatrick (ed.), *Ireland and the First World War* (Dublin, 1996), p. 32.
121 *War record of the St John's Ambulance Brigade and the British Red Cross Society in Leinster, Munster and Connaught, 1914–1918* (Dublin, 1919).
122 Catriona Clear, 'Fewer ladies, more women' in Horne (ed.), *Our war*, p. 165.
123 *LO*, 13 Mar. 1915. 124 Ibid., 21 Aug. 1915. 125 *LA*, 25 Nov. 1915.
126 Fionnuala Walsh, 'The impact of the Great War on women in Ireland' (PhD, TCD, 2015), p. 90.
127 *LO*, 26 June 1915. 128 *LA*, 24 Nov. 1915. 129 *LO*, 28 Oct. 1915.
130 *AC*, 13 May 1916.
131 Clare O'Neill, 'The Irish home front, 1914–1918, with particular reference to the treatment of Belgian refugees, prisoners-of-war, enemy aliens and war casualties' (PhD, NUI Maynooth, 2006), pp 88–9.
132 *LO*, 29 Aug. 1914. 133 *LA*, 5 Nov. 1914. 134 *LO*, 31 Oct. 1914.
135 *RH*, 24 Oct. 1914. 136 *LO*, 13 Mar. 1915. 137 *LA*, 1 Apr. 1915.
138 O'Neill, 'Home front', p. 17. 139 *LO*, 23 Oct. 1915.
140 Ibid., 22 Dec. 1916 141 *LA*, 28 Dec. 1916.
142 Ian Miller, *Reforming food in post-Famine Ireland: medicine, science and improvement, 1845–1922* (Manchester, 2014), p. 175.
143 *FH*, 28 Nov. 1914. 144 CI Leitrim, Apr. 1918 (TNA, CO 904/105).
145 *LO*, 30 Jan. 1915. 146 Ibid., 27 Feb. 1915. 147 *AC*, 21 Aug. 1915.
148 Press Censor's Office to editor of *Leitrim Observer*, 30 Dec. 1916 (NAI, 3/722/15).
149 Letter from HQ Irish Command to undersecretary Dublin Castle, 25 Jan. 1915 (TNA, CO 904/164).
150 Ross O'Carroll, 'The GAA and the First World War, 1914–18' in Gearóid Ó Tuathaigh (ed.), *The GAA and revolution in Ireland* (Cork, 2015), p. 87.
151 Ó Súilleabháin, *Leitrim GAA*, p. 21.
152 Dan Gallogly, *Ballinamore Seán O'Heslins', 1889–1984* (Cavan, 1984), p. 32; *Sunday Independent*, 25 Oct. 2015; *LO*, 4 Nov. 2015.
153 Ronan McGreevey, *Wherever the firing line extends: Ireland and the Western Front* (Dublin, 2016), p. 237.
154 *AC*, 28 Aug. 1915. 155 *LO*, 21 Aug. 1915. 156 Ibid., 1 July 1916.
157 Ibid. 158 Ibid., 10 July 1915. 159 Ibid., 30 Jan. 1915.
160 Ibid., 28 Oct. 1916. 161 Ibid., 18 Mar. 1916.

CHAPTER FOUR *'The people say they are tired of politics': the 1916 Rising and its aftermath*

1 *LO*, 20 Nov. 1915.   2 *LA*, 27 Apr. 1916.   3 Ibid., 4 May 1916.
4 *LO*, 13 May 1916.   5 Ibid., 20 May 1916.
6 CI Leitrim, Apr. 1916 (TNA, CO 904/99).   7 *LO*, 13 May 1916.
8 Ibid., 20 May 1916.   9 Ibid.   10 Ibid.
11 *LA*, 4 May 1916.
12 Colm O'Reilly, 'Bishop Joseph Hoare: a conflicted prelate and patriot', *Teathbha*, 4:4 (2017), 355–7.
13 *RH*, 29 Apr. 1916.   14 *LO*, 11 May 1916.
15 CI Leitrim, June 1916 (TNA, CO 904/100).   16 *LO*, 17 May 1916.
17 Charles Townshend, *Easter 1916: the Irish rebellion* (London, 2005), p. 308.
18 Alvin Jackson, *Home rule: an Irish history, 1800–2000* (Oxford, 2003), p. 174.
19 *LO*, 17 June 1916.   20 Ibid., 10 June 1916.   21 Ibid., 8 July 1916.
22 Ibid., 29 July 1916.   23 Ibid.   24 Ibid.
25 *RH*, 16 Sept. 1916.   26 UIL National Directory minute book (NLI, MS 708).
27 *LO*, 15 July 1916.   28 CI Leitrim, July 1916 (TNA, CO 904/100).
29 Jackson, *Home rule*, p. 172.   30 *LO*, 15 July 1916.
31 CI Leitrim, Aug. 1916 (TNA, CO 904/100).   32 *LO*, 16 Sept. 1916.
33 Ibid.   34 CI Leitrim, Dec. 1916 (TNA, CO 904/101).
35 Caoimhe Nic Dháibhéid, 'The Irish National Aid Association and the radicalization of public opinion in Ireland', *Historical Journal*, 55:3 (Sept. 2012), 705–29.
36 Ibid., 707.   37 *LO*, 29 May 1916.
38 CI Leitrim, July 1916 (TNA, CO 904/100).   39 *LO*, 22 July 1916.
40 Ibid.   41 Nic Dháibhéid, 'Irish National Aid', 709.
42 *LO*, 5 Aug. 1916.   43 *SC*, 9 Dec. 1916.   44 *LO*, 28 Oct. 1916.
45 CI Leitrim, Nov. 1916 (TNA, CO 904/101).
46 Redmond to Asquith, 30 Nov. 1916 (NLI, Redmond papers, MS 15,262/9).
47 *LO*, 30 Dec. 1916.   48 Ibid.

CHAPTER FIVE *'Thoroughly sound for the principle of self-determination': the triumph of Sinn Féin, 1917–18*

1 F.S.L. Lyons, *Culture and anarchy in Ireland, 1890–1939* (Oxford, 1982), p. 100.
2 *LO*, 13 Jan. 1917.   3 Ibid., 6 Jan. 1917.   4 Ibid., 10 Feb. 1917.
5 Ibid.   6 Ibid.
7 Inspector-General's report, Mar. 1917 (TNA, CO 904/102).
8 CI Leitrim, Feb. 1917 (TNA, CO 904/102).
9 CI Leitrim, Apr. 1917 (ibid.).
10 *SC*, 14 Apr. 1917.   11 Ibid., 21 Apr. 1917.
12 CI Leitrim, Apr. 1917 (TNA, CO 904/102).   13 *RH*, 26 May 1917.
14 *SC*, 14 July 1917.   15 CI Leitrim, July 1917 (TNA, CO 904/103).
16 *RH*, 21 July 1917.   17 *LO*, 8 Sept. 1917.   18 *RH*, 25 Aug. 1917.
19 *LO*, 8 Sept. 1917.   20 Ibid.
21 CI Leitrim, Sept. 1917 (TNA, CO 904/104).
22 Hugh Brady (BMH WS 1266, pp 1–2).
23 Patrick J. Hargaden (BMH WS 1268, p. 1).
24 CI Leitrim, Nov. 1917 (TNA, CO 904/104).
25 Charles Townshend, *The Republic: the fight for Irish independence* (London, 2013), p. 51.
26 Margaret Brady (BMH WS 1267, p. 2).
27 Bernard Sweeney (BMH WS 1194, pp 1–2).

28 Marie Coleman, *Longford and the Irish Revolution* (Dublin, 2002), p. 160.
29 Hugh Brady (BMH WS 1266, p. 1).
30 Interview by John Doyle with Lily Moffitt (Freyne) in *Iris*, Nov. 1982.
31 *RH*, 13 Oct. 1917.   32 *LO*, 20 Oct. 1917.   33 *SC*, 10 Nov. 1917.
34 *LO*, 10 Nov. 1917.   35 Coleman, *Longford*, p. 71.
36 *LO*, 24 Nov. 1917.   37 Ibid.   38 Ibid.
39 Ibid., 8 Dec. 1917.
40 Moore to John Dillon, 4 Mar. 1917 (NLI, Moore papers, MS 10,561/9).
41 *RH*, 24 Mar. 1917.   42 *LO*, 9 June 1917.   43 *RH*, 16 June 1917.
44 David Fitzpatrick, *Politics and Irish life, 1913–1921: provincial experiences of war and revolution* (Cork, 1977), p. 107.
45 *RH*, 9 June 1917.   46 *LO*, 29 Sept. 1917.   47 Ibid., 10 Nov. 1917.
48 Ibid., 17 Nov. 1917.   49 Ibid., 13 Oct. 1917.   50 Jackson, *Home rule*, p. 208.
51 *RH*, 21 July 1917.   52 *SC*, 17 Mar. 1917.   53 Ibid., 30 June 1917.
54 Ibid.   55 *RH*, 5 Jan. 1918.   56 *LO*, 13 Apr. 1918.
57 Paul Bew, 'Sinn Féin, agrarian radicalism and the War of Independence, 1919–1921' in D.G. Boyce (ed.), *The revolution in Ireland, 1879–1923* (Dublin, 1988), p. 225.
58 Fergus Campbell, *Land and revolution: nationalist politics in the west of Ireland, 1891–1921* (Oxford, 2005), p. 242.
59 E. Rumpf and A.C. Hepburn, *Nationalism and socialism in twentieth-century Ireland* (New York, 1977), p. 21.
60 Terence Dooley, *The decline of the big house in Ireland: a study of Irish landed families* (Dublin, 2001), p. 128.
61 *Nationality*, 8 Sept. 1917.   62 *SC*, 2 Mar. 1918.   63 *RH*, 23 Feb. 1918.
64 *LO*, 2 Mar. 1918.   65 Ibid.   66 Ibid.
67 CI Leitrim, Feb. 1918 (TNA, CO 904/105).   68 *LO*, 9 Mar. 1918.
69 Ibid., 23 Mar. 1918.   70 *SC*, 13 Oct. 1917.   71 *LO*, 21 Sept. 1918.
72 Ibid., 9 Nov. 1918.   73 CI Leitrim, Mar. 1919 (TNA, CO 904/108).
74 John Horne, *State, society and mobilisation in Europe during the First World War* (Cambridge, 1997), p. 14.
75 CI Leitrim, Jan.–Dec. 1917 (TNA, CO 904/102–105).
76 Ibid. No Leitrim police reports are available for the May–September 1918 period.
77 *SC*, 16 Feb. 1918.   78 *LO*, 9 Feb. 1918.   79 *SC*, 16 Mar. 1918.
80 *LO*, 9 Mar. 1918.   81 *SC*, 9 Mar. 1918; *RH*, 9 Mar. 1918.
82 *SC*, 16 Mar. 1918.   83 *RH*, 30 Mar. 1918.   84 *LO*, 30 Mar. 1918.
85 *SC*, 23 Mar. 1918.   86 Ibid.   87 Ibid.
88 CI Leitrim, Mar. 1918 (TNA, CO 904/105).   89 *LO*, 23 Mar. 1918.
90 Ibid., 4 May 1918.   91 Ibid., 27 Apr. 1918.
92 Eugene Kilkenny (BMH WS 1146, p. 2).   93 *LO*, 13 Apr. 1918.
94 Ibid., 20 Apr. 1918.   95 *RH*, 20 Apr. 1918.   96 Ibid., 4 May 1918.
97 *LO*, 20 Apr. 1918.   98 *RH*, 4 May 1918.   99 Ibid.
100 *SC*, 27 Apr. 1918.   101 Ibid.   102 *SC*, 11 May 1918.
103 Ibid.   104 CI Leitrim, Apr. 1918 (TNA, CO 904/105).
105 Ibid., Jan. 1918 (TNA, CO 904/104); ibid., May 1918 (TNA, CO 904/105).
106 Hugh Brady (BMH WS 1266, p. 2).   107 Ibid.
108 John Borgonovo, *The dynamics of war and revolution: Cork city, 1916–1918* (Cork, 2013), p. 186.
109 CI Leitrim, May 1918 (TNA, CO 904/105).   110 Ibid., June 1918 (ibid.).
111 *SC*, 15 June 1918.   112 *LO*, 15 June 1918.   113 Ibid., 22 June 1918.
114 *SC*, 15 June 1918.   115 *LO*, 6 July 1918.   116 *SC*, 22 June 1918.

117 Ibid., 10 July 1918. 118 *LO*, 17 Aug. 1918. 119 Ibid.
120 Ibid., 27 July 1918. 121 *RH*, 10 Aug. 1918. 122 *LO*, 24 Aug. 1918.
123 Ibid. 124 CI Leitrim, Aug. 1918 (TNA, CO 904/106).
125 Patrick Callan, 'Voluntary recruiting for the British army in Ireland during the First World War' (PhD, UCD, 1984).
126 *LO*, 5 Oct. 1918. 127 Ibid. 128 *RH*, 19 Oct. 1918.
129 CI Leitrim, Jan.–Apr. 1918, Oct. 1918 (TNA, CO 904/105; CO 904/107).
130 *LO*, 16 Nov. 1918. 131 *SC*, 16 Nov. 1918. 132 *Nationality*, 25 Aug. 1918.
133 Inspector-General's report, Jan. 1918 (TNA, CO 904/105).
134 *LO*, 9 Feb. 1918. 135 Ibid., 23 Feb. 1918. 136 Ibid., 4 May 1918.
137 Ibid., 21 Sept. 1918.
138 B.M. Walker (ed.), *Parliamentary election results in Ireland, 1801–1922* (Dublin, 1978), pp 359, 392.
139 *LO*, 24 Nov. 1918. 140 Ibid., 12 Oct. 1918. 141 Ibid.
142 Ibid., 16 Nov. 1918. 143 Ibid., 30 Nov. 1918.
144 *Irish Independent*, 2 Dec. 1918.
145 CI Leitrim, Nov. 1918 (TNA, CO 904/107).
146 *LA*, 5 Dec. 1918. 147 *LO*, 23 Nov. 1918. 148 Ibid., 30 Nov. 1918.
149 Ibid., 7 Dec. 1918. 150 *SC*, 7 Dec. 1918. 151 *LO*, 14 Dec. 1918.
152 *RH*, 14 Dec. 1918. 153 Borgonovo, *Dynamics of war*, p. 225.
154 Bridget Doherty (BMH WS 1193, pp 1–2); Margaret Brady (BMH WS 1267, p. 2).
155 *RH*, 7 Dec. 1918. 156 *LO*, 14 Dec. 1918. 157 Ibid., 21 Dec. 1918.
158 Ibid. 159 Patrick J. Hargaden (BMH WS 1268, p. 3).
160 Margaret Brady (BMH WS 1267, p. 2). 161 *LO*, 4 Jan. 1919.
162 Ibid.
163 Tom Garvin, *The evolution of Irish nationalist politics* (Dublin, 1981), p. 214; James McConnel, 'The franchise factor in the defeat of the Irish Parliamentary Party, 1885–1918', *Historical Journal*, 47:2 (2004), 355–77.

CHAPTER SIX *'On the last lap of the race for Liberty's goal': the Dáil counter-state, 1919–21*

1 *SC*, 25 Jan. 1919. 2 Ibid., 15 Feb. 1919. 3 *LO*, 15 Mar. 1919.
4 Ibid., 5 Apr. 1919. 5 Ibid., 8 Mar. 1919. 6 *RH*, 22 Mar. 1919.
7 *LO*, 15 Mar. 1919. 8 Ibid., 3 May 1919. 9 Ibid., 26 July 1919.
10 Ibid., 31 May 1919. 11 Ibid., 24 May 1919. 12 Ibid., 26 July 1919.
13 Ibid. 14 Ibid., 16 Aug. 1919. 15 Ibid., 6 Sept. 1919.
16 Hugh Brady (BMH WS 1266, p. 4); Arthur Mitchell, 'Making the case for Irish independence' in John Crowley, Donal Ó Drisceoil, Mike Murphy and John Borgonovo (eds), *Atlas of the Irish Revolution* (Cork, 2017), p. 476.
17 *LO*, 22 Nov. 1919. 18 *RH*, 15 Nov. 1919. 19 *LO*, 4 Oct. 1919.
20 CI Leitrim, Nov. 1919 (TNA, CO 904/110). 21 *RH*, 14 June 1919.
22 *LO*, 21 June 1919. 23 Townshend, *Republic*, p. 140.
24 *SC*, 7 Feb. 1920. 25 Laffan, *Resurrection*, p. 284.
26 Arthur Mitchell, *Revolutionary government in Ireland: Dáil Éireann, 1919–22* (Dublin, 1995), p. 72.
27 *LO*, 21 Feb. 1920. 28 Ibid., 15 May 1920. 29 Ibid., 1 May 1920.
30 Francis Costello, *The Irish Revolution and its aftermath, 1916–1923* (Dublin, 2003), p. 159.
31 Michael Laffan, '"Labour must wait": Ireland's conservative revolution' in Patrick J. Corish (ed.), *Radicals, rebels and establishments* (Belfast, 1985), p. 215.
32 *LO*, 12 June 1920. 33 Ibid., 5 June 1920. 34 Fitzpatrick, *Politics*, p. 143.

35 *LO*, 26 June 1920.
36 Minutes of meeting of Manorhamilton board of guardians, 24 June 1920 (Leitrim County Library).
37 *LO*, 19 June 1920.   38 Paul Mulvey (BMH WS 1265, p. 3).
39 Michael Farry, *Sligo: the Irish Revolution, 1912–23* (Dublin, 2012), p. 75.
40 *LO*, 10 July 1920.   41 Farry, *Sligo*, p. 75.   42 *RH*, 11 Sept. 1920.
43 Paul Mulvey (BMH WS 1265, p. 40).
44 Darrell Figgis, *Recollections of the Irish war* (London, 1927), p. 305.
45 *RH*, 24 July 1920; *LO*, 24 July 1920.   46 Laffan, *Resurrection*, p. 310.
47 *LO*, 10 July 1920.
48 Mary Kotsonouris, *Retreat from revolution: the Dáil courts, 1920–24* (Dublin, 1994), p. 12.
49 *SC*, 3 July 1920.   50 *LO*, 14 Aug. 1920.   51 *RH*, 14 Aug. 1920.
52 Costello, *Irish Revolution*, p. 197.
53 South Leitrim court registrar returns for quarter ending 31 December 1921, Dáil Éireann Courts Commission (NAI, DÉ 10/36).
54 *LO*, 2, 16 Oct. 1920.   55 Fitzpatrick, *Politics*, p. 152.
56 Costello, *Irish Revolution*, p. 197.
57 James Scott, *Domination and the arts of resistance: hidden transcripts* (London, 1990), p. 129.
58 *SC*, 1 Jan. 1921.   59 Ibid., 23 Apr. 1921.   60 *RH*, 6 Aug. 1921.
61 *Roscommon Journal*, 1 Jan. 1921.   62 *SC*, 15 Jan. 1921.
63 Dooley, *Land question*, p. 82.
64 Mitchell, *Revolutionary government*, p. 89.   65 *LO*, 27 Mar. 1920.
66 Mitchell, *Revolutionary government*, p. 89.   67 *LO*, 15 Nov. 1919.
68 Ibid., 1 May 1920.   69 CI Leitrim, Dec. 1919 (TNA, CO 904/110).
70 *LO*, 16 Aug. 1919.   71 Ibid., 11 Oct. 1919.   72 *RH*, 13 Aug. 1921.
73 Ibid., 4 June 1921.   74 Laffan, 'Labour must wait', p. 210.
75 *RH*, 11 Sept. 1920.   76 *LO*, 3 July 1920.   77 *SC*, 16 Apr. 1921.

CHAPTER SEVEN *'Vengeance was swift and very destructive': War of Independence, 1919–21*

1 Bernard Sweeney (BMH WS 1194, p. 5).
2 Marnie Hay, 'Fianna Éireann' in Crowley, Ó Drisceoil, Murphy and Borgonovo (eds), *Atlas of the Irish Revolution*, pp 173–6; Hay, *Na Fianna Éireann and the Irish Revolution, 1909–23: scouting for rebels* (Manchester, 2019), p. 98.
3 Prosecution of civilians, Charles Timoney (TNA, WO 35/105/24).
4 Peter Hart, *The IRA at war* (Oxford, 2003), p. 53.
5 CI Leitrim, Feb. 1920 (TNA, CO 904/111).
6 W.J. Lowe, 'The war against the RIC 1919–1921', *Éire-Ireland*, 37:3–4 (2002), 85.
7 Charles Pinkman (BMH WS 1263, p. 12).
8 Hugh Brady (BMH WS 1266, p. 5).
9 Bernard Sweeney (BMH WS 1194, pp 5–6).
10 *RH*, 29 May 1920; *FJ*, 30 May 1920.
11 Dan Gallogly, *Slieve an Iariann slopes: history of the town and parish of Ballinamore, Co. Leitrim* (Ballinamore, 1991), p. 218.
12 Register of crime, province of Connaught, Leitrim, 11 Aug. 1920 (TNA, CO 904/45).
13 Eugene Kilkenny (BMH WS 1146, p. 16).
14 *AC*, 11 Sept. 1920.
15 Register of crime, province of Connaught, Leitrim, 5 Sept. 1920 (TNA, CO 904/45).
16 Hugh Brady (BMH WS 1266, p. 6).   17 *LO*, 6 Mar. 1920.
18 Ibid., 13 Mar. 1920.   19 CI Leitrim, June 1920 (TNA, CO 904/120).

20 Ó Súilleabháin, *Leitrim's republican story*, p. 55.
21 *LO*, 24 Apr. 1920.
22 Brian Heffernan, *Freedom and the fifth commandment: Catholic priests and political violence in Ireland, 1919–21* (Manchester, 2014), p. 21.
23 Ibid., p. 36.   24 Hugh Brady (BMH WS 1266, p. 6).
25 *LO*, 10 Apr. 1920.   26 Lowe, 'The war against the RIC', 100.
27 *LO*, 10 Apr. 1920.   28 Patrick Doherty (BMH WS 1195, p. 11).
29 Conor Kostick, *Revolution in Ireland: popular militancy, 1917–1923* (Cork, 2009), pp 129–40.
30 *LO*, 17 Apr. 1920.   31 *RH*, 22 May 1920.
32 *Hansard (Commons)*, 27 Apr. 1920, vol. 128, cols. 1024–6; May 1920, vol. 128, cols 2216–17.
33 *LO*, 15 May 1920.   34 *SC*, 8 May 1920.
35 CI Leitrim, June 1920 (TNA, CO 904/112).
36 *Sligo Independent*, 12 June 1920; *Irish Bulletin*, 11 June 1920.
37 D.M. Leeson, *The Black and Tans: British police and Auxiliaries in the Irish War of Independence* (Oxford, 2011), pp 9–10, 28–30.
38 *LO*, 13 Mar. 1920.
39 William Sheehan, *Hearts and mines: the British 5th Division in Ireland, 1920–1922* (Cork, 2009), p. 184.
40 Ernest McCall, *The Auxiliaries, Tudor's toughs: a study of the Auxiliary Division Royal Irish Constabulary, 1920–1922* (Newtownards, 2013), p. 203.
41 Lowe, 'The war against the RIC', 110.
42 Harold McBrien (BMH WS 895, p. 4).
43 *Sligo Independent*, 5 June 1920; *LO*, 5 June 1920.   44 *RH*, 10 July 1920.
45 Hart, *IRA at war*, p. 44.
46 Post Office reports, Attacks on mails, 1 May 1920–31 Dec. 1920 (TNA, CO 905/158/1).
47 *RH*, 31 July 1920.
48 Hugh Brady (BMH WS 1266, p. 15); Register of crime, province of Connaught, Leitrim, 3 Sept. 1920 (TNA, CO 904/45).
49 Bernard Sweeney (BMH WS 1194, p. 8).
50 CI Leitrim, June 1920 (TNA, CO 904/112).
51 Ibid.; *RH*, 7 Aug. 1920.
52 Patrick J. Hargaden (BMH WS 1268, p. 7).
53 *Irish Bulletin*, 18 June 1920.
54 CI Leitrim, July 1920 (TNA, CO 904/112).
55 Mitchell, *Revolutionary government*, p. 149.
56 CI Leitrim, July 1920 (TNA, CO 904/112).
57 Lowe, 'The war against the RIC', 99.
58 Brian Hughes, 'Persecuting the Peelers' in David Fitzpatrick (ed.), *Terror in Ireland, 1916–1923* (Dublin, 2012), p. 207.
59 *Sligo Independent*, 19 June 1920.
60 Register of crime, province of Connaught, Leitrim, 21 July 1920 (TNA, CO 904/45).
61 Brian Hughes, *Defying the IRA?: intimidation, coercion, and communities during the Irish Revolution* (Liverpool, 2016), p. 149.
62 Ibid., pp 27–30.
63 Lieutenant E. Thorpe to O/C, A Branch, GHQ, 11 Apr. 1921 (TNA, WO 35/129/39).
64 *RH*, 14 Aug. 1920.   65 Patrick J. Hargaden (BMH WS 1268, pp 7–8).
66 Michael Hopkinson, *The Irish War of Independence* (Dublin, 2002), p. 79.
67 Michael Farry, *The aftermath of revolution: Sligo, 1921–23* (Dublin, 2000), p. 12.

68 *RH*, 18 Sept. 1920.   69 *LO*, 18 Sept. 1920.   70 Ibid.
71 Liam Ó Duibhir, *The Donegal awakening: Donegal and the War of Independence* (Dublin, 2009), p. 177; *Sligo Independent*, 2 Oct. 1920.
72 Register of crime, province of Connaught, Leitrim, 16 Sept. 1920 (TNA, CO 904/45).
73 *Sligo Independent*, 2 Oct. 1920.
74 *RH*, 25 Sept. 1920; *LO*, 25 Sept. 1920.   75 *LO*, 25 Sept. 1920.
76 *AC*, 25 Sept. 1920.   77 Ibid., 2 Oct. 1920.
78 *Sligo Independent*, 25 Sept. 1920.   79 *AC*, 2 Oct. 1920.
80 Ibid.   81 *LO*, 25 Sept. 1920.   82 *RH*, 2 Oct. 1920.
83 Ibid.
84 Prosecution of civilians, Michael McTierney (TNA, WO 35/116/31).
85 *LO*, 9 Oct. 1920.
86 Prosecution of civilians, James Gavin (TNA, WO 35/117/35).
87 *RH*, 16 Oct. 1920.   88 *LO*, 9 Oct. 1920.   89 Ibid., 16 Oct. 1920.
90 Ibid., 23 Oct. 1920.   91 *Irish Bulletin*, 12 Nov. 1920.
92 Hugh Brady (BMH WS 1266, p. 8); *LO*, 16 Oct. 1920.
93 Joost Augusteijn, 'Military conflict in the War of Independence' in Crowley, Ó Drisceoil, Murphy and Borgonovo (eds), *Atlas of the Irish Revolution*, pp 348–57.
94 *RH*, 15 Jan. 1921.   95 Ibid.
96 CI Leitrim, Nov. 1920 (TNA, CO 904/113).
97 Ibid., Oct. 1920 (ibid.).   98 *Westmeath Examiner*, 6 Nov. 1920.
99 *RH*, 6 Nov. 1920.   100 *FJ*, 11 Nov. 1920.   101 Ibid.
102 *Irish Bulletin*, 29 Nov. 1920.   103 *FJ*, 13 Nov. 1920.
104 *RH*, 13 Nov. 1920.   105 *RH*, 20 Nov. 1920; *SC*, 20 Nov. 1920.
106 *FJ*, 22 Nov. 1920.   107 Ibid.
108 Rumpf and Hepburn, *Nationalism and socialism*, p. 38.
109 Augusteijn, 'Military conflict', p. 354.
110 CI Leitrim, Nov. 1920 (TNA, CO 904/113).   111 Ibid.
112 William Murphy, *Political imprisonment and the Irish, 1912–1921* (Oxford, 2014), p. 194.
113 *RH*, 5 Feb. 1921.
114 Liam Ó Duibhir, *Prisoners of war: Ballykinlar internment camp, 1920–1921* (Cork, 2013), p. 67.
115 CI Leitrim, Dec. 1920 (TNA, CO 904/113).
116 Joost Augusteijn, *From public defiance to guerrilla warfare: the experience of ordinary volunteers in the Irish War of Independence, 1916–1921* (Dublin, 1996), p. 126.
117 Townshend, *Republic*, p. 182.
118 Bernard Sweeney (BMH WS 1194, p. 10).
119 Townshend, *Republic*, p. 182.
120 Hopkinson, *War of Independence*, p. 143.   121 Ibid.
122 Francis Davis (University College Dublin Archives (hereafter UCDA), Ernie O'Malley papers, P17b/131).
123 Ibid.   124 CI Leitrim, Jan. 1921 (TNA, CO 904/114).
125 *AC*, 19 Feb. 1921.
126 Charles Townshend, 'The Irish Republican Army and the development of guerrilla warfare, 1916–21', *English Historical Review*, 94 (1979), 321–2.
127 Marie Coleman, *The Irish Revolution, 1912–1923* (London, 2014), p. 79.
128 Peter Hart, 'The geography of the Irish Revolution, 1917–1923', *Past and Present*, 155:1 (1997), 142–76.
129 Ernie O'Malley, *Rising out: Seán Connolly of Longford* (Dublin, 2007), p. 166.
130 Bernard Sweeney (BMH WS 1194, p. 16); Hugh Brady (BMH WS 1266, p. 11); Patrick J. Hargaden (BMH WS 1268, p. 14).

131 Francis Davis (UCDA, O'Malley papers, P17b/131). 132 *RH*, 29 Jan. 1921.
133 *Irish Catholic*, 5 Feb. 1921. 134 Bernard Sweeney (BMH WS 1194, p. 11).
135 Ibid., pp 11–12. 136 Ibid.
137 Francis Davis (UCDA, O'Malley papers, P17b/131).
138 O'Malley, *Rising out*, p. 149.
139 *History of Bedfordshire and Hertfordshire Regiment* (File 6, Leitrim County Library), p. 13.
140 Manuscript memoir, Leitrim County Library, McGoohan papers.
141 *Bedfordshire and Hertfordshire Regiment*, p. 14.
142 Patrick Doherty (BMH WS 1195, p. 20); Ó Súilleabháin, *Leitrim's republican story*, pp 72–5.
143 O'Malley, *Rising out*, p. 151.
144 Manuscript memoir, Leitrim County Library, McGoohan papers.
145 *Bedfordshire and Hertfordshire Regiment*, p. 14.
146 Irish Office and Irish Branch, Heroism of Nurse Alice Gray at ambush, Sheemore Hill, County Leitrim (TNA, HO 351/87).
147 Macready to undersecretary, War Office, 4 Apr. 1921 (TNA, HO 351/87).
148 Eugene Kilkenny (BMH WS 1146, pp 12–13).
149 Patrick J. Hargaden (BMH WS 1268, p. 11).
150 *SC*, 20 Mar. 1921. 151 O'Malley, *Rising out*, p. 152.
152 Michael Whelan, 'Selton Hill', *Leitrim Guardian* (1970), 30–40; O'Malley, *Rising out*, p. 155.
153 Whelan, 'Selton Hill', 31.
154 Courts of inquiry in lieu of inquest: deaths of Michael Baxter, Joseph Beirne, John Connolly, John J. O'Reilly, J.J. Wrynne, and an unknown man (Joseph Nangle?) (TNA, WO 35/160/3).
155 Bernard Sweeney (BMH WS 1194, p. 14).
156 *Bedfordshire and Hertfordshire Regiment*, p. 18.
157 William H. Kautt, *Ambushes and armour: the Irish rebellion, 1919–21* (Dublin, 2010), pp 152–85.
158 Courts of inquiry in lieu of inquest: deaths of Michael Baxter, Joseph Beirne, John Connolly, John J. O'Reilly, J.J. Wrynne, and an unknown man (Joseph Nangle?) (TNA, WO 35/160/3).
159 CI Leitrim, Mar. 1921 (TNA, CO 904/114).
160 *Roscommon Journal*, 19 Mar. 1921; *Strokestown Democrat*, 12 Mar. 1921.
161 CI Leitrim, Mar. 1921 (TNA, CO 904/114). 162 *AC*, 21 May 1920.
163 Ibid. 164 Ibid., 19 Mar. 1920.
165 *Longford Leader*, 19 Mar. 1920 166 Gallogly, *Kilmore*, p. 286.
167 Ibid., pp 286–7. 168 Charles Pinkman (BMH WS 1263, pp 7–8).
169 Ibid.; Ó Súilleabháin, *Leitrim's republican story*, p. 79. 170 Ibid., p. 9.
171 CI Leitrim, Mar. 1921 (TNA, CO 904/114).
172 Irish Distress Committee and Irish Grants Committee: Isabella Latimer (TNA, CO 762/4/4).
173 Townshend, *Republic*, p. 293.
174 Patrick J. Hargaden (BMH WS 1268, p. 12).
175 Francis Davis (UCDA, O'Malley papers, P17b/131).
176 Francis Davis (BMH WS 496, pp 31–2).
177 Coleman, *Longford*, p. 130; Francis Davis (BMH WS 496, p. 38).
178 Bernard Sweeney (BMH WS 1194, p. 16).
179 O'Malley, *Rising out*, pp 139, 142.
180 Bernard Sweeney (BMH WS 1194, p. 18); Hugh Brady (BMH WS 1266, p. 12).
181 Intelligence Officer to GHQ, 13 Aug. 1921 (UCDA, Richard Mulcahy papers, P7A/18).
182 Court of inquiry in lieu of inquest: death of James McGlynn (TNA, WO 35/154/52).

183 Hughes, *Defying the IRA*, p. 7.
184 *RH*, 11 Sept. 1920; Register of crime, province of Connaught, Leitrim, 4 Sept. 1920 (TNA, CO 904/45).
185 Patrick J. Hargaden (BMH WS 1268, p. 9).
186 Margaret Brady (BMH WS 1267, p. 4).
187 Fanny Barry application file (IMA, MSPC, MSP34REF60172); Catherine Flynn application file (IMA, MSPC, MSP34REF60079); Rose Ann Geoghegan application file (IMA, MSPC, MSP34REF60007); Bridget Doherty (BMH WS 1193, p. 5); Louise Ryan and Margaret Ward (eds), *Irish women and nationalism: soldiers, new women and wicked hags* (Kildare, 2004); Margaret Ward, *Unmaneagable revolutionaries: women and Irish nationalism* (London, 1989), p. 104.
188 Margaret Brady (BMH WS 1267, p. 3).
189 Cal McCarthy, *Cumann na mBan and the Irish Revolution* (Cork, 2014), p. 120.
190 Townshend, *Republic*, pp 250–1.
191 Bridget Doherty (BMH WS 1193, p. 4).
192 Manuscript memoir (Leitrim County Library, McGoohan papers).
193 Court of inquiry in lieu of inquest: death of Constable Wilfred Jones (TNA, WO 35/151B/24).   194 *RH*, 23 Apr. 1921; *AC*, 23 Apr. 1921.
195 Hugh Brady (BMH WS 1266, pp 8–9).
196 O'Malley, *Rising out*, p. 167.
197 Bernard Sweeney (BMH WS 1194, p. 160).
198 Hugh Brady (BMH WS 1266, p. 17).
199 Court of inquiry in lieu of inquest: death of John Harrison (TNA, WO 35/151A/35).
200 Ibid.
201 Anne Dolan, '"Spies and informers beware"' in Diarmaid Ferriter and Susannah Riordan (eds), *Years of turbulence: the Irish Revolution and its aftermath* (Dublin, 2015), p. 162.
202 Ó Súilleabháin, *Leitrim's republican story*, p. 83; *AC*, 15 Oct. 1921.
203 *FJ*, 18 May 1921.   204 *RH*, 20 Aug. 1921.   205 *SC*, 21 May 1921.
206 Eunan O'Halpin, 'Counting terror: Bloody Sunday and the dead of the Irish Revolution' in David Fitzpatrick (ed.), *Terror in Ireland, 1916–1923* (Dublin, 2012), p. 153.
207 Sheehan, *Hearts and mines*, p. 75.
208 Prosecution of James Moran, Michael Moran, Michael Early, Thomas McGarty, James Doonan (TNA, WO 35/128/14).
209 Patrick Doherty (BMH WS 1195, p. 28).
210 Irish Distress Committee and Irish Grants Committee: Revd George Ingham (TNA, CO 762/53/12).
211 Bernard Sweeney (BMH WS 1194, p. 18).
212 Report of raids on channels of communication employed by IRA (TNA, WO 35/35/86b).
213 CI Leitrim, Feb. 1921, Mar. 1921 (TNA, CO 904/114).
214 *RH*, 11 June 1920.
215 Bernard Sweeney (BMH WS 1194, p. 16); Sheehan, *Hearts and mines*, p. 232.
216 W.H. Kautt, *Ground truths: British army operations in the Irish War of Independence* (Sallins, 2014), p. 159.
217 *FJ*, 14 June 1921.   218 Ibid., 28 June 1921.   219 *RH*, 2 July 1921.
220 Coleman, *Irish Revolution*, p. 78.
221 Army of Ireland, Administrative and Easter Rising records, Sinn Féin activists, James N. Dolan (TNA, WO 35/206/62).
222 O'Malley, *Rising out*, p. 166.
223 Peter Hart, *The IRA and its enemies: violence and community in Cork, 1916–1923* (Oxford, 1998), p. 106.

224 Charles Townshend, *Political violence in Ireland* (Oxford, 1984), pp 335–6.
225 Fitzpatrick, *Politics*, p. 179.

CHAPTER EIGHT 'The opportunity of being mistress in their own house': the transition to self-government, 1921–2

1 *SC*, 16 July 1921. 2 Ibid. 3 *RH*, 2 July 1921.
4 Mitchell, *Revolutionary government*, p. 160.
5 Mary E. Daly, *The buffer state: the historical roots of the Department of the Environment* (Dublin, 1997), p. 89.
6 *RH*, 5 Nov. 1921. 7 Hughes, *Defying the IRA*, p. 71.
8 Daly, *Buffer state*, p. 89. 9 *RH*, 5 Nov. 1921. 10 Ibid., 19 Nov. 1921.
11 Ibid., 3 Dec. 1921. 12 *SC*, 4 Mar. 1922.
13 Hughes, *Defying the IRA*, pp 71–3. 14 *RH*, 15 Apr. 1922.
15 Ibid. 16 Ibid., 17 June 1922. 17 Ibid., 3 Sept. 1921.
18 Coleman, *Longford*, p. 98. 19 Daly, *Buffer state*, p. 75.
20 *RH*, 5 Nov. 1921. 21 Ibid., 24 Sept. 1921. 22 Ibid., 22 Oct. 1921.
23 Farry, *Sligo*, p. 82; Coleman, *Longford*, p. 100. 24 *RH*, 4 Feb. 1922.
25 Daly, *Buffer state*, p. 85. 26 *RH*, 27 Aug. 1921. 27 Ibid., 5 Nov. 1921.
28 Daly, *Buffer state*, p. 120.
29 Summaries of reports of criminal offences and breaches of the truce in Leitrim, 1921 (TNA, CO 904/153).
30 Elaine Byrne, *Political corruption in Ireland, 1922–2010: a crooked harp?* (Manchester, 2012), p. 31.
31 *SC*, 8 Apr. 1922. 32 Mitchell, *Revolutionary government*, p. 327.
33 *RH*, 10 Dec. 1921. 34 *SC*, 8 Oct. 1921. 35 Ibid., 22 Oct. 1921.
36 Murphy, *Imprisonment*, p. 245. 37 *RH*, 17 Dec. 1921.
38 Ibid. 39 *SC*, 17 Dec. 1921. 40 *RH*, 31 Dec. 1921.
41 Ibid., 7 Jan. 1922. 42 Ibid. 43 Ibid., 14 Jan. 1922.
44 Ibid. 45 *SC*, 18 Mar. 1922.
46 *Roscommon Messenger*, 14 Jan. 1922. 47 *RH*, 25 Mar. 1922.
48 Ibid., 29 Apr. 1922. 49 *Roscommon Messenger*, 10 June 1922.
50 *RH*, 18 Feb. 1922. 51 Ibid., 22 Apr. 1922. 52 Ibid., 13 May 1922.

CHAPTER NINE 'There is this particular type of madness amongst a section of the people': Civil War, 1922–3

1 Nollaig Ó Gadhra, *Civil War in Connacht, 1922–1923* (Cork, 1999), p. 13.
2 *FJ*, 28 Jan. 1922. 3 *RH*, 18 Mar. 1922. 4 Farry, *Sligo*, pp 89–90.
5 *RH*, 11 Mar. 1922. 6 Farry, *Aftermath of revolution*, p. 165.
7 Hopkinson, *Civil War*, p. 90. 8 *LA*, 9 Feb. 1922. 9 Ibid., 27 Apr. 1922.
10 *FJ*, 11 May 1922. 11 Ibid.
12 Michael Hopkinson, 'The Craig–Collins pacts of 1922: two attempted reforms of the Northern Ireland government', *Irish Historical Studies*, 27:106 (1990), 156.
13 John M. Regan, *The Irish counter-revolution, 1921–1936* (Cambridge, 1999), p. 61.
14 *Ulster Herald*, 18 Feb. 1922; *Donegal Democrat*, 3 June 1922; Robert Lynch, *The northern IRA and the early years of partition* (Dublin, 2006), pp 154–6.
15 *FH*, 11 Feb. 1922; Lynch, *Northern IRA*, pp 100–6.
16 Interview with Bernard Sweeney, *Leitrim News*, 22 Apr. 1971.
17 *RH*, 18 Mar. 1922; *AC*, 18 Mar. 1922; *FJ*, 14 Mar. 1922.
18 *FH*, 18 Mar. 1922.

19 Manuscript memoir, Leitrim County Library, McGoohan papers.
20 *FH*, 15 Apr. 1922.   21 Hopkinson, *Civil War*, p. 90.
22 Des Guckian, *Deported: an undesirable alien* (Dromod, 1986).
23 *AC*, 6 May 1922.   24 *RH*, 6 May 1922.   25 *FH*, 22 Apr. 1922.
26 Campbell, *Land and revolution*, p. 303.
27 https://www.cso.ie/en/census/censusvolumes1926 to1991/historicalreports/census1926 reports/census1926volume2-occupations/ (accessed 4 May 2016).
28 Dooley, *Land question*, p. 235.   29 *RH*, 13 May 1922.
30 Ibid., 6 May 1922.   31 Dooley, *Land question*, pp 50–1.
32 Eunan O'Halpin, *Defending Ireland: the Irish state and its enemies since 1922* (Oxford, 1999), p. 31.
33 *FJ*, 10 May 1922.   34 Ibid.   35 *LA*, 1 June 1922.
36 Gemma Clark, *Everyday violence in the Irish Civil War* (Cambridge, 2014), p. 7.
37 Francis White, *Glenfarne – a history* (Glenfarne, 2014), p. 25.
38 O'Halpin, *Defending Ireland*, p. 33.
39 Reports of prisoners arrested by 'A' Coy., Second Battalion, Special Infantry Corps, 17 May 1923 (IMA, Athlone Command papers, CW/P/02/02/02).
40 Dooley, *Decline of the big house*, p. 42.   41 *FH*, 24 June 1922.
42 Ibid.   43 Farry, *Aftermath of revolution*, p. 93.
44 Ibid., p. 54.   45 *RH*, 29 Apr., 2 May 1922.
46 *LA*, 6 July 1922.   47 *RH*, 1 July 1922.
48 Ó Súilleabháin, *Leitrim's republican story*, p. 138.
49 Jim Gallagher (Leitrim County Library, Local Studies oral history collection, audio 263).
50 Paul Bew, *Ireland: the politics of enmity, 1789–2006* (Oxford, 2007), pp 438–9.
51 Tom Garvin, *1922: the birth of Irish democracy* (Dublin, 1996), p. 39; Joe Lee, *Ireland, 1912–1985: politics and society* (Cambridge, 1989), p. 67; Dorothy Macardle, *The Irish Republic: a documented chronicle* (London, 1968); P.S. O'Hegarty, *The victory of Sinn Féin* (Dublin, 1924); John M. Regan, *Myth and the Irish state: historical problems and other essays* (Dublin, 2013).
52 Gavin Foster, *The Irish Civil War and society: politics, class and conflict* (New York, 2015), p. 7; Paul Bew, 'Agrarian radicalism' in Boyce (ed.), *The revolution in Ireland*, pp 229–34; Dooley, *Land question*, p. 50.
53 Bew, *Ireland: politics of enmity*, p. 439.
54 Bill Kissane, *The politics of the Irish Civil War* (Oxford, 2005), p. 8.
55 *RH*, 18 Feb. 1922.   56 Ibid., 18 Mar. 1922.
57 Hart, 'Geography', 142–76.
58 *Donegal News*, 22 July 1922.   59 *FJ*, 8 July 1922.   60 *LA*, 6 July 1922.
61 Farry, *Aftermath of revolution*, p. 79.
62 Daily intelligence report, 4 Aug. 1922 (IMA, Western Command papers, CW/Ops/02/01/01).
63 Farry, *Aftermath of revolution*, p. 80.
64 *FJ*, 11 July 1922; *Donegal News*, 13 July 1922.   65 *FJ*, 19 July 1922.
66 Ibid.   67 Ibid., 20 July 1922.
68 *Fermanagh Herald*, 15 July 1922; *Donegal News*, 15 July 1922.
69 Farry, *Aftermath of revolution*, p. 80.
70 Hegarty Thorne, *Roscommon*, p. 142.
71 Command intelligence officer to director of intelligence GHQ, 8 Sept. 1922 (IMA, Western Command papers, CW/Ops/02/01/01).
72 Foster, *Civil War*, p. 5.   73 Lynch, *Northern IRA*, pp 194, 208.
74 *FJ*, 6 Sept. 1922; *LA*, 7 Sept. 1922; *AC*, 9 Sept. 1922.

75 *AC*, 26 Aug. 1922.
76 J. Fearin and D. Laitin, 'Ethnicity, insurgency and civil war', *American Political Science Review*, 97:1 (2003), 81, quoted in Kissane, *Politics of the Irish Civil War*, p. 9.
77 Hopkinson, *Civil War*, p. 215; Farry, *Aftermath of revolution*, p. 83.
78 Calton Younger, *Ireland's Civil War* (London, 1968), p. 467.
79 *LA*, 21 Sept. 1922.
80 *FJ*, 20 Sept. 1922; Younger, *Civil War*, p. 467.
81 *FH*, 23 Sept. 1922.
82 Unsigned statement, n.d. (IMA, Western Command papers, CD 333/36).
83 *SC*, 30 Sept. 1922. 84 *Fermanagh Times*, 30 Sept. 1922.
85 *FJ*, 17 Oct. 1922.
86 Operations report, Western Command, 5 Oct. 1922 (IMA, Western Command papers, CW/Ops/02/01/04).
87 *RH*, 4 Nov. 1922. 88 *FJ*, 27 Oct. 1922.
89 Patrick Murray, *Oracles of God: the Roman Catholic Church and Irish politics, 1922–37* (Dublin, 2000), pp 72–4.
90 *Irish Independent*, 6 Nov. 1922. 91 *FH*, 11 Nov. 1922.
92 *RH*, 11 Nov. 1922. 93 *FJ*, 21 Nov. 1922; *AC*, 25 Nov. 1922.
94 Farry, *Aftermath of revolution*, p. 172.
95 Fearghal McGarry, *Eoin O'Duffy: a self-made hero* (Oxford, 2005); Conor Brady, *Guardians of the peace* (Dublin, 2000), p. 103.
96 *RH*, 30 Sept. 1922. 97 Ibid., 28 Oct. 1922. 98 Ibid., 7 Oct. 1922.
99 *AC*, 7 Oct. 1922. 100 *FH*, 28 Oct. 1922. 101 *AC*, 14 Oct. 1922.
102 Vicky Conway, *Policing twentieth-century Ireland: a history of an Garda Siochána* (Oxford, 2014), p. 37.
103 *AC*, 25 Nov. 1922. 104 *RH*, 6 Jan. 1923. 105 *FH*, 10 Mar. 1923.
106 Brian McCarthy, *The Civic Guard mutiny* (Cork, 2012), p. 197.
107 McGarry, *O'Duffy*, p. 123.
108 *RH*, 14 Oct., 11 Nov., 16 Dec. 1922.
109 *Irish Independent*, 23 Dec. 1922.
110 *FJ*, 22 Jan. 1923; Brady, *Guardians*, p. 137.
111 *FJ*, 5 Dec. 1922; *AC*, 9 Dec. 1922; *RH*, 9 Dec. 1922.
112 Ó Súilleabháin, *Leitrim's republican story*, p. 149.
113 Ibid.; *FJ*, 14 Dec. 1922.
114 Peter Hart, 'The Protestant experience of revolution in Southern Ireland' in Richard English and Graham Walker (eds), *Unionism in modern Ireland: new perspectives on politics and culture* (New York, 1996), pp 81–99.
115 *FH*, 27 May 1922. 116 Clark, *Everyday violence*, p. 152.
117 Miriam Moffitt, 'The Protestant experience of revolution in County Leitrim, 1911–1928', *Breifne*, 12:46 (2011), 303–23.
118 Andy Bielenberg, 'Exodus: the emigration of southern Irish Protestants during the Irish War of Independence and the Civil War', *Past & Present*, 218:1 (2013), 199–233; David Fitzpatrick, 'Protestant depopulation and the Irish Revolution', *Irish Historical Studies*, 38:152 (2013), 643–61.
119 Moffitt, 'Protestant experience', 315, 323. 120 Ibid., 310.
121 Ibid., 315–16.
122 Rural deans' reports 1921 (Representative Church Body Library, D3/1/19–24).
123 Reports of Revd Austin Sweetman, Revd Matthew Porteus and Revd S.J. Haylett, 1923 (Representative Church Body Library, D3/1/22).
124 Farry, *Aftermath of revolution*, p. 200.

125 Evidence of Thomas Scott and Revd Thomas Walmsley, 29 Apr. 1925, Boundary Commission papers (NLI, MS 6,515).
126 Moffitt, 'Protestant experience', 323; R.B. Mc Dowell, *Crisis and decline: the fate of southern unionists* (Dublin, 1995), p. 120, quoted in Farry, *Aftermath of revolution*, p. 201.
127 Adjutant General to Major General Mac Eoin, 7 Jan. 1923 (IMA, Western Command papers, CW/OPS 02/03/01).
128 Colonel Pádraig Woods to Major General Mac Eoin, 7 Jan. 1923 (IMA, Western Command papers, CW/OPS/02/03/01).
129 *Irish Independent*, 8 Jan. 1922; Hegarthy Thorne, *Roscommon*, p. 153.
130 *FH*, 3 Feb. 1923. 131 *FJ*, 10 Feb. 1923. 132 Ibid.
133 *LO*, 10 Feb. 1923. 134 *FJ*, 2 Feb. 1923. 135 *LO*, 10 Feb. 1923.
136 *RH*, 10 Feb. 1923. 137 *Dáil Éireann debates*, 8 Feb. 1923.
138 Ibid. 139 O'Halpin, *Defending Ireland*, pp 29–30.
140 *Dáil Éireann debates*, 7 Feb. 1923.
141 Hopkinson, *Civil War*, pp 239–45.
142 *FJ*, 15 Feb.; *RH*, 17 Feb. 1923.
143 O/C Carrick Garrison to O/C Boyle Garrison, 20 Feb. 1923 (IMA, Athlone Command papers, CW/Ops/02/03/01).
144 *LO*, 3 Mar. 1923. 145 Ó Súilleabháin, *Leitrim's republican story*, p. 151.
146 Weekly appreciation report, Athlone Command, 5 Mar. 1923 (IMA, Athlone Command papers, CW/Ops/02/03/02).
147 *LO*, 3 Mar. 1923. 148 *Irish Independent*, 5 Mar. 1923.
149 O'Halpin, *Defending Ireland*, p. 30.
150 Lynch, *Revolutionary Ireland*, p. 126.
151 O'Halpin, *Defending Ireland*, p. 31. 152 *FH*, 17 Feb. 1923.
153 *RH*, 17 Feb. 1923. 154 *LO*, 17 Feb. 1923. 155 Ibid.
156 Gallogly, *Kilmore*, p. 290. 157 *FH*, 10 Mar. 1923; *Irish Independent*, 8 Mar. 1923.
158 *RH*, 17 Mar. 1923; *LO*, 17 Mar. 1923.
159 *FJ*, 15 Mar. 1922. 160 *Irish Independent*, 14 Mar. 1923.
161 *FJ*, 13 Mar. 1923.
162 Seán and Sile Murphy, *The Comeraghs, gunfire and civil war: the story of the Déise Brigade IRA, 1914–1924* (Kilmacthomas, 2003), pp 161–5; Hopkinson, *Civil War*, p. 236.
163 Hopkinson, *Civil War*, p. 236. 164 *RH*, 31 Mar. 1923.
165 Eric Hobsbawm, *Bandits* (London, 2005), p. 25.
166 General weekly return, Athlone Command, 5 Apr. 1923 (IMA, Athlone Command papers, CW/OPS 02/03/07).
167 *FJ*, 9 Apr. 1923. 168 Ibid., 27 Mar. 1923. 169 Ibid., 28 Mar. 1923.
170 *RH*, 24 Mar. 1923. 171 *Irish Times*, 13 Feb., 10 May 1923.
172 Ó Súilleabháin, *Leitrim's republican story*, pp 152–3.
173 Leitrim County Library, Local Studies Collection, Muldoon file (502).
174 Ibid.
175 Ibid.; Ken Boyle and Tim Desmond, *The murder of Dr Muldoon: a suspect priest, a widow's fight for justice* (Cork, 2019), p. 192.
176 *Irish Independent*, 4 Apr. 1923; *FJ*, 5 Apr. 1923.
177 Hegarty Thorne, *Roscommon*, p. 196.
178 *FJ*, 2 May 1923; *RH*, 5 May 1923.
179 *RH*, 5 May 1923; *Irish Independent*, 3 May 1923.
180 *FJ*, 16 May 1923. 181 *LO*, 2 June 1923.
182 Patrick Keville application file (IMA, MSPC, DP 24313).
183 Brady, *Guardians*, p. 137.

CHAPTER TEN *Revolution?*

1 Wheatley, *Nationalism*, pp 24–7.　　　　　　2 Ibid.
3 Fitzpatrick, *Ireland and the First World War*, p. vii; Coleman, *Longford*, p. 4.
4 Trinity College Dublin Library, Samuels papers, box 3.
5 *Sligo Nationalist*, 20 May 1916.
6 Nic Dháibhéid, 'Irish National Aid', p. 707.
7 Fitzpatrick, 'Collective sacrifice', p. 1030; Martin Staunton, 'Kilrush, Co. Clare and the Royal Munster Fusiliers', *Irish Sword*, 15:65 (1986), 268–72; Dungan, *Distant drums*, p. 54.
8 CI Leitrim, July 1918 (TNA CO 904/106).
9 Laffan, *Resurrection*, pp 186–8.
10 Costello, *Irish Revolution*, p. 197.　　　　　11 Coleman, *Longford*, p. 111.
12 Lowe, *The war against the RIC*, p. 85; Hughes, 'Persecuting the Peelers', p. 207.
13 Hopkinson, *Civil War*.　　14 Brady, *Guardians*, p. 137.
15 Clark, *Everyday violence*, p. 199.
16 Fitzpatrick, *The two Irelands* (Oxford, 1998), p. 69.

Select bibliography

PRIMARY SOURCES

A. MANUSCRIPTS

Ballinamore
Leitrim County Library
Absent voters' register, October 1918.
Andrew Mooney papers.
Charles Eddie McGoohan papers.
Daniel Gallogly papers.
Leitrim war dead.
Local Studies oral history collection, audio 263.
Minute books of Ballinamore Rural District Council.
Minute books of Carrick-on-Shannon District Council.
Minute books of Kinlough District Council.
Minute books of Manorhamilton District Council.
Minute books of Mohill Rural District Council.
Muldoon files.

Belfast
Public Record Office of Northern Ireland
J.M. Wilson papers.

Dublin
Military Archives
Bureau of Military History witness statements.
Civil War operation and intelligence files: Athlone and Western Commands.
Military Service Pensions Collection.

National Archives of Ireland
Colonial Office, CO 904/, Dublin Castle Special Branch files.
County Inspectors' monthly confidential reports.
Sinn Féin and republican suspects, 1899–1921.
Damage to Property Compensation Act 1923, Register of claims.
Dáil Éireann Local Government papers.

National Library of Ireland
Count Plunkett papers.
John Redmond papers.
Maurice Moore papers.
Robert Brennan papers.

Representative Church Body Library
Archives of the Diocese of Kilmore, Elphin and Ardagh.

Diocesan reports.
Records relating to diocesan clegy and officers, 1819–2000.
Rural deans' reports and visitations.

University College Dublin Archives
Éamon de Valera papers.
Eoin O'Duffy papers.
Ernie O'Malley notebooks.
Ernie O'Malley papers.
Richard Mulcahy papers.
Seán Mac Eoin papers.

London
National Archives
Colonial Office papers.
Home Office papers.
Irish Distress Committee and Irish Grants Committee records.
War Office papers.

Longford
Archives of the Diocese of Ardagh and Clonmacnoise (Roman Catholic)
Clergy parochial records.

B. OFFICIAL RECORDS

Census of Ireland, 1911.
Dáil Éireann debates.
Hansard 5 *(Commons), The parliamentary debates, fifth series, 1909–81.*

C. NEWSPAPERS AND PERIODICALS

An Claidheamh Soluis
Anglo-Celt
An tÓglach
Donegal Democrat
Donegal News
Fermanagh Herald
Fermanagh Times
Freeman's Journal
Iris
Irish Bulletin
Irish Catholic
Irish Independent
Irish Times

Leitrim Advertiser
Leitrim Guardian
Leitrim News
Leitrim Observer
Longford Leader
Roscommon Herald
Roscommon Messenger
Sinn Féin
Sligo Independent
Sligo Nationalist
Strokestown Democrat
Ulster Herald
Weekly Freeman's Journal

D. CONTEMPORANEOUS PRINTED PRIMARY MATERIAL

Breen, Dan, *My fight for Irish freedom* (Dublin, 1924).
Dixon McDougall, Margaret, *The letters of Norah on her tour through Ireland* (Montreal, 1882).
Figgis, Darrell, *Recollections of the Irish war* (London, 1927).
MacGiolla Choille, Brendán (ed.), *Intelligence notes, 1913–16* (Dublin, 1966).
O'Hegarty, P.S., *The victory of Sinn Féin* (Dublin, 1924).
O'Malley, Ernie, *On another man's wound* (London, 1936).
War record of the St John's Ambulance Brigade and the British Red Cross Society in Leinster, Munster and Connaught, 1914–1918 (Dublin, 1919).

SECONDARY SOURCES

E. PUBLISHED WORKS

Augusteijn, Joost, *From public defiance to guerrilla warfare: the experience of ordinary Volunteers in the Irish War of Independence, 1916–1921* (Dublin, 1996).
——, (ed.), *The Irish Revolution, 1913–1923* (London, 2002).
Barry, Tom, *Guerrilla days in Ireland* (Tralee, 1962).
Becker, Jean-Jacques, *The Great War and the French people* (Paris, 1985).
Bew, Paul, 'Sinn Féin and agrarian radicalism, 1919–1921' in D.G. Boyce (ed.), *The revolution in Ireland, 1879–1923* (Dublin, 1988), pp 217–34.
——, *Ideology and the Irish question: Ulster unionism and Irish nationalism, 1912–1916* (New York, 1994).
——, *Ireland: the politics of enmity, 1789–2006* (Oxford, 2007).
——, 'The politics of war' in John Horne (ed.), *Our war: Ireland and the Great War* (Dublin, 2008), pp 95–129.
Bielenberg, Andy, 'Exodus: the emigration of southern Irish Protestants during the Irish War of Independence and the Civil War', *Past & Present*, 218:1 (2013), 199–233.
Borgonovo, John (ed.), *Spies, informers and the Anti-Sinn Féin Society: the intelligence war in Cork city, 1920–1921* (Dublin, 2007).
——, *The dynamics of war and revolution: Cork city, 1916–1918* (Cork, 2013).
Bowman, Tim, 'Propaganda, political rhetoric and identity' in Bertrand Taithe and Tim Thornton (eds), *War: identities in conflict, 1300–2000* (Stroud, 1999), pp 227–43.
Boyce, D.G., '"That party politics should divide our tents": nationalism, unionism and the First World War' in Adrian Gregory and Senia Pašeta (eds), *Ireland and the Great War: 'A war to unite us all?'* (Manchester, 2002), pp 190–222.
Boyle, Ken, and Tim Desmond, *The murder of Dr Muldoon: a suspect priest, a widow's fight for justice* (Cork, 2019).
Brady, Conor, *Guardians of the peace* (Dublin, 2000 [1974]).
Bull, Philip, *Land, politics and nationalism: a study of the Irish land question* (Dublin, 1996).
——, 'Land and politics, 1879–1903' in D.G. Boyce (ed.), *The revolution in Ireland, 1879–1923* (Dublin, 1998), pp 23–46.

Byrne, Elaine, *Political corruption in Ireland, 1922–2010: a crooked harp?* (Manchester, 2012).
Callan, Patrick, 'Recruiting for the British army in Ireland during the First World War', *Irish Sword*, 17:66 (1987), 42–56.
Campbell, Fergus, *Land and revolution: nationalist politics in the West of Ireland, 1891–1921* (Oxford, 2005).
Casey, P.J., K.T. Cullen and J.P. Duignan (eds), *Irish doctors in the First World War* (Sallins, 2015).
Clark, Gemma, *Everyday violence in the Irish Civil War* (Cambridge, 2014).
Clear, Caitríona, 'Fewer ladies, more women' in John Horne (ed.), *Our war: Ireland and the Great War* (Dublin, 2008), pp 157–71.
Codd, Pauline, 'Recruiting and responses to the War in Wexford' in David Fitzpatrick (ed.), *Ireland and the First World War* (Dublin, 1986), pp 15–26.
Coleman, Marie, *Longford and the Irish Revolution* (Dublin, 2002).
——, 'Mobilization: the South Longford bye-election and its impact on political mobilization' in Joost Augusteijn (ed.), *The Irish Revolution, 1913–1923* (Hampshire, 2002), pp 53–69.
——, *The Irish Revolution, 1912–1923* (London, 2014).
——, 'Violence against women during the Irish War of Independence, 1919–21' in Diarmaid Ferriter and Susannah Riordan (eds), *Years of turbulence: the Irish Revolution and its aftermath* (Dublin, 2015), pp 137–55.
Conway, Vicky, *Policing twentieth-century Ireland: a history of an Garda Siochána* (Oxford, 2014).
Coogan, Oliver, *Politics and war in Meath, 1913–1923* (Dublin, 1983).
Costello, Francis, *The Irish Revolution and its aftermath, 1916–1923* (Dublin, 2003).
Cousins, Mel, 'The creation of association: the National Insurance Act, 1911 and approved societies in Ireland' in J. Kelly and R.V. Comerford (eds), *Associational culture in Ireland and abroad* (Dublin, 2010), pp 155–212.
Crowley, John, Donal Ó Drisceoil, Mike Murphy & John Boganovo (eds), *Atlas of the Irish Revolution* (Cork, 2017).
Curtis, Maurice, *The splendid cause: the Catholic social movement in Ireland in the twentieth century* (Dublin, 2009).
——, *A challenge to democracy: militant Catholicism in modern Ireland* (Dublin, 2010).
Daly, Mary E., *The buffer state: the historical roots of the Department of the Environment* (Dublin, 1997).
De Bromhead, Alan, Alan Fernihough & Enda Hargaden, 'Representation of the people: franchise extention and the 'Sinn Féin' election in Ireland, 1918', Queen's University Centre for Economic History, working paper, 2018–08.
Dewey, P.E., 'Nutrition and living standards in wartime Britain' in Richard Wall & Jay Winter (eds), *The upheaval of war: family, work and welfare in Europe, 1914–1918* (Cambridge 1988), pp 197–220.
Dolan, Anne, '"Spies and informers beware"' in Diarmaid Ferriter and Susannah Riordan (eds), *Years of turbulence: the Irish Revolution and its aftermath* (Dublin, 2015), pp 157–72.
Dooley, Tom, 'Politics, bands and marketing: army recruitment in Waterford city, 1915–1915', *Irish Sword*, 18:72 (1991), 205–19.

Dooley, Terence, *The decline of the Big House in Ireland: a study of Irish landed families, 1860–1960* (Dublin, 1999).
——, *'The land for the people': the land question in independent Ireland* (Dublin, 2004).
Dougan, Quincey, *Leitrim: a county at war* (Carrick-on-Shannon, 2015).
Downes, Margaret, 'The civilian voluntary aid effort' in David Fitzpatrick (ed.), *Ireland and the First World War* (Dublin, 1986), pp 27–37.
Dunbar, Holly, 'Women and alcohol during the First World War in Ireland', *Women's History Review*, 25:6 (2016), 379–96.
Dungan, Myles, *Distant drums: Irish soldiers in foreign armies* (Belfast, 1993).
Fanning, Ronan, *Fatal path: British government and Irish Revolution, 1910–1922* (London, 2013).
Farrell, Brian, *The founding of Dáil Éireann: parliament and nation building* (Dublin, 1971).
Farry, Michael, *Sligo, 1914–1921: a chronicle of conflict, 1914–1921* (Trim, 1992).
——, *The aftermath of revolution, Sligo, 1921–23* (Dublin, 2000).
——, *Sligo: the Irish Revolution, 1912–23* (Dublin, 2012).
Fearin, J., and D. Laitin, 'Ethnicity, insurgency and Civil War', *American Political Science Review*, 97:1 (2003), 75–90.
Ferguson, Niall, *The pity of war* (London, 1998).
Ferriter, Diarmaid, *A nation and not a rabble: the Irish Revolution, 1913–1923* (London, 2015).
Fitzpatrick, David, *Politics and Irish life, 1913–1921: provincial experiences of war and revolution* (Cork, 1977).
——, 'The geography of Irish nationalism, 1910–1921', *Past and Present*, 78 (1978), 113–44.
——, (ed.), *Revolution?; Ireland, 1917–1923* (Dublin, 1990).
——, 'The logic of collective sacrifice: Ireland and the British army, 1914–1918', *Historical Journal*, 38:4 (1995), 1017–30.
—— (ed.), *Ireland and the First World War* (Dublin, 1996).
——, *The two Irelands* (Oxford, 1998).
——, 'Home front and everyday life' in John Horne (ed.), *Our war: Ireland and the Great War* (Dublin, 2008), pp 131–42.
——, 'Protestant depopulation and the Irish Revolution', *Irish Historical Studies*, 38:152 (2013), 643–61.
Foster, Gavin, 'Class dismissed? The debate over a social basis to the Irish Civil War', *Saothar: Journal of the Irish Labour History Society*, 33 (2008), 73–86.
——, '"No Wild Geese this time"? IRA emigration after the Irish Civil War', *Éire-Ireland*, 47:1 (2012), 94–122.
——, *The Irish Civil War and society: politics, class and conflict* (New York, 2015).
Gallogly, Daniel, *Ballinamore Seán O'Heslins', 1889–1984* (Cavan, 1984).
——, *Slieve an Iariann slopes: history of the town and parish of Ballinamore, Co. Leitrim* (Ballinamore, 1991).
——, *The diocese of Kilmore, 1800–1950* (Cavan, 1999).
Garton, Stephen, 'The dominions, Ireland and India' in Robert Gerwarth and Erez Manela (eds), *Empires at war* (Oxford, 2014), pp 152–77.
Garvin, Tom, *The evolution of Irish nationalist politics* (Dublin, 1981).

——, *1922: the birth of Irish democracy* (Dublin, 1996).
Gerwarth, Robert, and Erez Manela (eds), *Empires at war* (Oxford, 2014).
Gerwarth, Robert, *The vanquished: why the First World War failed to end, 1917–1923* (London, 2016).
Gilley, Sheridan, 'The Catholic Church and revolution' in D.G. Boyce (ed.), *The revolution in Ireland, 1879–1923* (Dublin, 1988), pp 157–72.
Grayzel, Susan R., *Women's identities at war: gender, motherhood, and politics in Britain and France during the First World War* (London, 1999).
Gregory, Adrian, *The last great war: British society and the First World War* (Cambridge, 2002).
Guckian, Des, *Deported: an undesirable alien* (Dromod, 1986).
Hart, Peter, 'The Protestant experience of revolution in Southern Ireland' in Richard English and Graham Walker (eds), *Unionism in modern Ireland: new perspectives on politics and culture* (New York, 1996), pp 81–99.
——, 'The geography of the Irish Revolution, 1917–1923', *Past and Present*, 155:1 (1997), 142–76.
——, *The IRA and its enemies: violence and community in Cork, 1916–1923* (Oxford, 1998).
——, *The IRA at war, 1916–1923* (Oxford, 2003).
Hay, Marnie, 'The foundation and development of Na Fianna Éireann, 1909–16', *Irish Historical Studies*, 36:141 (2008), 53–71.
——, *Bulmer Hobson and the nationalist movement in twentieth-century Ireland* (Manchester, 2009).
——, *Na Fianna Éireann and the Irish Revolution, 1909–23: scouting for rebels* (Manchester, 2019).
Heffernan, Brian, *Freedom and the fifth commandment: Catholic priests and political violence in Ireland, 1919–21* (Manchester, 2014).
Hegarty Thorne, Kathleen, *They put the flag a'flyin: the Roscommon Volunteers, 1916–1923* (Oregon, 2005).
Hepburn, A.C., 'The Ancient Order of Hibernians in Irish politics, 1905–1914', *Cithara*, 10 (1971), 5–18.
——, *A past apart: studies in the history of Catholic Belfast, 1850–1950* (Belfast, 1996).
Hopkinson, Michael, *Green against green: the Irish Civil War* (Dublin, 1988).
——, 'The Craig-Collins pacts of 1922: two attempted reforms of the Northern Ireland government', *Irish Historical Studies*, 27:106 (1990), 145–58.
——, *The Irish War of Independence* (Dublin, 2002).
Horne, John, 'Social identity in war: France, 1914–1918' in T.G. Fraser and K. Jeffery (eds), *Men, women and war* (Dublin, 1993), pp 119–35.
——, *State, society and mobilization in Europe during the First World War* (Cambridge, 1997).
—— (ed.), *Our war: Ireland and the Great War* (Dublin, 2008).
Hoschild, Adam, *To end all wars: a story of loyalty and rebellion, 1914–1918* (Boston, 2011).
Hughes, Brian, 'Persecuting the Peelers' in David Fitzpatrick (ed.), *Terror in Ireland, 1916–1923* (Dublin, 2012), pp 206–18.
——, *Defying the IRA? Intimidation, coercion, and communities during the Irish Revolution* (Liverpool, 2016).

Jackson, Alvin, *Home rule: an Irish history, 1800–2000* (Oxford, 2003).
Jeffery, Keith, *Ireland and the Great War* (Cambridge, 2000).
Kadel, Bradley, *Drink and culture in nineteenth-century Ireland: the alcohol trade and the politics of the Irish public house* (London, 2015).
Kalyvas, Stathis N., *The logic of violence in civil war* (Cambridge, 2006).
Kautt, William H., *Ambushes and armour: the Irish rebellion, 1919–21* (Dublin, 2010).
——, *Ground truths: British army operations in the Irish War of Independence* (Kildare, 2014).
Kelly, Jennifer, 'Popular attitudes to formal medical care in early-nineteenth-century County Leitrim', *Breifne: Journal of Cumann Seanchais Bhreifne*, 11:44 (2008), 573–86.
Kelly, M.J., *The Fenian ideal and Irish nationalism, 1882–1916* (Woodbridge, 2006).
Kissane, Bill, *The politics of the Irish Civil War* (Oxford, 2005).
Kostick, Conor, *Revolution in Ireland: popular militancy, 1917–1923* (Cork, 2009).
Kotsonouris, Mary, *Retreat from revolution: the Dáil Courts, 1920–24* (Dublin, 1994).
Laffan, Michael, '"Labour must wait": Ireland's conservative revolution' in Patrick J. Corish (ed.), *Radicals, rebels and establishments* (Belfast, 1985), pp 203–22.
——, *The resurrection of Ireland: the Sinn Féin party, 1916–1923* (Cambridge, 1999).
Lawson, Kay, and Peter H. Merkl (eds), *When parties fail: emerging alternative organizations* (Princeton, 1988).
Lee, Joe, *Ireland, 1912–1985: politics and society* (Cambridge, 1989).
Leeson, D.M., *The Black and Tans: British police and Auxiliaries in the Irish War of Independence* (Oxford, 2011).
Leonard, Jane, 'Getting them at last: the IRA and ex-servicemen' in David Fizpatrick (ed.), *Revolution? Ireland, 1917–1923* (Dublin, 1990), pp 118–29.
Lowe, W.J., 'The war against the RIC, 1919–1921', *Éire-Ireland*, 37:3–4 (2002), 79–117.
Lynch, Robert, *The northern IRA and the early years of partition* (Dublin, 2006).
——, *Revolutionary Ireland, 1916–1923* (London, 2015).
Lyons, F.S.L., *The Irish Parliamentary Party, 1890–1910* (London, 1951).
——, 'The two faces of home rule' in Kevin B. Nowlan (ed.), *The making of 1916* (Dublin, 1969), pp 99–127.
——, *Culture and anarchy in Ireland, 1890–1939* (Oxford, 1982).
Macardle, Dorothy, *The Irish Republic: a documented chronicle* (London, 1968).
MacAtasney, Gerard, *Seán Mac Diarmada: the mind of the revolution* (Manorhamilton, 2004).
Marwick, Arthur, *The deluge: British society and the First World War* (London, 1965).
Maume, Patrick, *The long gestation: Irish nationalist life, 1891–1918* (Dublin, 1999).
McCall, Ernest, *The Auxiliaries, Tudor's toughs: a study of the Auxiliary Division Royal Irish Constabulary, 1920–1922* (Newtownards, 2013).
McCarthy, Brian, *The Civic Guard mutiny* (Cork, 2012).
McCluskey, Fergal, *Tyrone: the Irish Revolution, 1912–23* (Dublin, 2014).
McConnel, James, 'The franchise factor in the defeat of the Irish Parliamentary Party, 1885–1918', *Historical Journal*, 47:2 (2004), 355–77.
——, 'Recruiting sergeants for John Bull? Irish nationalist MPs and enlistment during the early months of the Great War', *War in History*, 14:4 (2007), 408–28.
——, *The Irish Parliamentary Party and the third home rule crisis* (Dublin, 2013).

——, '"*Après la guerre*": John Redmond, the Irish Volunteers and armed constitutionalism, 1913–1915', *English Historical Review*, 131:553 (2016), 1445–70.
McConville, Seán, *Irish political prisoners, 1848–1922: theatre of war* (London, 2002).
McDowell, R.B., *Crisis and decline: the fate of southern unionists* (Dublin, 1995).
McGarry, Fearghal, *Eoin O'Duffy: a self-made hero* (Oxford, 2005).
McGreevy, Ronan, *Wherever the firing line extends: Ireland and the Western Front* (Dublin, 2016).
McMahon, Timothy G., *Grand opportunity: the Gaelic Revival and Irish society, 1893–1910* (Syracuse, 2008).
McNamara, Conor, 'A Tenants' League or a Shopkeepers' League?: urban protest and the Town Tenants' Association in the West of Ireland, 1909–1918', *Studia Hibernica*, 36 (2009–10), 135–60.
Malcolm, Elizabeth, *The Irish policeman, 1822–1922: a life* (Dublin, 2006).
Miller, David W., *Church, state and nation in Ireland, 1898–1921* (Dublin, 1973).
Miller, Ian, *Reforming food in post-Famine Ireland: medicine, science and improvement, 1845–1922* (Manchester, 2014).
Mitchell, Arthur, *Revolutionary government in Ireland: Dáil Éireann, 1919–22* (Dublin, 1995).
Moffitt, Miriam, 'The Protestant experience of revolution in County Leitrim, 1911–1928', *Breifne*, 12:46 (2011), 303–23.
Morrison, Eve, 'Kilmichael revisited: Tom Barry and the "false surrender"' in David Fitzpatrick (ed.), *Terror in Ireland, 1916–1923* (Dublin, 2012), pp 158–80.
Mullin, Katherine, 'Irish chastity? British Social Purity Associations and the Irish Free State' in J. Kelly and R.V. Comerford (eds), *Associational culture in Ireland and abroad* (Dublin, 2010), pp 141–54.
Mulvagh, Conor, *The Irish Parliamentary Party at Westminster, 1900–18* (Manchester, 2016).
Murphy, Seán and Síle Murphy, *The Comeraghs, gunfire and Civil War: the story of the Déise Brigade IRA, 1914–1924* (Kilmacthomas, 2003).
Murphy, William, 'The GAA during the Irish Revolution' in Mike Cronin, William Murphy and Paul Rouse (eds), *The Gaelic Athletic Association, 1884–2009* (Dublin, 2009), pp 61–76.
——, 'Enniscorthy's revolution' in Mícheál Tóibín and Colm Tóibín (eds), *Enniscorthy: a history* (Wexford, 2010), pp 399–423.
——, 'A various and contentious country' in Paul Daly, Ronan O'Brien and Paul Rouse (eds), *Making the difference? The Irish Labour Party, 1912–2012* (Cork, 2012), pp 4–16.
——, *Political imprisonment and the Irish, 1912–1921* (Oxford, 2014).
Murray, Patrick, *Oracles of God: the Roman Catholic Church and Irish politics, 1922–37* (Dublin, 2000).
Newell, Úna, *The West must wait: County Galway and the Irish Free State, 1922–32* (Manchester, 2015).
Nic Dháibhéid, Caoimhe, 'The Irish National Aid Association and the radicalization of public opinion in Ireland, 1916–1918', *Historical Journal*, 55:3 (2012), 705–29.
Novick, Ben, 'Propaganda 1: advanced nationalist propaganda and moralistic revolution, 1914–18' in Joost Augusteijn (ed.), *The Irish Revolution, 1913–1923* (New York, 2002), pp 34–52.

——, *Conceiving revolution: Irish nationalist propaganda during the First World War* (Dublin, 2001).
Nowlan, Kevin B. (ed.), *The making of 1916* (Dublin, 1969).
O'Callaghan, John, *Revolutionary Limerick: the republican campaign for independence in Limerick, 1913–1921* (Dublin, 2010).
O'Callaghan, Micheál, *For Ireland and freedom: Roscommon's contribution to the fight for independence, 1917–21* (Boyle, 1991).
O'Carroll, Ross, 'The GAA and the First World War, 1914–18' in Gearóid Ó Tuathaigh (ed.), *The GAA and revolution in Ireland* (Cork, 2015), pp 85–104.
O'Day, Alan, *Irish home rule, 1867–1921* (Manchester, 1998).
Ó Duibhir, Ciarán, *Sinn Féin: the first election 1908* (Manorhamilton, 1993).
Ó Duibhir, Liam, *The Donegal awakening, Donegal and the War of Independence* (Dublin, 2009).
——, *Donegal and the Civil War* (Dublin, 2011).
——, *Prisoners of War, Ballykinlar Internment Camp, 1920–1921* (Cork, 2013).
O'Farrell, Padraic, *The Seán Mac Eoin story* (Dublin, 1981).
Ó Fearaíl, Pádraig, *The story of Conradh na Gaelige* (Dublin, 1975).
Ó Gadhra, Nollaig, *Civil War in Connacht, 1922–1923* (Cork, 1999).
O'Halpin, Eunan, *Defending Ireland: the Irish state and its enemies since 1922* (Oxford, 1999).
——, 'Counting terror: Bloody Sunday and the dead of the Irish Revolution' in David Fitzatrick (ed.), *Terror in Ireland, 1916–1923* (Dublin, 2012), pp 141–57.
——, 'Problematic killing during the War of Independence and its aftermath' in James Kelly and Mary Ann Lyons (eds), *Death and dying in Ireland, Britain and Europe: historical perspectives* (Sallins, 2013), pp 317–48.
O'Malley, Ernie, *Rising out: Seán Connolly of Longford* (Dublin, 2007).
O'Neill, Clare, 'Unity in adversity: associational culture in Ireland during the First World War' in J. Kelly and R.V. Comerford (eds), *Associational culture in Ireland and abroad* (Dublin, 2010), pp 165–78.
O'Reilly, Colm, 'Bishop Joseph Hoare: a conflicted prelate and patriot', *Teathbha*, 4:4 (2017), 355–7.
O'Riordan, Maeve, 'Titled women and voluntary war work in Ireland during the First World War: a case study of Ethel, Lady Inchiquin', *Women's History Review*, 27:3 (2016), 360–78.
Ó Súilleabháin, Cormac, *Leitrim's republican story, 1900–2000* (Ballinamore, 2014).
Ó Súilleabháin, Seán, *History of Leitrim GAA, 1886–1984* (Ballinamore, 1985).
O'Sullivan, Donal J., *The Irish constabularies, 1822–1922: a century of policing in Ireland* (Dingle, 1999).
Orr, Phillip, *The road to the Somme: men of the Ulster Division tell their story* (Belfast, 2008).
——, '200,000 volunteer soldiers' in John Horne (ed.), *Our war: Ireland and the Great War* (Dublin, 2008), pp 63–77.
Osborne, John M., *The voluntary recruiting movement in Britain, 1914–1918* (London, 1982).
Panikos, Panayi, *Prisoners of Britain: German civilian and combatant internees during the First World War* (Manchester, 2012).

Pennell, Catriona, *A kingdom united: popular responses to the outbreak of the First World War in Ireland and Britain* (Oxford, 2012).
Regan, John M., *The Irish counter-revolution, 1921–1936: treatyite politics and settlement in independent Ireland* (Cambridge, 1999).
—— , 'The "Bandon Valley massacre" as a historical problem', *History: The Journal of the Historical Society*, 97:325 (2012), 70–98.
—— (ed.), *Myth and the Irish state: historical problems and other essays* (Dublin, 2013).
Reid, Colin, 'The Irish Party and the Volunteers: politics and the home rule army, 1913–1916' in Caoimhe Nic Dháibhéid and Colin Reid (eds), *From Parnell to Paisley: constitutional and revolutionary politics in modern Ireland* (Dublin, 2010), pp 33–55.
Reilly, Eileen, 'Cavan in the era of the Great War, 1914–1918' in Raymond Gillespie (ed.), *Cavan: essays on the history of an Irish County* (Kildare, 1995), pp 177–97.
—— , 'Women and voluntary war work' in Adrian Gregory and Senia Pašeta (eds), *Ireland and the Great War: 'A war to unite us all '?* (Manchester, 2002), pp 49–72.
Rooney, Dominic, 'Manorhamilton's Irish Volunteers 1914', *Leitrim Guardian* (2001), 47–9.
Rumpf, E., and A.C. Hepburn, *Nationalism and socialism in twentieth-century Ireland* (New York, 1977).
Ryan, Louise, and Margaret Ward (eds), *Irish women and nationalism: soldiers, new women and wicked hags* (Kildare, 2004).
Scott, James C., *Domination and the arts of resistance: hidden transcripts* (London, 1990).
Seth Jones, David, *Graziers, land reform and political conflict in Ireland* (Washington, 1995).
Sheehan, Aideen, 'Cumann na mBan' in David Fitzpatrick (ed.), *Revolution?: Ireland, 1917–1923* (Dublin, 1990).
Sheehan, William, *Hearts and mines: the British 5th Division in Ireland, 1920–1922* (Cork, 2009).
Smith, John, 'The Oldcastle prisoner of war camp, 1914–1918', *Ríocht na Midhe*, 12 (2010), 212–50.
Staunton, Martin, 'Kilrush, Co. Clare and the Royal Munster Fusiliers', *Irish Sword*, 15:65 (1986), 268–72.
Swiftcork, Roger, *Irish migrants in Britain, 1815–1914: a documentary history, 1815–1914* (Cork, 2002).
Taylor, Paul, *Heroes or traitors: experiences of southern Irish soldiers returning from the Great War, 1919–1939* (Liverpool, 2015).
Tilly, Charles, *Rebellious century, 1830–1930* (London, 1975).
—— , 'From mobilization to revolution' in Ernesto Castenada and Cathy Lisa Scheider (eds), *Collective violence, contentious politics and social change* (New York, 2017), pp 71–91.
Townshend, Charles, 'The Irish Republican Army and the development of guerrilla warfare, 1916–21', *English Historical Review*, 94 (1979), 318–45.
—— , *Easter 1916: the Irish rebellion* (London, 2005).
—— , *The Republic: the fight for Irish independence* (London, 2013).
Vaughan W.E., and A.J. Fitzpatrick (eds), *Irish historical statistics: population, 1821–1971* (Dublin, 1978).

Verley, Jeffrey, *The spirit of 1914: militarism, myth and mobilization in Germany* (Cambridge, 2000).
Walker, B.M. (ed.), *Parliamentary election results in Ireland, 1801–1922* (Dublin, 1978).
Walsh, Fionnuala, '"Every human life is a national importance": the impact of the First World War on attitudes to maternal and infant health' in David Durnin and Ian Miller (eds), *Medicine, health and Irish experiences of conflict, 1914–45* (Manchester, 2017), pp 15–27.
Ward, Margaret, *Unmanageable revolutionaries: women and Irish nationalism* (London, 1989).
Watson, J.S.K., 'Khaki girls, VADs and Tommy's sisters: gender and class in First World War Britain', *International History Review*, 19:2 (1997), 32–51.
Whearity, Peter, '"Come and find sanctuary in Éire": the experiences of Ireland's Belgian refugees during the First World War', *Historical Studies in Ethnicity, Migration and Diaspora*, 34:2 (2016), 192–209.
Wheatley, Michael, *Nationalism and the Irish Party: provincial Ireland, 1910–1916* (Oxford, 2005).
Whelan, Michael, 'Selton Hill', *Leitrim Guardian* (1970), 30–40.
White, Francis, *Glenfarne: a history* (Glenfarne, 2014).
Wilk, Gavin, *Transatlantic defiance: the militant Irish republican movement in America, 1923–1945* (New York, 2014).
Younger, Calton, *Ireland's Civil War* (London, 1966).

F. THESES AND UNPUBLISHED WORK

Cahalan, Peter, 'The treatment of Belgian refugees in England during the Great War' (PhD, McMaster University, 1977).
Callan, Patrick, 'Voluntary recruiting for the British army in Ireland during the First World War' (PhD, UCD, 1984).
McCaul, Oliver Patrick, 'The divided political landscape of County Cavan, 1912–1922' (MA, NUI Maynooth, 2002).
McEvoy, John Noel, 'A study of the United Irish League in King's County, 1899–1918' (MA, NUI Maynooth, 1992).
McNamara, Conor, 'Politics and society in East Galway, 1914–1921' (PhD, St Patrick's College/DCU, 2009).
O'Neill, Clare, 'The Irish home front, 1914–1918 with particular reference to the treatment of Belgian refugees, prisoners-of-war, enemy aliens and war casualties' (PhD, NUI Maynooth, 2006).
Walsh, Fionnuala, 'The impact of the Great War on women in Ireland' (PhD, TCD, 2015).
White, John, 'Revolution in counties Carlow, Kildare and Wicklow? A regional study' (MA, Mater Dei Institute/DCU, 2010).

G. INTERNET SOURCES

https://www.cso.ie/en/census/censusvolumes1926to1991/historicalreports/census1926reports/census1926volume2–occupations/ (4 May 2016).

Index

Aiken, Frank, 112, 130
Aliens Restriction Act, 31
Allen, Elsie, 30
Allen, Richard, 30
An tÓglach, 87, 155
Ancient Order of Hibernians (AOH), 3, 5–6, 8, 14, 19, 21, 22, 27, 38, 40, 44, 47, 50, 51, 53, 54, 56, 61, 62, 80; growth of membership, 5; North Leitrim by-election, 9–10; rivalry with UIL, 10; Volunteer formation, 15; Sinn Fein support, 48–9
Anderson, Bertie, 56
Anglo-Celt, 3, 17, 78, 86, 87, 92, 113
Anglo-Irish Treaty, 103, 106–11, 115–16, 134
Anglo-Irish truce 103; breaches of, 105
Annaduff, 5, 47, 88, 93
anti-Treaty IRA, *see* Arigna column, 110, 111, 112, 114, 115, 116, 124, 127, 128, 130
Ardagh and Clonmacnoise (Diocese), 8
Ardcarne, Co. Roscommon, 117
Ardrum, 77
Arigna, 1, 30, 46, 74, 106
Arigna column, 117–19, 120, 122–3, 125–8, 130, 134; *see* anti-Treaty IRA
Armstrong, Dr Samuel, 28
Arvagh, Co. Cavan, 92
Ashe, Thomas, 47
Ashley, Wilfred, 80
Asquith, Herbert Henry, 12, 16, 18, 22, 38, 41
Athlone, County Westmeath, 89, 116, 119
Aughavas, 3, 66, 78–9, 88, 90
Aughawillan, 57, 62
Aughnasheelin, 46, 56, 58, 108
Austin, Sergeant A.M., 94
Auxiliaries, *see* RIC

Balbriggan, Co. Dublin, 86
Ballaghameehan, 121
Ballinaglera, 41, 44, 45, 101
Ballinamore, 2, 3, 6, 8, 17, 24, 29, 30, 44–6, 49, 59, 61, 65, 74, 76–8, 80, 82–4, 87–8, 92–3, 95, 100, 104–5, 121–2, 125–6, 128
Ballinawig, 93
Ballyconnell, Co. Cavan, 124–6
Ballykinlar, Co. Down, 90–1
Banks, James, 119
Baxter, Captain, 126–7
Baxter Michael, 95
Bayly, Revd Thomas, 101
Beirne, Joe, 95
Belcoo, Co. Fermanagh, 112, 120
Belfast boycott, 98–9, 102, 111, 134
Belgian refugees, 29–30
Belgian Relief Fund, 29–30
Belgium, 18, 23–4, 35, 54
Benbulben mountains, 119
Benson, Harry, 120
Bere Island, Co. Cork, 90
Beresford, Revd, 87
Black and Tans, *see* RIC
Blacklion, Co. Cavan, 112
Bofin, Edward (Ned), 117, 119, 124
Bofin, Paul, 128
Boland, Harry, 45, 47
Bornacoola, 22, 55
Boundary Commission, 124
Boylan, Matthew, 93, 97
Boyle, Co. Roscommon, 23, 81, 83, 96, 114–18, 121, 125–6
Brady, Fr John, 117
Brady, Hugh, 46, 47, 77, 88, 92, 100
Brady, Margaret, 62, 99
Brady, Private Phillip, 118
Brennan, Michael, 110
Briody, Patrick, 13, 18–19, 87
British army: recruiting campaigns, 22, 24–5, 27, 58–9; arrival in 1920, 80; Sheemore ambush, 93–4; Selton Hill, 95–6; countywide searches, 101;

165

withdrawal, 108, 110; Bedfordshire and Hertfordshire Regiment, 81, 93, 94; East Yorkshire Regiment, 80, 81, 83, 85; Royal Irish Regiment, 24; Royal Munster Fusiliers, 21; Royal Sussex Regiment, 81, 110; Royal Army Medical Corps, 28; Royal Dublin Fusiliers, 34; Sherwood Foresters, 37
British Nationality and Status of Aliens Act, 31
Brown, Judge, 25, 57, 67, 88
Bruree, Co Limerick, 74
Bundoran, Co. Donegal, 17, 34, 116
Bush Hotel, 44, 62, 84, 115

Cahill, Fr Philip, 41
Callaghan, Private Andrew, 126
Calry, Co. Sligo, 56
Campbell, Patrick, 122
Canning, Hugh, 111
Canon Donohue hall, 35, 48
Carrigallen, 6, 16, 18–19, 47, 66, 87, 121–2
Carrick-on-Shannon (Carrick), 2, 3, 6, 13, 15, 17, 20, 22, 25–30, 32–4, 36–40, 43–5, 47–8, 51–2, 55–9, 62, 65, 67–8, 70–1, 73–9, 81, 83, 85, 86, 87–9, 91–6, 100, 104, 105, 107–8, 112–13, 115–19, 121, 123, 126, 128
Carroll, Paddy, 119
Carson, Edward, 12, 16, 39
Carter, Michael, 10, 14, 51
Carter, Tom, 118
Casement, Roger, 36
Casey, Fr John, 120
Cashel, 51
Catholic Church: 1, 8, 23, 30, 35, 44, 132; anti-GAA, 6; anti-Parnell, 8; AOH, 8; dioceses, 8; involvement in Volunteer formation, 15; clerical support for recruiting, 23; condemnation of 1916 Rising, 37; condemnation of post-1916 Rising repression, 38; clerical support for Sinn Féin, 44, 79; anti-conscription campaign, 55–6; condemation of IRA violence, 68, 93, 96; condemnation of anti-Treaty IRA violence, 129
cattle drives, 13, 108, 112, 113

Cavan, County, 3, 5, 16, 25, 41, 54, 101, 112, 124, 126
census 1911, 1
census 1925 (Northern Ireland), 124
Central Council for the Organisation of Recruiting in Ireland (CCORI), 23, 26
Cheevers, Captain, 25
Church of Ireland, 1, 8, 41, 87
Civic Guard, 111, 116, 121–2
Civil Service Commission, 106
Civil War, 1, 110–30, 134; *see also* National Army; Irish Republican Army (IRA)
Clancy, Fr Patrick, 23
Clare, County, 45, 110
Clarke, Thomas J., 33
Clones, Co. Monaghan, 112
Cloone, 40, 46, 49, 54, 59, 76, 8, 80, 90, 130, 132
Clooneagh, 64
Clyne, Jimmy, 34
Collins, Michael, 45, 84, 97, 107, 110–11, 118, 130
Collinstown, Co. Dublin, 90
Commercial Hotel, 28
Conboy, Jane, 31
Conefrey, Pat, 87
Congested District Board, 114
Connolly, Bernard, 44, 68
Connolly, James (1916 Rising leader), 36
Connolly, James (Senior), 86
Connolly, James (Junior), 86, 116
Connolly, Seán, 91, 95, 102
conscription, 17, 19, 20, 21–2, 25–7, 30, 34–5, 37, 41, 43, 59, 63, 131–2; conscription crisis 1918, 52–6
Cork, County, 90
Cork Examiner, 12
Cormongan, 126
Cosgrave, William, 45, 47, 103, 117
Coulter, Revd Issac, 16
Craig–Collins pact, 111
Criminal Investigation Division, 129
Crimlin, 84
Crofton, Amy, 29
Crofton, Captain Duke, 17, 22, 30, 31
Crofton, Major James, 15
Crowther, Lieutenant, 71

Index

Cull, Michael, 124–5
Cull, Owen, 128
Cull, Séamus, 126
Cumann na mBan, 46, 47, 62, 67, 95, 98, 99, 129
Curragh, Co. Kildare, 90
Curragh mutiny, 24
Curran, Francis, 79
Curran Michael, 79, 88

Dáil Commission of Inquiry, 71
Dáil Éireann, 64, 66, 69, 70–2, 75, 79, 98, 103, 105 107, 110–11, 126
Dáil loan, 66
Daly, John, 37
Davis, Frank, 91
de Valera, Éamon, 45, 47, 48, 107
Defence of the Realm Act, 31, 33
Dennison, Carson, 123
Dennison, Thomas, 123
Devanny, Sergeant Hugh 77
Devine, Thomas, 43
Devins, Séamus, 83, 111, 119, 120
Devlin, Joe, 5, 9, 14
Dillon, John, 13, 53, 60
Dobson, Parke, 21
Dockery, Michael, 116
Dockery, Thomas, 34
Dolan, Charles, 9, 10
Dolan, James, 37, 44–6, 48, 50, 56, 60–1, 63–7, 102, 104, 107–8, 117, 119, 134
Donnelly, Patrick, 53
Doonan, James, 101
Doorly, Dr Patrick, 39
Doris, William, 27
Dowd, Murtagh, 92
Dowra, Co. Cavan, 3, 124
Doyle, Annie, 40
Doyle, Edward, 69
Dromahair, 23, 50, 52, 54, 56, 58, 72, 75–6, 98, 119, 123, 129
Dromod, 6, 44, 47, 55, 76, 88, 113, 118
Drumalease, 56, 77
Drumkeeran, 6, 8, 15, 19, 60–1, 65, 121, 123, 134
Drumlea, 83
Drumlion, 44, 51, 108
Drumshanbo, 2, 6, 10, 15, 23, 34, 37, 44, 49, 61–2, 65–6, 76, 79, 83, 85, 87, 93, 98, 111, 119–20, 123, 125–6
Drumsna, 5, 6, 40, 49, 57, 76, 79, 85, 88, 100, 104, 113, 116, 118, 120–2, 126
Dublin, County, 86, 90
Duignan, Michael, 114
Duignan, Thomas, 51
Dunkineely, Co. Donegal, 86
Dunne, John, 89
Dunne, Patrick, 3, 37, 87

Earley, Michael, 101
Early, Thomas, 92
Easter Rising 1916, 28, 30, 34, 36–7, 39–42, 69, 131–2, 135
Edentenny, 92
elections: 1910 general election, 1, 12; North Leitrim by-election, 9–10; 1918 general election, 59–64, 76, 131, 133; 1920 local elections, 68–9; 1922 general election, 108; East Cavan by-election, 46, 58; East Clare by-election, 45; East Tyrone by-election, 53; North Roscommon by-election, 42–4; South Armagh by-election, 52–3; South Longford by-election, 44–5, 48, 132; Waterford city by-election, 52–3
Elliott, Bishop Alfred, 16
Elphin, Co. Roscommon, 52–3
emigration, 1, 19, 22, 50, 124, 133
Emlagh, 51
Enniskillen, Co. Fermanagh, 112

Fallon, Martin, 115
Fallon, Thomas, 6, 10, 23, 24, 26–7, 37, 49, 57, 61
Farmers' Protection Association, 14
Farnaught, 80
Farrell, Gerald, 61–2
Farrell, J.P., 61
Farrell, Matt, 62
Fenagh, 13, 45, 73, 80, 88, 93, 124
Fermanagh, County, 16, 41, 112, 118, 120, 124, 134
Fermanagh Herald, 3, 28
Fianna Éireann, 76
Figgis, Darrell, 47
Finegan, Bishop Patrick, 30, 96, 127

Finn, James, 89
Finner, Co. Donegal, 116, 119
First World War, 11, 12, 19, 21, 33, 35, 54, 64; effect on Irish Parliamentary Party (IPP), 131; GAA, 34; Irish Volunteers, 18–9; recruitment, 20–7, 58; suspension of home rule, 16; separation women/allowances, 31; spy scare, 32; voluntary associations, 29–30
Fivemilebourne, 77, 83
flying columns, see Irish Republican Army (IRA)
Flynn, Fr Charles, 9
Flynn, James, 95
Flynn, Patrick, 3, 9, 27, 32, 36, 40, 43, 58, 51, 57, 65
Flynn, Thomas, 38, 67
Foley, Mary, 31
Four Courts, 114–16, 123
Freeman's Journal, 74, 90, 110, 116, 120, 125, 129–30
Freyne, Lily, 47
Frongoch internment camp, 41, 44

Gaelic Athletic Association (GAA), 6, 34, 58, 88
Gaelic League, 8, 12, 36, 67, 70
Gaffney, John, 77
Gaffney, Pat, 14
Gallagher, Jim, 115
Galligan, Fr Peter, 52–3
Galligan, Paul, 54, 56
Gallogly, Con, 58
Gallogly, Mary Kate, 129
Galway, County, 72,–3, 113, 117, 124
Garrison, Co. Fermanagh, 112, 124
Gavin, James, 88
Geelan, Edward, 28, 129
Geevagh, Co. Sligo, 118
Geoghegan, James, 14
Geoghegan, Michael, 93, 97
Geraghty, Revd, 29
Germany, 16–17, 23
Gilgunn, Phil, 121
Gilgunn, Thomas, 37
Gilhooley, Bernard, 113
Gilhooley, Patrick, 113
Gill, Pat, 85

Ginnell, Laurence, 26–7, 45, 49
Glasson, Co. Westmeath, 89
Glenade, 28, 80
Glenfarne, 85, 114, 118, 120–1, 128–9
Godley, Anna, 16, 78
Gorby, Robert, 122
Gordon, Justice, 64
Gordon, Captain Thomas, 28
Gore Booth, Constance (Countess Markievicz), 36
Gore Hickman, District Inspector Thomas, 96–7, 100–1
Gortlettragh, 22, 58
Gorvagh, 5, 22, 41, 45, 76, 80, 88, 95, 97, 101, 111
Government of Ireland (Amendment) Act, 16
Government of Ireland Act, 72
Gowel, 40, 45, 73, 89, 93, 94, 108, 114
Gralton, Jim, 73, 108, 112–14
Gray, Alice, 94
Greenwood, Sir Hamar, 101
Griffin, John, 112
Griffith, Arthur, 9, 10, 44, 46–7, 58
Guckian, Paddy, 95
Guinan, Fr Joseph, 55

Hargaden, Patrick J., 46, 62, 84, 85, 92, 98
Harlech, County Lieutenant, 29
Harrison, Colonel, 31
Harrison, Jane, 100
Harrison, John, 100
Hart, Constable Leonard, 100
Harte, John, 90
Hay, Constable Colin, 100
Haylett, Revd S.J., 124
Healy, Katie, 40, 46
Healy, Sergeant, 93
Heslin, Patrick, 33
Hewson, George, 17
Higgins, J.J., 86
Hoare, Bishop Joseph, 35, 37, 79, 127, 129
Hobson, Bulmer, 9
Hogan, Patrick, 113, 114, 127
Holt, Sam, 37, 53, 127
home rule, 1, 5, 8, 9, 10, 16–18, 21, 25, 35, 36, 39, 40, 53, 57, 66, 68, 69, 72,

Index

79, 124, 131; home rule bill, 11–12, 14–16, 18–19, 22, 38, 55; home rule crisis, 15–16, postponement of, 16; post-1916 Rising talks, 38–9
House of Lords, 12, 16
Hunt, Jack, 95–6

internment, 32, 88, 90, 102
Irish Bulletin, 81, 84, 89
Irish Convention, 49, 57
Irish Farmers' Union (IFU), 73–4
Irish Free State, 67, 110–11, 119, 124, 133
Irish Independent, 38, 122
Irish National Aid Association, 40
Irish National Aid and Volunteer Dependants' Fund (INAAVDF), 40–2, 132
Irish National Foresters (INF), 5, 6, 47, 55
Irish National Volunteers (National Volunteers), 18, 21–2, 24, 48
Irish Parliamentary Party (IPP), 1–3, 5–6, 8–12, 19, 22, 23, 27, 37–45, 48–9, 53–4, 57, 59, 67, 68, 106, 131–3, 135; declining support, 39; 1918 general election, 60–3; Irish Volunteers, 14–15; support for army recruitment, 21
Irish Republican Army (IRA), 70, 81, 83, 86, 88, 90, 98, 99, 101, 102, 104–5, 108, 110–12, 114–16, 122, 128, 130, 133, 134; arms raids, 77–8; barrack burnings, 79–81; Belfast boycott, 98–9; formation in county, 76; Crimlin ambush, 84; flying column (ASU), 91–3; GHQ criticism, 91; intimidation of RIC and state officials, 84–5; internment, 90–1; Selton Hill ambush, 95–6; Sheemore ambush, 93–4; North Longford Brigade, 91; North Roscommon Brigade, 115–16; North Sligo Brigade, 76, 83; South Donegal Brigade, 76, 86; South Tipperary Brigade, 76; Western Division, 104; Third Western Division, 111, 115
Irish Republican Brotherhood (IRB), 6, 8–9, 15, 33, 36
Irish Transport and General Workers' Union (ITGWU), 52, 68–9, 74
Irish Unionist Alliance, 15

Irish Volunteers, 12, 15, 18, 21, 36, 40, 67, 78
Irish White Cross, 114
Irwin, Councillor, 81

Jamestown, 22, 73
Johnston, William, 77
Johnstonsbridge, 130
Jones, Constable Wilfred, 99, 100

Keaney, Peadar, 70–1
Keaveney, John, 39–40
Keaveney, Thomas, 51
Kellegher, Captain J.F., 124
Kelly, Captain, 27
Kelly, Fr Michael, 101
Kelly, Fr Thomas, 15
Kelly, James, 98
Kelly's Hotel 28
Kerry, County, 127
Keville, Patrick, 130
Kiernan, James, 26
Kiernan, J.A., 88
Kiernan, John, 112
Kilkenny, County, 45
Kilkenny, Eugene, 78, 94, 128
Killargue, 76, 83, 117
Killavoggy, 76
Killegar, 16, 78
Killenumery, 62
Kiltoghert, 50–1, 70, 94
Kiltubrid, 60, 77
Kiltyclogher, 1, 41, 80, 119–20, 128
King, Fr Philip, 41
King, George V, 16
Kinlough, 8, 76, 85–6, 118–19
Kinlough Farmers' Union, 104
Knocklong, Co. Limerick, 74

labour movement, 52, 68–9, 74
Labour Party, 80
Lambert, Brigadier C.S., 88
Land Acts (1903, 1909), 1, 2, 13, 50
land agitation, 2–3, 6, 50–1, 73, 113–14
Langan, Tom, 120
Larkin, Constable Sydney, 89
Latimer, Isabella, 97
Latimer, William, 97–8

Lavin, Andrew, 107–8
Leitrim Advertiser, 3, 18–22, 29, 33, 36–7, 61, 115
Leitrim County: demography, 1; diocesan structures, 8; local government structures, 8–9; parliamentary constituencies, 7, 9; socio-economic conditions, 1–2
Leitrim County Committee of Agriculture, 105
Leitrim County Council, 14, 23, 26, 30, 32, 36, 48, 61, 65, 67–70, 72–3, 89, 103, 105, 107
Leitrim Observer, 3, 12, 14, 16, 18–20, 22, 25, 28, 32–4; 36–9, 42–4, 49, 51, 53, 58, 60–2, 65, 69, 80–1, 125; Crown forces burning of printing works, 89
Leitrim–Roscommon North constituency, 107
Lloyd George, David, 38, 42, 49, 107
Local Appointments Commission, 106
Local Government (Ireland) Act (1898), 8
Local Government Board (LGB), 8, 70, 133
Logue, Cardinal Michael, 127
Londsdale, Robert, 71
Longford, County, 2, 5–6, 10, 31, 47, 61, 81, 83, 90, 92, 96, 98, 100, 105, 110, 112, 126
Longford Leader, 3, 9, 96
Lough Allen, 5, 9, 78, 126
Lough Derg, 17
Louth, County, 3
Lynch, Liam, 122, 128, 130
Lynch, Michael, 51

McAviney, Patrick, 58
McCabe, Fr Bartle, 15, 22, 81, 91, 107
McCabe, Fr Matthew, 58, 65, 81
McCabe, Patrick, 77
McCarron, Francis, 123
McCarthy, Charles, 108
McCormack, Joe, 69, 88
McCullough family, 95, 97
McDaid, Patrick, 25
MacDermott, Patrick, 68
McDermott, Pee, 95
Mac Diarmada, Seán, 9, 33, 36, 41, 67, 107
McDonagh, Mary, 31
McDonald, John, 54–5
McDougall, Margaret Dixon, 1
Mac Eoin, General Seán, 92, 98, 104, 108, 110, 112, 115, 119–20, 124, 134
McGarty, Tom, 101
McGauran, Dr Arthur, 130
McGee, Patrick, 20
McGivney, Thomas, 48, 61
McGlynn, James, 98
McGoey, P.J., 28
McGoldrick, Michael, 77
McGoohan, Charles, 93, 99, 112, 120, 128
McGorrin, James, 72
McGovern, Thomas, 15, 68, 98
McGowan, Kathleen, 8
McGowan, Martin Bernard, 76
McGrath, Michael, 3, 6, 13, 40, 57, 68
McGrath, Seán, 125
McGuinness, Frank, 55
McGuinness, J.P., 18, 28
McGuinness, Joe, 44–6, 49
McGuinness, John, 33
McGuire, Patrick, 130
McGuire, Philip, 130
McHugh, Michael, 58
McHugh, P.A., 9
McKenna, Myles, 19
McKenna, Patrick, 111
McKeon, Commandant Harry, 93, 109, 113, 118
McKiernan, Hugh, 118
McLoughlin's Hotel, 87
McLoughlin, James, 114
McManus, Fr Daniel, 117
McManus, Pat, 10
McManus, Private Michael, 125
McNabola, Captain, 121
McNabola, T.P., 51
McNasser, William, 78
MacNeill, Brian, 111, 115, 117, 119–20
McNeill brothers, 3
McPartland, Andy, 95
McPartlin, John, 87
Macready, General Sir Nevil, 94
MacSwiney, Terence, 89, 107

Index

McTierney, Michael, 87, 89
Magee, Bernard, 87
Maguire, Ben, 37, 44, 61, 69, 72, 102, 106–7
Maguire, Fr John, 8
Manning, Eliza, 31
Manning, Mary, 31
Mannion, Delia, 95
Manorhamilton, 2–3, 6, 8, 9–10, 15, 18, 21, 23–6, 28–9, 33, 37, 44, 47, 50–3, 57, 67–8, 71–2, 78–9, 83, 104–5, 107, 113, 119, 121, 123–4, 128
Martin, Michael, 93
Masterson, Canon, 129
Maxwell, General Sir John, 34
Mayo, County, 73, 112, 117, 124
Meehan, Francis, 5, 9–10, 13–15, 21, 23–4, 27, 30, 39, 44, 49, 51, 54, 62
Methodism, 1, 8, 29, 41, 123
Military Service Act, 132
Military Service bill, 52, 54
Mitchell, Commandant Seán, 92, 93, 114
Mohill, 2, 8–9, 16, 28–9, 45–8, 81–4, 125
Monaghan, County, 110, 112.
Mooney, Andrew, 91
Moore, Colonel Maurice, 48, 71
Moore, Justice, 78
Moran, James, 101
Moran, Michael, 101
Morrissey, Captain Paddy, 97
Mountjoy Jail, 47, 80
Mugan, Constable Thomas, 100
Mulcahy, General Richard, 110, 125–6
Muldoon, Dr Paddy, 129
Mullane, Brigid, 46
Mulligan, John, 48
Murphy, Major James, 22, 24, 26
Murphy, Michael 46, 48, 57, 67, 73
Murray, J., 51
Meath, County, 32
Meath County Council, 68

Nangle, Joe, 93
National army, 114, 116–17, 119–20, 122, 124–9
National Insurance Act, 5
National Land Bank, 73
Newbridge, 22

Newtowngore, 122
Newtownmanor, 49, 76
Nire Valley, Co. Waterford, 128
North Sligo constituency, 9
Northern Bank, 28, 111
Northern Command (Ulster Council), 112
Northern Ireland, 111, 124
Notley, Evelyn, 29
O'Beirne, Bernard, 85–6
O'Beirne, Rice, 61
O'Boyle, Patrick, 125
O'Brien, William, 2
O'Connell, J.J., 110
O'Connell, John, 81
O'Connor, Rory, 54, 114
O'Connor, T.P., 101
O'Conor, Major Maurice, 108
O'Donel, John, 10, 15, 22, 25, 27, 31–2, 34, 51, 58, 113
O'Donnell, James, 128
O'Duffy, Eoin, 110, 115, 121
O'Dwyer, Bishop Edward, 38
O'Farrell, Fr, 73
O'Hara, County Inspector Charles, 84
O'Higgins, Kevin, 114, 126–7
O'Kelly, James J., 42–3
O'Leary, Lieutenant Michael, 26
O'Malley, Ernie, 92, 94, 100, 102
O'Neill Clarke, Eugene, 65, 105–6
O'Reilly, Canon Thomas, 6, 23, 39, 55, 59, 62, 73, 87, 93
O'Reilly, John Joe (Derrinkeher), 95
O'Reilly, John Joe (Miskawn), 95
O'Reilly, Thomas, 92–3
O'Rourke, John (Ballinamore), 77
O'Rourke, John (Manorhamilton), 10
Ó Ruadháin, Seán, 8
Oldcastle, Co. Meath, 32
Orange Order, 5
Ormsby Lawder, J.A., 51
Owens, William, 125
Owens and Richardson hardware shop, 124–5

Parliament Act (1911), 12
Parnell, Charles Stewart, 8
Pearse-Connolly hall, 113–14
Pentland, Dr Charles, 28, 97

Peters, F.R.S., 28
Pettigo, Co. Donegal, 112
Pettit, John A., 96
Peyton, George, 30
Phillips, Captain, 59
Phillips, John, 44
Pilkington, Billy, 111, 117, 119
Pim, Justice, 71
Pinkman, Charles, 97–8
Pinkman, Fr John, 37, 78
Plumb, Constable Edwin, 112
Plunkett, Count George, 43–4, 66, 107
Plunkett, Joseph Mary, 43
Porteus, Revd Matthew, 124
Prince of Wales Relief Fund, 29
Prior, Fr Francis, 53, 56
Prior, Myles, 104
Protestants: 134; anti-conscription, 55–6; arms raids against homes, 78; Belfast riots, 111; demography, 1; diocesan structure, 8; intimidation, 97, 123; migration, 124; supporting home rule, 16; supporting army recruitment, 23
Provisional government, 111, 114, 116, 120–1, 127

Quinn, Ellen, 31
Quinn, John, 86

Rahelly House, 117, 119
Rainsford, County Inspector Ross, 3, 14, 51, 53, 78, 93
Ranch War, 2
Rantogue, 61, 79–80
Ratepayers' Protection Association, 14
rates: anti-rates campaigns, 14; attacks on rate collectors, 114; non-payment, 103–4, 133
Red Cross, 29–30, 34
Redmond, Captain William, 53
Redmond, John, 2, 12, 19, 21–2, 27, 41, 53, 131; home rule crisis, 15–16; First World War, 18; National Volunteers, 18
Reilly, William, 52, 68, 74
Representation of the People Act (1918), 60, 68
Restoration of Order in Ireland Act, 72,

85, 102
Reynolds, Bernard, 26
Reynolds, Charlie, 112
Reynolds, Joe, 112
Reynolds, Michael, 130
Riverstown, Co. Sligo, 128
Roddy, Fr James, 118
Rooney, Dr P.J., 28
Rooney, Philip, 128
Roscommon, County, 2, 5, 10, 22, 23, 42, 45, 47, 49, 51, 53, 73, 74, 81, 91, 92, 93, 110, 113, 115–19, 124, 134
Roscommon County Council, 70
Roscommon Herald, 3, 17, 19, 32, 37, 39, 62, 84–5, 87, 88, 90, 93, 103, 106, 107–108, 115–16, 120, 125, 128–30
Rowan, Lord Justice, 33
Royal Irish Constabulary (RIC), 1, 3, 9–10, 12, 15, 20, 22, 26–8, 32, 39, 40, 44, 51, 54, 56, 59, 70–1, 77–8, 83, 93, 97, 101, 105, 130; Auxiliaries, 83; Black and Tans, 81, 83, 89, 99, 100; reprisals, 86–90, 94; barrack burnings, 79–81; boycott by IRA, 84–5; disbandment and departure, 110–11
Royal Ulster Constabularly (RUC), 112, 120
Ryan, Bernard, 90
Ryan, Frank, 90
Ryan, William, 125
Ryans, Fr Edward, 66, 90, 129

Sadlier, Margaret, 99
Scott, Thomas, 124
Selton Hill, 95, 97, 98, 102, 134
separation allowances, 20, 31
separation women, 31
Shannon, river, 34, 43, 89, 110, 116, 118, 120
Sharp, Lieutenant Colonel, 83
Sheehan, Canon Patrick, 13
Sheelan, Denis, 85
Sheemore, 92–5, 99
Sigerson, George, 40
Sinn Féin (SF), 3, 11, 37, 39–41, 43, 46–8, 57, 58, 64, 73, 75, 77, 79, 80, 86, 87, 88, 89, 90, 105, 106, 108, 113, 116, 120, 131–3, 135; agrarian agitation, 50–1;

Index

Anglo-Irish Treaty, 106–9; anti-conscription, 52–6; clerical support, 65–6, 79; counter-state, 69–72; North Leitrim by-election, 9–10; transfer of support from AOH, 48–9, 79; 1918 general election, 59–63; 1920 local elections, 68–9
Slevin, Frank, 128
Slieve an Anerin mountains, 101
Sligo Champion, 3, 10, 28, 45, 53, 58–9, 64, 68, 72, 103, 106, 108
Sligo, County, 2, 5, 10, 15, 22, 36, 39, 41, 51, 53, 77–8, 81, 90, 105–6, 110–11, 114–15, 117–21, 124, 128, 134
Sligo Independent, 3, 81, 83, 87
Sligo Nationalist, 132
Smyth, Thomas, MP, 3, 6, 9, 14, 21–4, 44–6, 49, 54, 61
Soldiers' and Sailors' Families Association, 20
Special Infantry Corps (SIC), 114
Spike Island, Co. Cork, 90
Stanley, Venetia, 16
Streamstown, Co. Westmeath, 89
Sweeney, Bernard, 46, 77, 84, 91–3, 95, 98, 112
Sweeney, Commandant Joe, 119
Sweeney, Frank, 91
Sweeney, Michael, 77
Sweetman, Revd Austin, 124

Tarmonbarry, Co. Longford, 31
Tasker, Constable Thomas, 100
Taylor, Richard, 77
Teague, James, 57
Templemore, Co. Tipperary, 32
Tennant, Harold, 27
Thompson, Robert, 55
Timoney, Charles, 57, 76–7
Tipperary, County, 32
Town Tenants' League (TTL), 6, 13
Tullaghan, 51, 76, 116, 119
Tully, Jasper, 3, 9, 43
Turbett, Hugh, 64
Turner, Robert, 3
Tymon, Paddy, 126

Ulster Bank, 98

Ulster Volunteer Force (UVF), 12, 16, 131
United Irish League (UIL), 2, 13–4, 19, 21, 49, 131; agrarian agitation, 2–3, 8, 51; North Leitrim by-election, 9–10; rivalry with AOH, 10; reorganization 1915, 13; supporting army recruitment, 27; Irish Volunteers, 15; declining support, 39–40; anti-conscription, 54

Vanston William, 78
Vaugh, Wilton, 113
voluntary associations, 29–30

Wallace, Lieutenant, 86
Walmsley, Revd Thomas, 124
Walsh, Archbishop William, 39
War of Independence, 76, 82, 87–8, 98–9, 101–2, 115, 120, 123, 129, 130, 134; arms raids, 77–8; Auxiliaries, 83; barrack burnings, 79–81; Belfast boycott, 98–9; Black and Tans, 81 83, 89, 99, 100; Crimlin ambush, 84; Crown forces' reprisals, 86–90, 94; flying column (ASU) formation, 91–3; intimidation of RIC and state officials, 84–5; Selton Hill, 95–6; Sheemore ambush, 93–4; shooting of alleged informers, 97, 100
Ward, Tim, 58, 70, 104
Waterford, County, 128
Westmeath, County, 89
Westmeath County Council, 68
Whyte estate, 6
Wilson, Justice, 112
Wilson, Lieutenant C.E., 93–5
Wimborne, Lord, 26
Winter, William, 32
Woodbrook, 51
Woodenbridge, Co. Wicklow, 18
Woodlock, Bishop Bartholemew, 8
Woods, Brigid, 31
Woods, Colonel Pádraig, 124
Woods, Kathleen, 31
Woods, Patrick, 25
Woods, Patrick (Councillor), 48, 53
Wrynne, Séamus, 92, 95